PIPELINE
to the PROS

How D3, Small-College Nobodies Rose to Rule the NBA

Ben Kaplan
and Danny Parkins

TRIUMPH
BOOKS

Library of Congress Cataloging-in-Publication Data

Names: Kaplan, Ben, author. | Parkins, Danny, author.
Title: Pipeline to the pros: how D3, small-college nobodies rose to rule
   the NBA / Ben Kaplan and Danny Parkins.
Description: Chicago, Illinois: Triumph Books, [2023]
Identifiers: LCCN 2023058005 (print) | LCCN 2023058006 (ebook) | ISBN
   9781637274347 (hardcover) | ISBN 9781637274354 (epub)
Subjects: LCSH: National Basketball Association. | National Collegiate
   Athletic Association. Division III. | Basketball players—United States.
   | Basketball coaches—United States. | Basketball managers—United
   States. | Professionalism in sports—United States.
Classification: LCC GV885.515.N37 K37 2023 (print) | LCC GV885.515.N37
   (ebook) | DDC 796.323/640973—dc23/eng/20240104
LC record available at https://lccn.loc.gov/2023058005
LC ebook record available at https://lccn.loc.gov/2023058006

This book is available in quantity at special discounts for your group or organization. For further information, contact:

Triumph Books LLC
814 North Franklin Street
Chicago, Illinois 60610
(312) 337-0747
www.triumphbooks.com

Printed in U.S.A.
ISBN: 978-1-63727-433-0
Design by Patricia Frey

In loving memory of those we lost during the process of writing this book:

My dad, Jimmy, who encouraged me to stick with it
—B.K.

My dad, Tom, who took me to every big game, and my brother, Brad, who was the best man I've ever known
—D.P.

We're swept up, are we not, by the large events and forces of our time?

—A.W. Merrick, *Deadwood* (2006)

To win the game is great...
To play the game is greater...
But to love the game is greatest of all.

—Plaque inside The Palestra

CONTENTS

Foreword *by Jeff Van Gundy*. ix

Prologue xi

PART I: PRE-D3

1 Head West, Old Man 3

2 Coaching Spectrum 13

3 Mergers and Expansion 25

4 Jersey Guys. 39

5 Lifer vs. Convert. 55

6 Open Borders. 73

PART II: MAIN BRANCHES

7 A Coaching Family. 89

8 Spurs Culture 113

PART III: SIDE DOORS

9 With a Little Help 145

10 Hoosiers 161

11 G League 185

PART IV: PIPELINE COMPLETE

12 D3 Player Empowerment. 199

13 Got Next 215

Epilogue 241

Acknowledgments. 245

Sources 247

FOREWORD

College athletics are changing at such a rapid rate that it is difficult to keep track of the new NCAA rules and new league affiliations. What has not changed and never will change is my joy and pride in having played D3 basketball at Nazareth University. The best five minutes of life are the first five minutes in the locker room after a great road win. When I told my daughters that, they pushed back and asked, "Better than when we were born?"

After a moment or two, I told them they would understand if they were in the locker room at the College of Staten Island in the spring of 1984. Every once in a while, I reflect back on the elation and euphoria we felt in that cramped visiting locker room after upsetting the host team to advance to the Elite Eight in the D3 NCAA Tournament. Nor will I ever forget our crushing home loss to Clark University a week later that would have advanced us to the Final Four. Both are forever seared into my mind and helped shape my basketball core beliefs. And what most people don't understand is that the pain of losing and the joy of winning are no different in the NBA or D3.

I was fortunate to grow up in a family where my dad coached small-college basketball. I didn't realize until I was an adult all the life lessons that I was taught by my dad and being around his teams on car rides to scout and on van trips to games and practices. I saw firsthand how my dad's guidance and my mom's care influenced the young players, how lifetime relationships were established and kept over the years, and how players gravitated to my parents for help and advice through challenging times in their lives. The joy my parents felt when they could celebrate the successes of these players and their families made me beam with pride. And to think these relationships were formed on basketball courts where very few watched and even fewer noticed shows the true value of small-college sports. If you didn't play or coach at the D3 level, you most likely have no idea just how good the players and coaches are. But that almost misses the point. Playing D3 basketball was such a great forum to teach the values necessary to break into and succeed in any profession.

After bouncing around to four colleges in five years, I found my basketball home at Nazareth. I will always be indebted to my dad and brother for all they taught me about the game and the profession. But my gratitude to my coaches at Nazareth is immense. Bill Nelson, Bob Ward, and Jim Emery found the sweet spot of pushing my teammates and me to reach our basketball potential, while also showing us great empathy and concern. My coaches and many others involved in Division III basketball have achieved great things professionally and done so many things to help positively alter the trajectory of others' lives. In their book, authors Ben Kaplan and Danny Parkins highlight a number of those people who have found great success in the NBA. But I guarantee that even with all their NBA successes they will look back on their Division 3 experiences with both fondness and gratitude for all it taught them along the way—even the most painful losses. I hope you enjoy this book as much as I loved my time at Nazareth University and my D3 basketball experience.

—*Jeff Van Gundy*

PROLOGUE

Standing alone at the host stand, the man considered his options. He could continue waiting just inside the doorway, hoping a staff member would soon appear to ask him his name and how many. Or he could just pick an empty table and seat himself. The man, for that type of restaurant in that type of neighborhood, was as non-descript as it gets—early 30s, close-cropped brown hair, and a few days of stubble. He had his hands tucked into the pockets of his gold and blue quarter-zip windbreaker, which did little to protect him from the lion of a March day. The short walk from his swanky downtown Chicago hotel to the neighborhood corner tap had reddened his cheeks and ears. He slipped his right hand into the pocket of his black joggers, grabbed his phone, and glanced at the home screen: 12:29 PM, Tuesday, March 10.

Half of the tables were unoccupied, and two out of every three stools at the bar were cool to the touch. The very next day—March 11, 2020—Tom Hanks would announce from Australia that he was recovering from the new novel coronavirus, and Utah Jazz center Rudy Gobert's positive test would force the NBA to suspend the season indefinitely.

On March 10, though, life in Chicago was still lurching forward. It was a combination of the Tuesday lull and the crummy weather—not any sort of capacity mandate—that was responsible for the restaurant's empty seats. To most Americans Covid-19 was a joking excuse to bump elbows and avoid sharing their fries, not an unstoppable force well on its way to bringing the country, and the NBA season along with it, to its knees.

After finally attracting the host's attention, the man was led to an empty outdoor patio, still covered and heated to combat the wind whipping off Lake Michigan. Maybe one or two diners glanced at the man as he walked by. None of them stared or did a double take. He presented no real reason for any of the patrons to divert their attention away from their beer or their menu or their phone. If, say, he had arrived on a sunny Friday, to a busier incarnation of the restaurant, the host wouldn't have made any special accommodations for him. Same as anyone else, he would've had to shout his name over the lunchtime chatter of tourists and coworkers. Then he would've had to wait for a table or two to pay the check and for a busser to clear away the backwash-filled glasses and gnawed chicken bones until it was finally his turn.

The man took his seat at the table and told the server he would wait for the rest of his party before ordering. His phone buzzed. Expecting a message from the friend he was meeting, he instead saw a text from an old teammate. It described a controversy amongst fans of small-college basketball. Apparently, three weeks earlier, a *Sports Illustrated* tweet referred to the leading scorer in NCAA men's basketball as a "D3 Nobody."

The term "nobody" didn't sit well with the Division III community, a group who proudly represented the nation's smallest colleges. In response to the tweet, they cited how talented and hardworking D3 athletes are. They lauded the passion necessary to play a game when very few, if any, people are watching. Eventually, SI yielded and removed the word "nobody" from the post. Putting the phone down, the man chuckled to himself. He knew better than most that even a small-school somebody was still, in the grand scheme of things, a D3 nobody.

Judging from the complete lack of attention paid to him, not a soul in that Chicago restaurant recognized the man as one of the most decorated college basketball players of the 21st century. Even if he walked up to every patron and introduced himself—"Hi, I'm Andrew Olson, nice to meet you"—no one in that restaurant would have recognized his name. They'd all be ignorant to the fact that, in a few short hours, he'd be stepping onto the floor at the United Center, home of the Chicago Bulls, to prepare for an NBA game.

That same afternoon—March 10, 2020—most NBA teams unwittingly prepared for what would be their final game for at least four months. The Los Angeles Lakers, gearing up to host the underdog Brooklyn Nets, sat atop the Western Conference standings. LeBron James, in his second season with the Lakers, appeared to be on yet another collision course with the NBA Finals.

The prior year, a groin injury sidelined the usually indestructible James, rendering him helpless to stop the Lakers' uncharacteristic playoff drought from stretching to a sixth season. By March of 2020, though, Lakers fans had slipped back into the comfortable groove of supporting a winner. The team wasn't some reincarnation of the fast-paced, flashy Showtime Lakers—new coach Frank Vogel instilled them with a gritty, defensive identity that was more Rust Belt than Tinseltown.

The Lakers were Vogel's third stop as a head coach. His first stint calling the timeouts—at any level, not just the NBA—came in 2011 with the Indiana Pacers. He was just 37, the youngest coach in the league at the time. He reluctantly took over on an interim basis for his freshly fired mentor, Jim O'Brien, the man who, Vogel said, "was responsible for giving me opportunities and moving me up the ranks."

Vogel steered the Pacers to the playoffs in his first half season, convincing team brass to scrap the "interim" title and officially name him head coach. In five of Vogel's six seasons in Indianapolis, the team finished top 10 in the league in defensive efficiency. They reached the Eastern Conference Finals twice, losing on both occasions to James' Miami Heat. In his fifth season, the team began to regress. Pacers president of basketball operations Larry Bird, a firm believer that even the best coach's voice grows stale over time, dismissed Vogel.

The young coach had established himself as a worker and a defensive tactician. It wasn't long before the Orlando Magic came calling. Vogel only lasted two seasons in Orlando before their new leadership decided to send him packing. Leaving the Happiest Place on Earth and finding a new home would take time. The NBA is a small world, after all. There are just 30 head coaching jobs. One bad stint can cause the clock to strike midnight, revealing the wunderkind to be nothing more than a common retread. And retreads, who don't excite fanbases or win press conferences, aren't the hires that general managers and owners are eager to make.

After taking a gap year to sit in on college and pro practices across the country, Vogel was ready to coach again. Rarely does a new coach take over a team with legitimate championship aspirations. But just such an opportunity arose in 2019, when the Lakers missed the playoffs and subsequently canned their coach, Luke Walton. The Lakers were the overwhelming favorites to acquire Anthony Davis that offseason, which would transform them into immediate title contenders.

After a very public breakdown in negotiations with James' preferred candidate, Tyronn Lue, the team turned to Vogel. They did their best to Euro step past the very awkward reality that he was not their first choice. Unlike Lue, Vogel hadn't played for the Lakers. In fact, he hadn't played for any professional team. Not counting his short stint with the University of Kentucky's junior varsity squad, Vogel's playing days ended at Pennsylvania's Juniata College, a Division III school with an enrollment of fewer than 1,500.

To assist Vogel, the Lakers tabbed Jason Kidd, a Hall of Fame player and former NBA head coach. Most expected Kidd to usurp Vogel sooner rather than later, likely with a nudge from James. Instead, Vogel sat down with Kidd prior to the season to clear the air and align on responsibilities, one of many instances where the Lakers' new head coach demonstrated confidence and a steady hand. By early March, it appeared as though it was going to take an act of God to keep the Lakers from postseason success. An act of God is what they got.

ON MARCH 10, 2020, Mike Budenholzer and the Bucks needed a break. They were back in Milwaukee, recuperating after a disastrous road trip. The three-game jaunt was a homecoming of sorts for Budenholzer, the Bucks' head coach. The first game—a loss to Vogel's Lakers—was played just 40 miles due west of Pomona College, Budenholzer's alma mater. Then the second loss—this one at the hands of the inferior Phoenix Suns—brought Budenholzer back to Arizona, the state where he grew up in the shadow of six older siblings, a politician mother, and a high school basketball coach father.

Fortunately, the schedule gods had the Bucks' collective back: two days off, followed by a four-game homestand tipping off on March 12. There were rumors that, due to the new virus, they'd have to start playing games without fans. *Oh well,* Budenholzer figured. *I played Division III. I'm used to empty stands.*

Even after the losing streak, Budenholzer and the Bucks still had the NBA's best record, thanks in large part to their star forward, Giannis Antetokounmpo. It had been only eight years since the Bucks plucked the gangly teenager from Athens, Greece, with the 15th pick in the 2013 NBA Draft. League commissioner David Stern pronounced his name carefully, enunciating each syllable: "The Milwaukee Bucks select...YAH-nus Ah-det-oh-KOOM-bo." Draft analyst Fran Fraschilla called him "the most mysterious" prospect selected that evening.

John Hammond, the Bucks general manager at the time, made the call to select the raw, relatively unskilled Antetokounmpo, betting on his size and his almost tangible desire to be great. At the post-draft press conference, Hammond told the media, "I do think this kid has potential All-Star talent." Team officials, intoxicated on the promise of tomorrow, do not generally temper expectations at those media sessions. So when Antetokounmpo became the league's MVP in 2019, it wowed even Hammond, the man who put his job on the line to draft the so-called "Greek Freak."

In the 2010s, it was en vogue for teams to avoid mediocrity and lean into losing. Bad teams got higher draft picks, higher draft picks had a greater probability of becoming stars, and stars won championships. So-so teams drafted so-so players and stayed so-so. Bucks ownership committed to winning as many games as possible, despite having no real shot at a championship. Their approach was so novel, ESPN's Kevin Arnovitz wrote a profile of the team entitled, "What's up with the Milwaukee Bucks?" Mediocrity, according to the league executives Arnovitz interviewed, was a treadmill. Hammond and the Bucks were pumping away, dripping sweat and gasping for air while their position in the league's standings remained unchanged.

Antetokounmpo, who came into the league more Bambi on ice than graceful Buck, improved drastically from year to year. By his fourth season, the 22-year-old fulfilled Hammond's prophecy, earning a trip to the NBA All-Star Game. The Bucks, however, were still on that treadmill. Through Antetokounmpo's first five seasons, Milwaukee failed to advance beyond the first round of the playoffs.

In 2017, Hammond left the Bucks for the Orlando Magic. The following year, the Bucks finally hopped off the treadmill. With his spread offense and innovative defensive framework, new head coach Mike Budenholzer unlocked Antetokounmpo's unique gifts. Both player and team took the leap almost immediately. The Bucks finished Budenholzer's first season with the league's best record. Antetokounmpo was named the NBA's Most Valuable Player, and Budenholzer collected his second Coach of the Year trophy.

That first season ground to a halt with a loss in the Eastern Conference Finals. The disappointing end reminded NBA fans of Budenholzer's tenure in Atlanta, where he overachieved in the regular season but fell flat in the playoffs. In year two, the Bucks continued to dominate, but it would all be for nought without at least a trip to the NBA Finals. Unexpected success in the NBA quickly morphs into heightened expectations, and heightened expectations can prove dangerous for a coach.

In July of 2020, the NBA relocated to Disney World to hold the playoffs in the safety of the so-called "Bubble." Outside the Bubble it was a summer of great civil unrest. When, in the middle of the first round, footage surfaced of a police officer shooting a Black man named Jacob Blake in Kenosha, Wisconsin, members of the Bucks led a boycott that suspended play for three days.

Shortly after returning to the court, the Bucks fell in the second round to the underdog Miami Heat. Budenholzer didn't make any excuses, even though there were plenty to go around due to the pandemic and the protests. It was widely understood that, should the Bucks underwhelm in the playoffs one more time, the organization would be forced to make a coaching change.

Unlike the Bucks, the Lakers regained their pre-pandemic form. They eventually toppled James' former team, the Heat, to win the franchise's 17th NBA championship. One of the league's most iconic organizations, led by one of history's most legendary players, was back on top. And Frank Vogel was the coach who got them there.

It was a season full of unpredictable winds and bumps, a journey befitting Vogel's coaching career. His third stint as an NBA coach was finally the charm. Twenty-some years earlier, Vogel, a pre-med student at Juniata College in Huntingdon, Pennsylvania, did what most college students do in mid-December: he went home for a nice, long winter break. Juniata's basketball coach told Vogel and his teammates to return to campus shortly after the New Year. They'd have just one tune-up practice before a game on January 4. Vogel couldn't stand it. "I was really blown away at how little commitment there was to really winning," he said.

During the long layoff, the Division III point guard enviously watched his Division I counterparts on TV. His jealousy stemmed not from the fanfare, cheerleaders, or the television coverage but from their level of devotion. When an episode of *SportsCenter* covered University of Kentucky coach Rick Pitino's decision to hold double sessions on Christmas Day, Vogel thought to himself, *I'm more like that guy. I want to be that committed to basketball.* So he took action.

AS AN ENCORE to their disappointing run in the Bubble, Budenholzer and the 2020–21 Bucks finished third in the Eastern Conference, falling short of Vegas' expected win total by three-and-a-half games. According to those same oddsmakers, the Bucks had only about a 10 percent chance of winning the title when the playoffs began. The odds reflected the consensus sentiment that the Bucks' star player and head coach were not equipped to replicate their regular season success in the playoffs.

Antetokounmpo and Budenholzer emphatically proved their doubters wrong. In the face of rumors that he was on the chopping block, which persisted, and persisted, and persisted seemingly up until the moment he hoisted the 2021 championship trophy into the air, Budenholzer architected an impressive come-from-behind Finals victory. He was, and forever will be, an NBA champion.

When Budenholzer was interviewed during the trophy presentation, he deflected credit to the players, namely the two franchise pillars: Antetokounmpo and Khris Middleton. "Khris and Giannis, they built this," Budenholzer said. "I'm just glad to be a part of what Khris and Giannis have done."

Even though John Hammond was no longer with the team, he watched with pride at the culmination of his work in Milwaukee. The man who refused to tank managed to acquire Antetokounmpo, likely to go down as one of the greatest players in league history, in the middle of the first round. Then he snagged Middleton, a former second-round draft pick, as a trade throw-in.

In the postgame press conference, a champagne-soaked Antetokounmpo went out of his way to thank the Bucks' former general manager. "John Hammond drafted me, believed in me, believed in my family, brought them over here," Antetokounmpo said. "He made me feel comfortable. He made me feel like I was his son when I was homesick and alone in the hotel."

Many years before he was a talent evaluator, Hammond was a high school hooper with dreams of his own. That all came to an end one evening in 1971. Lying in a hospital bed, Hammond reckoned with the fact that there was no way the compound fracture in his leg would heal in time. He would miss his entire senior season, and the best small-college programs would look elsewhere. Heartbroken, he decided instead to follow his best friend, Scott Burgess, to tiny Greenville College in central Illinois. Maybe, if his leg healed, he could play basketball there.

That evening, when the doctor reset the bones in Hammond's leg, Budenholzer was just two years old, doing his best to keep up with his older siblings. He eventually grew to be 6'1" and, like his brothers before him, excelled on the hardwood. By his senior year in high school, Budenholzer dreamt of playing for his home state Arizona Wildcats. But Arizona's coach, Lute Olson, was busy recruiting future NBA players, not scrappy coaches' sons like Budenholzer. So Budenholzer decided to follow in his older brothers' footsteps and play Division III basketball at Pomona College.

Before he arrived on campus, the coach who recruited him, a former member of the Air Force by the name of Gregg Popovich, resigned to take a job with the San Antonio Spurs. Little did the teenage Budenholzer know, this string of disappointments set off a chain of events that would end with him coaching in the NBA.

IN 2020, VOGEL became the first former Division III basketball player to win an NBA championship as a head coach. The very next season, Budenholzer became the second. After a 37-year streak of championship-winning coaches with either NBA or Division I playing experience, D3 alums reigned supreme.

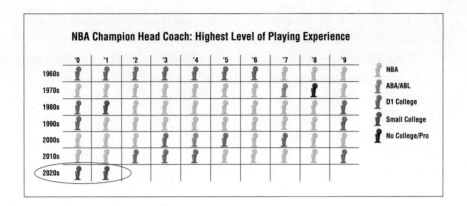

Former Division III players aren't just making their mark as head coaches. Six men, including Sam Presti, Koby Altman, and Leon Rose, are running teams' basketball operations, deciding which players to draft, negotiating trades, and determining overall basketball strategy.

The small-college dominance of the NBA peaked during the 2020–21 season, when 12 of the 30 teams had a former D3 player either running the front office or serving as head coach. A confluence of factors, both within the league and on America's small-college campuses, led to that point, where nearly half of the NBA teams are entrusted to a person whose abilities on the court only took them so far but, due to love or stubbornness or faith or lack of a better option, refused to give up on the game.

While the infiltration of D3 nobodies has only recently reached unprecedented levels, former small-college hoopers have been influencing the NBA throughout its 75-plus year history. They've executed some of the biggest trades, drafted MVPs, and guided teams to championships. They've given birth to new franchises and revolutionized the way the game is played and teams are managed.

In fact, the D3 pipeline's origin can be traced back to a time when "Division III" didn't even exist, when small-college alums lacked the collective banner under which to band together. From the 1950s through the 1980s, a few men who graduated from small colleges—institutions that would one day join Division III—managed to sneak into the NBA as general managers or head coaches. They did so by acquiring valued skills and establishing key connections with an owner, GM, or head coach—someone with the power to pluck a small-college grad from the hinterlands and welcome them into basketball's most exclusive rooms.

These pioneers—the first former small-college players to reach the NBA's front offices and coaching staffs—helped prime the league for Vogel, Budenholzer, Hammond, and dozens of others. Their unlikely tales of success, which either established or personified GM and coaching archetypes that pervade today, made the pipeline possible.

PART I:
PRE-D3

CHAPTER 1

HEAD WEST, OLD MAN

*How a small-college superhero helped the Lakers
survive and then thrive in Los Angeles*

When Andrew Olson's family moved from Phoenix to San Diego in 1994, he was four years into a lifelong love affair with basketball. The romance began when he and a friend ignored the Arizona heat and spent their days outside playing dunk context on a Little Tikes hoop. The five-year-old boys begged their moms to sign them up for the local YMCA league, even though it was for seven-year-olds. When Olson received his uniform, the shorts hung down to his ankles, and the shirt reached his knees. Despite playing the entire season with his uniform held together by clothespins, he competed admirably. He scored four points that season. But his friend scored eight, a fact that stuck with Olson throughout his playing career.

After the family relocated, Olson could comfortably shoot outdoors 12 months a year. He had a 10-foot hoop for serious practice and then a mini hoop for dunking. The mini hoop had a custom plywood backboard, on to which Olson painted the Phoenix Suns' orange and purple logo. When he wasn't busy shooting or dunking outside, he collected Suns trading cards—everyone from Charles Barkley to Danny Schayes—familiar faces in an unfamiliar new home.

It wasn't long before he picked up the San Diego slang and knew where to find the best burrito. Many of the other transients, drawn from all over the country to San Diego's beaches and laid-back lifestyle, shed their previous sports allegiances like a molting snake wiggling out of ill-fitting skin. But Olson never strayed from the Suns. With

Michael Jordan retired and out of the way, his team was a legitimate title contender. The local sports channel, Prime Ticket, aired the Los Angeles Lakers, so Olson could only watch a handful of Suns games. His friends loved the Lakers, especially point guards Sedale Threatt and Nick Van Exel. Deep down, he knew they were no match for Suns floor general Kevin Johnson. The Lakers were like a religion in Southern California, but the local hoopheads, despite their best efforts, could never convert Olson.

When the NBA formed shortly after World War II, a franchise wasn't all that it is today—an alternative investment that doubles as a tax shelter and triples as a vanity project, complete with courtside seats. Back then, NBA ownership was a possibility for ordinary men with an extraordinary love of the game. Owners were a blend of promoters and businessmen. Many served as their team's general manager. Some even coached.

In the early years, bankruptcy circled the league's franchises like a bony vulture. By 1954, three of the 11 original teams had shuttered. Drawing fans sometimes required scheduling doubleheaders with the Harlem Globetrotters, and teams learned the hard way that they darn well better put that Globetrotters game second, lest the audience walk out whistling "Sweet Georgia Brown" before the NBA game even tipped.

The Minneapolis Lakers' first general manager, Max Winter, knew firsthand just how popular the Globetrotters were. Promoting their games was one of the many jobs he held after graduating from Hamline University in Saint Paul, Minnesota. At Hamline, Winter played basketball and football. He was a small-college athlete in every sense of the word—the school had fewer than 1,000 students, and he stood just 5'4".

Winter attended Hamline in the 1920s—50 years before the NCAA created the Division III umbrella, home to small colleges that do not grant athletic scholarships. He was the first of several NBA general managers and head coaches who attended a future Division III school prior to the Division's genesis in 1973. Winter's lofty position with the Lakers came as a result of his knack for promotion, as well as the connections he built as a restaurateur.

In the early NBA, where the grandstands were half-full and the profit margins razor thin, public relations and promotional ability could be more critical than an eye for basketball talent. Some owners hired promoters, others turned to relatives, and some just did the jobs themselves. Throughout the league's first full decade, experience playing the game at a high level was not a prerequisite for running a team. Most NBA general managers hadn't played organized basketball beyond high school.

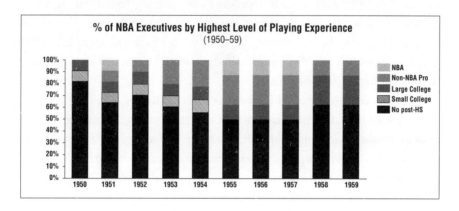

Thanks in part to Winter, who was instrumental in signing the league's first dominant star, George Mikan, the Lakers won five championships by 1954. It was but a blissful honeymoon period in the doomed marriage between team and city. Mikan retired, Winter sold out his stake to help found the NFL's Minnesota Vikings, and the franchise was, according to *Sports Illustrated*, "cultivating about as much Minnesota excitement as a YWCA canasta tournament."

Bob Short, a graduate of the College of St. Thomas (a Division III school from 1973 to 2021) organized a group to buy the team in 1957. After playing some successful exhibition games in San Francisco and Seattle, he had an idea. Minneapolis was already the westernmost city in the NBA, why not move a little farther? Perhaps the burgeoning L.A. sports scene would welcome a basketball team.

To replant the franchise and establish strong roots in Los Angeles, Short, who had business to attend to in Minneapolis, needed a leader capable of running both the team's business and basketball operations. He hired a fellow St. Thomas alum, Lou Mohs, making Mohs the second small-college basketball player to serve as general manager in Lakers (and NBA) history. Short sent Mohs to Los Angeles with $5,000 in seed money and specific instructions: "Go out there and don't let me hear from you. If you have any money left, send it back to me. If you need any money, forget where you came from."

When Mohs took the helm of the moribund Lakers in 1960, the NBA was still young. Mohs, however, was not. The 64-year-old—broad and fit, his wavy hair only slightly receding—was nearing retirement age. His decision to move to warmer climes was an age-appropriate one. The reason behind that move, however, was a bit abnormal. Mohs had spent his entire career in newspapers. Why move halfway across the country to work long hours running a basketball team?

The answer can be traced back to his time at the College of St. Thomas. Mohs demonstrated an unrivaled capacity for work during his college days, a man on a mission to single-handedly eradicate idle time. He was a rare four-letter athlete: football captain, starting basketball center, baseball left fielder, and high hurdler. Somehow, he managed to find enough time between practices and games to both edit the student newspaper and serve as guardian of the funds for the Sigma Tau Delta fraternity. All the while, he remained an exemplary student, the valedictorian of the 1921 graduating class.

Mohs' athletic excellence caught the attention of media both local and national. *The Minneapolis Star*, who at that time devoted valuable sports section real estate to the local small colleges, routinely covered Mohs' exploits on the gridiron and the hardwood. It wasn't just the local yokels who followed Mohs. A nationally syndicated cartoon called "Strange as it Seems," a precursor to *Ripley's Believe it or Not*, featured Mohs, labeling him a "College Superman." Mohs carried the clipping with him late into his life, occasionally showing it to Los Angeles sports columnists who were skeptical of his tales of past athletic glory.

The interest between Mohs and the press was mutual. Armed with his experience editing the college paper, he kicked off his career in the *St. Paul Pioneer Press and Dispatch*'s advertising department. He rose to president of the Northern States Circulation Managers Association, a role that had him traveling the country to implement cost-effective strategies and save struggling newspapers. Wherever he went, Mohs hung around the sports desk, hoping to overhear some inside info that would help him pull one over on his bookie.

Despite his busy professional life, Mohs stayed active with St. Thomas. He led alumni associations, planned homecomings, and played in alumni basketball and football scrimmages well into his 40s. The last record of Mohs' impressive athletic career was from a 1947 St. Thomas alumni game, where he was one of 27 graduates—both recent and, in his case, not-so-recent—who suited up against the varsity. The 51-year-old Mohs didn't attempt a field goal in what observers, according to the St. Thomas student newspaper, "laughingly called a basketball game."

Through his St. Thomas ties, Mohs met two men who would become influential in the Lakers organization—Short, the owner to be, as well as John Kundla, the Lakers' first head coach. Right before joining the Lakers, Kundla coached one season at St. Thomas, which was plenty of time to get to know Mohs, the ever-present alum. At the 1946 alumni game, Kundla joked with the 50-year-old Mohs, who proudly donned a tank top, that he should try to come back to school under the G.I. Bill.

Prior to the team's move to L.A., Mohs started doing some scouting for the Lakers. The work eventually led to his unexpected jump from newspaper executive to NBA general manager. When Mohs arrived in L.A., he hopped out of his maroon Buick, unfolded his black horn-rimmed spectacles, and started the painstaking process of building a fanbase. While perched on a chair he had borrowed from the arena—he wasn't going to waste the little cash he had on furniture—he studied a copy of the Los Angeles Dodgers' season ticket holder list. He spent the first week or two mailing blank ticket order forms to potential buyers.

Mohs knew not to spend a dime unless it would quickly yield a quarter. When the subject of money came up, he'd jut out his chin and grin and say, "Ask anybody around here. They'll tell you how tight I am." Enough of the blank order forms came back with enclosed checks to stave off bankruptcy, at least for another few weeks. He splurged, buying himself an office desk and a chair. With a little financial breathing room, Mohs could turn his attention to the roster. Even though player personnel piqued Mohs' interest more than the business side, he knew ownership was only concerned with the former in relation to how it impacted the latter. Without a quick influx of cash, it didn't really matter how many good players he signed—the team would be bankrupt.

Since the Lakers finished their final season in Minneapolis with the second-worst record in the league, they would pick second in the upcoming college draft. Although a losing season came with the reward of a high draft pick, the concept of tanking—losing games intentionally to secure a higher pick in the draft—didn't really exist back then. Teams couldn't afford the decreased gates and loss of playoff revenue, as the Lakers' moving vans could attest.

Short preferred that the Lakers go the more conventional route and select Los Angeles-born center Darrall Imhoff, who played collegiately at Cal. The Lakers were still trying to replace the Mikan-sized hole in the middle of their lineup, and having a local product would help sell some tickets. Mohs successfully pushed his boss to instead draft West Virginia's Jerry West. The Lakers GM then signed West to a two-year contract instead of the usual one-year commitment, telling reporters that "West would have been in a position after his first year of pro basketball to do a pretty good job of dickering with us for his second year's salary."

The first NBA team to put their fate in the hands of Manifest Destiny found salvation in a man named West. After just two seasons, Mohs was bragging to local journalist Wells Twombly of the *Valley Times* that West was "worth eight Imhoffs, give or take an Imhoff or two." West became one of the era's superstars, a Lakers legend, and a player so iconic that the NBA used his silhouette as their logo.

That first season in L.A., the Lakers brass worried more about the turnstiles than the scoreboard. Mohs' youngest daughter, Martha Higgins, remembered Mohs and the players' families sitting in the stadium together and praying, "not necessarily for the team but watching the counter mark for each fan's arrival. Once it had marked 4,000, we knew we had made it into the black for the game, and sometimes that was a struggle."

Mohs wasn't above enlisting some help to ensure his team didn't stink... literally. After games, Mohs' wife, Alice, could be found at the family's kitchen sink, where she sudsed and scrubbed the team's tanks and shorts, single-handedly guaranteeing star forward Elgin Baylor and company would be fresh for their next contest.

To sell enough tickets, Mohs resorted to outlandish schemes to raise the team's profile, like running a "Seven Footers Get in Free" promotion when 7'1" Wilt Chamberlain and the Philadelphia Warriors first played in Los Angeles. Whenever the Lakers did something extraordinary on the court, Mohs' first thought was how to best parlay it into revenue. Early in the season, the team traveled east on a pilgrimage to the basketball Mecca, Madison Square Garden. Baylor couldn't miss. He twitched and herky-jerkied his way to 71 points, a new NBA single-game scoring record. When Coach Schaus spoke with Mohs after Baylor's historic night, the Lakers GM groused: "Too bad he didn't score five fewer points. Then we could have gotten Phillips 66 as a sponsor."

When it came to payroll, Mohs knew to do whatever was necessary to keep West and Baylor happy. By taking care of his stars financially and limiting roster turnover, he kept the boat steady. "The salaries you pay the Jerry Wests and Elgin Baylors don't hurt at all," Mohs said. "If it's your last breath, you can pay for a good doctor."

It was a different story for the rest of the roster. Nearly half of all Americans in the early 1960s agreed that their country was trending toward socialism. The same could not be said about the Lakers. When it came to the players not named West or Baylor, Mohs took advantage of the weak pre-union basketball labor force. Under his watch the Lakers were, as Sam Feldman of *The San Bernadino County Sun* put it, not "noted for participating in the War on Poverty." Free agency was still over twenty years away. Signing players for less than their worth was, unfortunately for said players, easy in those days. If the team offered a contract and the player didn't like it, he had two options: hope for a trade, or go find a job outside of basketball.

Even though teams mostly built their rosters through trades and the draft, Mohs' commitment to scouting was borderline revolutionary. Most teams formed opinions on draft prospects by word of mouth and the annual collegiate All-Star Games. Not Mohs. He took every opportunity to watch draft prospects in action. When presumptive top pick Bill Bradley's Princeton Tigers traveled west for the NCAA Tournament in 1965, Mohs hopped a plane to Portland, Oregon, to see him in person.

Mohs was an analytical talent evaluator. He was one of the first basketball executives to understand the importance of wingspan, and not just height, in determining a players' potential. At the Lakers' facility, he measured players' reach to create a benchmark, making notches on a wall for stars like Bill Russell, Chamberlain, Nate Thurmond, and West. "Don't sign anyone," he told his scouts, "until you measure his wingspan." He scoured the few statistics that were kept in that era, which inspired him to acquire a young Don Nelson, the future Boston Celtics role player and Hall of Fame coach. "His statistics last year showed what a hustler Don is," Mohs told the *Los Angeles Evening Citizen News*. "He went to the free throw line about once every four minutes, showing that he liked to get in there and mix it up."

Mohs' ability to identify talent, paired with his business savvy and the inherent advantage he held at the negotiating table, helped the Lakers' value soar. In the summer of 1965, Short sold the team to Canadian media mogul Jack Kent Cooke for a whopping $5.175 million dollars. In just five years, Mohs had transformed an organization that was hundreds of thousands of dollars in debt into the most valuable franchise in basketball. The dynastic Boston Celtics sold the same year for $2 million less than the Lakers. It would mark the only time that decade that the Lakers got the better of their hated rivals.

With the league and its franchises on more solid financial footing, owners were more prone to handing over control to basketball experts. Nobody was going bankrupt, so it made sense to divert resources and attention away from ticket sales and toward roster construction. As a general manager without major collegiate playing experience, Mohs suddenly found himself in the minority. He was eager to prove he could identify talent just as well, if not better, than his counterparts who played professionally.

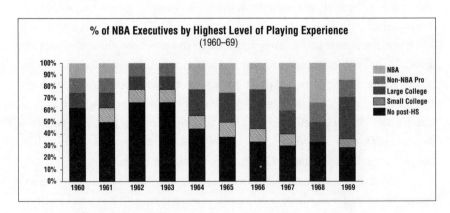

Unfortunately, around that time, Big Lou's lifetime of labor finally caught up to him. In 1967, Mohs died in his sleep from an apparent heart attack. He was 71 years old. Baylor and West, whose brilliance on the court carried Mohs' Lakers, were pallbearers.

In their six-plus years under Mohs, the Lakers never did catch that elusive championship trophy, but they still bagged their fair share of framers. They reeled in a franchise icon in West, built a vibrant fanbase, and sold the team for a record amount. When asked about Mohs in 2016, West told Frank Rajkowski of the *St. Cloud Times*, "Age deteriorates everything, and back then, people didn't write about the front office the way they do today. So a lot of people probably don't know about him. But the people he brought in know what he contributed to the success the Lakers had... He did all the little things that needed to be done to put a franchise on the court that was successful."

West wasn't alone in his belief that Mohs was crucial to the team's success. Chick Hearn, who became basketball's first Hall of Fame broadcaster only after Mohs put him on the Lakers mic in 1961, agreed. "That son of a gun came in with literally nothing to work with," Hearn said. "He worked out of a desk and did it all: tickets, money, everything else. He saved the franchise, no question about it. Literally threw his heart and soul into it."

Mohs' small-college background, while unique amongst his peers, played a significant role in his NBA career. His time at St. Thomas taught him how to fold his athletic passions into an already busy schedule. And, thanks to his connection to the college, he ran in the same social circles as Lakers leadership, who ultimately hired him.

When Mohs led the Lakers' successful relocation to L.A., he helped propel the NBA's maturation from a tenuous business into an growing one. Expansion begat new franchises, which then created opportunities for more small-college alums to join the NBA.

CHAPTER 2

COACHING SPECTRUM

How Bill Fitch carved a niche on his path from
small-college player and coach to NBA Hall of Famer

As Andrew Olson's obsession with basketball grew, so did he…only not as much as he would've hoped. From kindergarten to elementary school to high school, San Diego's biggest Phoenix Suns fan was almost always the shortest player on his team. If he wasn't the shortest, he was the thinnest. Topping out at 5'10" (but listed at 5'11"), he still had to contend with oversized jerseys and shorts, but at least they stayed up without clothespins.

The point guard's hard work in the driveway and hours spent watching Kevin Johnson, Jason Kidd, and Stephon Marbury paid off. As a freshman at Rancho Bernardo High, he played up on the varsity team. Some playmakers default to a pass-first, unselfish style because they struggle to score themselves. Olson wasn't one of them. He looked for his teammates because he believed that was the right way to play. If the defense sagged off of him too much or if he sensed a chance to swing the momentum and involve the crowd, he'd pull up and drain one from well beyond the three-point line. Local newspapers started taking interest in him, asking him for quotes after games. He followed the media relations rules an older teammate passed down: "Don't say 'I' and always say that you couldn't have done anything without your teammates."

Earlier in high school, form recruiting letters poured in from name-brand Division I programs: Stanford. UNC. Clemson. When coaches started calling his house, the names on the Caller ID didn't quite stack up to the letters' return addresses: Colorado College. Pomona College. University of Chicago. The lack of legitimate interest from the big-time D1 programs splashed cold water on the hoop dreams of the self-described "short, White, and unathletic" point guard. During spring and summer AAU tournaments, he kept waiting for that one life-changing conversation, that gum-chomping, steely-eyed coach in the school-branded polo shirt who would march up to him after a particularly impressive game, smile, and tell him, "We've been watching you, we like your game, and all of us at The University would love to have you join our program."

It was almost like he was always playing two games—the one against the other team on the court and the one against the preconceived notions of coaches and scouts. The on-the-court one he could manage. Solving pick-and-roll coverages and picking apart zone defenses was doable, even sometimes downright easy. The other one… well, that one weighed heavily. He couldn't figure out how to prove to all those polo-clad coaches that a sub-six-footer without eye-popping athleticism could hold his own with the very best. The short White gym rat was a stereotypical Division III player profile, so, naturally, he caught the eye of the few D3 coaches watching. The D1 coaches seemed to almost look through him. He decided to focus his attention on his senior season, hoping a successful campaign would revive his D1 hopes. Any campus visits and decisions on where to matriculate would wait until spring.

During his final high school campaign, some low-level D1 scholarship offers trickled in late from nearby state schools like UC Irvine and UC Riverside. If the offers felt last-minute, that's because they were. There was a very real possibility that the coaches would recruit over him the next year, making the prospect of playing time, even as an upperclassman, unlikely. "D1 or bust" seemed foolish when the reality of that D1 dream meant riding pine for a team that would likely never qualify for the NCAA Tournament.

When the desired scholarship offers didn't materialize, Olson started to consider opportunities across the Mississippi. Most Division III schools sit in the central and eastern time zones. Many are concentrated in the Mid-Atlantic and Northeast. Olson would've loved to use his basketball ability as a ticket to a world class education and to do so close to his beloved Southern California. Unfortunately, his options out West were limited. The college world had him pegged as a D3 talent, and as a D3 talent, he would most likely need to head east.

Before immortalization in the Basketball Hall of Fame, before the NBA jobs from the Great Lakes to the Atlantic to the Gulf to the Pacific, and before the stints at colleges across the Midwest, Bill Fitch was just an Iowa kid who wanted to stay home. The 6'1" All-State guard considered other college options—including an alleged offer from the University of Kansas— before ultimately deciding on Coe College, a small school located in a tidy campus on the east edge of Cedar Rapids, Iowa. Cedar Rapids was home to the sandlots where Fitch and his pals spent summers playing baseball. Home to the bakeries and butcher shops where the Czech immigrants sold kolaches and snapdogs. Home to his brothers, bonded not biologically, but through a love of sport.

Fitch was the only child of a Marine drill instructor who made scratch in civvie life as an auto mechanic. The family moved to Cedar Rapids in 1941, when Bill was nine. He quickly fell in with a group of neighborhood boys who played baseball, basketball, and football together. For Fitch and his friends, the college conversation wasn't always a question of where but a condition of if. There was no talk of ACT scores or magazine rankings or Division I, II, or III. None of those things existed in the late 1940s.

Nearby Coe offered Fitch an athletic scholarship and a chance to play both basketball and baseball. At Coe, he would team up with several Cedar Rapids chums, including his childhood neighbor and high school teammate, a 6'7" center named Jack Fulton. "The world was small for these guys," explained Fulton's son, Otis. "They were really small-town kids. They were very comfortable with their social network and the people that they knew there."

Fitch led a full life at Coe. He played basketball and baseball, ran for and won the student council presidency for the rising sophomore class, and even competed against five other students in the 1952 Ugliest Man Contest, where candidates took pictures while donning goofy hats and distorting their faces to raise money for March of Dimes. He lost that Ugliest Man

Contest, which, to paraphrase Rosie Perez in *White Men Can't Jump*, might be one of those losses where you really win.

By his senior year, Fitch, who as a coach would go on to be arguably the greatest turnaround artist in NBA history, got his first taste of transforming a frog into a prince. Coe won just three games in the season before Fitch's freshman year. By the time Fitch was a senior co-captain, Coe won the 1952 conference championship, its third in school history.

The ultimate goal for future D3 schools like Coe was a spot in the NAIA Tournament, which crowned the nation's top small-college team. Coe lost in the Iowa state qualifiers, one game away from making it into the 32-team field. For most of Fitch's classmates, that loss marked the end of their days in competitive basketball. For Fitch, it was only the beginning.

Once Fitch reached the pro ranks, he liked to share his coaching origin story with reporters. According to his version of events, he walked into the Coe College administrative office and told the career counselor sitting across from him, "I have half a mind I want to become a coach."

"Then that is the way you should go," the counselor replied, "because half a mind is what it takes."

The story is trademark Fitch. During practice, he'd channel his inner drill sergeant, barking at his players and accepting nothing less than perfection. Then he'd step off the court and schmooze with the press, winning them over with witty one-liners and charming anecdotes.

When he enrolled at Coe in 1950, Fitch didn't have a master plan to reach the NBA in 20 years. Hell, the NBA barely even existed in 1950. Fitch had his career ambitions narrowed down to four options: doctor, lawyer, minister, or coach. "He had the makings of a coach right from the start," Fitch's college coach, Tommy Thomsen told *The Bismarck Tribune*. "He was a coach on the floor and he knew the game. He was smart and he was always trying to figure out a better way to do something."

After graduation and a stint in the Army, Fitch followed Thomsen to Creighton University, where he worked as an assistant basketball coach and head baseball coach. His teams rarely lost. One of his pitchers, a big right-hander from Omaha, Nebraska, named Bob Gibson, went on to win two World Series rings with the St. Louis Cardinals. Gibson was the first future Hall of Famer Fitch had the pleasure of coaching. He would not be the last.

Following two years at Creighton, Fitch returned to Coe with his college sweetheart and their daughters in tow. At a small school like Coe, "head basketball coach" wasn't a job in and of itself. Fitch also coached freshman football and golf and taught physical education. He eventually became head baseball coach as well.

Fitch began penning his own mythology, the story of a man who could take whatever ragtag bunch the Good Lord dropped in his lap and drill them into tough, disciplined winners. Speaking after his first season, Fitch, according to the *Coe College Cosmos*, told the audience at a high school athletic banquet, "When we started the season I felt like a guy that had entered a donkey in the Kentucky Derby…But we finished the season with an 11–9 record. Not because we had good basketball players but because they had the desire."

The ugly side of the Fitch experience emerged in year three, a trope that would plague his coaching life. At halftime, he once lined up the starters and, one after another, slapped them across the face. On a team trip to California, he held a practice immediately following a loss. Players were anonymously quoted in the student paper, calling the late-night session "bush" and "rinky-dink." The general consensus was that Fitch emphasized winning too much for a small-college program, accusations to which Fitch, it's safe to presume, would have gladly pled guilty.

In the weeks leading up to his fourth and final season coaching at his alma mater, a desperate Fitch took to the student paper. Sandwiched between the student radio station's ad for disc jockeys and engineers and the student council's ad for an assistant treasurer, Fitch placed his own notice: "WANTED—seven-foot basketball players for Coach Bill Fitch. Any one *[sic]* 6'5" or over may apply."

There's a version of Fitch's story where he swallows his pride, softens around the edges, and spends his entire professional life coaching at Coe. Maybe he turns them into a small-college basketball or baseball power. Or maybe he just continues to chug along, overachieving each year, even if that occasionally means dragging subpar players to a .500 record. No national notoriety, no spot in the Basketball Hall of Fame, no NBA championship, but a beloved legacy and deep roots in his hometown. Instead, he left for the University of North Dakota, an undesirable job where the coach who preceded him quit after just one day.

North Dakota was the first of three increasingly prestigious college jobs Fitch took on his unfathomable eight-year ride from Coe to the NBA. In the three years immediately following Lou Mohs' death in 1967, the NBA ballooned from 10 teams to 17. Cleveland was home to one of the new franchises, thanks to a push by Nick Mileti, a proud Bowling Green alum and owner of the Cleveland Arena. Fitch, during the one season he spent at Bowling Green, executed his patented program turnaround before jumping to the University of Minnesota. All of that winning made an impression on Mileti. He told reporters that, of the 100 coaching candidates on his list, Fitch was the only one in all caps.

The great irony for coaches, many of whom are control freaks who try to dictate every little detail of a game, is that they never actually touch the ball. Their work is crucial, their decisions matter, but, ultimately, so much of what happens is literally out of their hands. Very few coaching success stories are inevitable. Even those who are more than capable of reaching great heights need a break here or a break there, especially if they start from a meager or unconventional point of origin. Spending a season coaching at Bowling Green, the alma mater of the future owner of the Cavaliers, was exactly the break Fitch needed.

"People act like coaching is a straight meritocracy, and the best 30 coaches in the world are coaching in the NBA," said former NBA head coach Stan Van Gundy, a Division III alum who also coached at both small and large colleges. "Then you've got Europe and the NCAA, and that's the next best coaches. C'mon, that's not what happens at all. There's guys at the high school level, Division III level, Division II level, every international level, who are every bit as good or better than people coaching in the NBA or the NCAA high-majors."

Throughout his college career, Fitch leapt from one job to the next, often leaving a stable environment for one very much in flux. He exhibited faith in his abilities and took comfort in the uncertainty. If the next step failed to work out, there would always be another job, maybe even a better one than what he left behind in the first place. Not only did the job-hopping do wonders for his resume, it also expanded his network, which created new opportunities, like the dual head coach/GM role with the Cavaliers.

The NBA was in its adolescent stage in 1970, growing quickly but still very much figuring out how to best navigate the world. A new franchise handing over their entire basketball operation to a young outsider like Fitch didn't raise any eyebrows, especially in an expansion market. Longtime Cavs announcer Joe Tait wrote about the Fitch hiring in his 2011 autobiography, *It's Been a Ball.* "Today, some in the media would ask: 'Why are you turning over the entire franchise to a guy with zero background in the NBA? You are going to let him draft the players, make trades, and coach?' But that question wasn't raised in 1970. The Cavs were new, and Cleveland was not familiar with the ways of the NBA."

So what, exactly, were the ways of the NBA? There's an old coaching adage, "It's not the X's and O's but the Jimmys and Joes." In other words, it's not the coach's play calling and strategy that wins games, it's the players on the floor. The motto can be repurposed as a spectrum of sorts. On one end sits X's & O's, representing the marks a coach uses when drawing up plays. On the other is Jimmys and Joes, the living, breathing manifestation of those coach's scribbles. Those firmly in the X's and O's camp believe a coach's pen is basically a magic wand, enabling them to perform miracles regardless of the talent their players might possess. The Jimmys and Joes acolytes contend that players, not schemes, win games. To them, a barking coach is just an expensive hot air machine in a cheap suit.

Professional basketball in the late 1940s and 1950s sat on the far-right side of the spectrum, firmly in the Jimmys and Joes camp. Pro ballplayers knew what they were doing. What was a coach going to teach *them?* The pages of NBA history books are crawling with quotes from players in the 1950s and 1960s belittling their coaching. When Lenny Wilkens started playing in the NBA in 1960, he expected to find a robust support system like the one he had at Providence College. Instead, he encountered terrain he'd have to navigate without a guide. "I didn't realize that the NBA of the 1950s and early 1960s had so little hands-on coaching," Wilkens wrote in his autobiography, *Unguarded.* "There was little individual instruction, little scouting, little of anything that would help a rookie adapt to the NBA."

So where *did* NBA franchises source these coaches, whom the players held in such high esteem? Most played the game professionally. Some were recently retired former stars. When management didn't want to wait for the best player to hang 'em up, or hoped to save on salary, they would assign a player/coach. The popular phrase describing a minimalist coach is that "they just roll the balls out." It's not hard to imagine that, in those days, some coaches just sat on the bleachers and told the players to get their own damn balls.

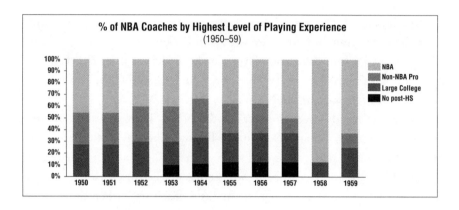

As the pool of retired NBA players grew, the share of coaches with NBA playing experience boomed. During each season in the 1960s, at least two out of every three teams were coached by a former NBA player.

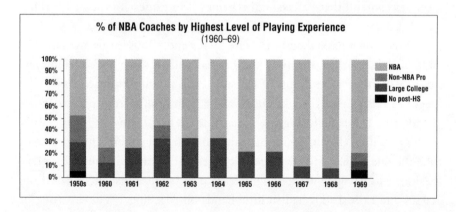

But by the back end of the '60s, teams hunting for an edge started turning to X's and O's mavens from the college ranks. "Dick Motta, Cotton Fitzsimmons, Bill Fitch, and John MacLeod—when they came into the NBA in the late '60s and early '70s—had an impact on the league," wrote former NBA executive and coach Jerry Reynolds in his autobiography *Reynolds Remembers.* "They were good college coaches who changed what coaching was at the pro level."

The league was sliding along the spectrum, away from "Jimmys and Joes," a trend that continued into the 1970s. Fitch, however, was unique. The leap from major university to the NBA had been done. But Fitch was the first NBA coach whose playing career topped out at the small-college level. He managed to cross that chasm thanks to his successful turnarounds at North Dakota and Bowling Green and his connection to Mileti.

FITCH STARTED IN Cleveland less than two months before the 1970 Expansion Draft, so he had no chance to scout the league in person. There were no databases from which to pull stats, no video libraries from which to cut clips, and no scouting services from which to solicit reports. There was, however, bubble gum.

Assistant coach Jim Lessig noticed that the basketball cards his son collected had each player's stats on the back. Fitch and company quickly realized that the packs of gum with those cards enclosed were going to be their best draft resource. The new Cavs coach sent Lessig out with $20 to buy up all of the bubble gum he could. They cobbled together the cards of nearly 100 of the league's 120 active players (and enough bubble gum to supply all of Greater Cleveland's Little League teams). With the cards laid out on the floor, stats side up, the Cavaliers started to build their roster.

The ragtag bunch then lived out the nightmare that was life as an expansion team. They hemorrhaged money, drew an average of 5,000 fans a game, and won no more than 32 games in each of their first four seasons. When they traded for a frustrated, past-his-prime Lenny Wilkens, the former All-Star guard viewed Fitch with a great deal of skepticism. "How would I react," Wilkens wrote, "to a coach whose playing experience was limited to little Coe College?"

Fitch won Wilkens over by inviting him to his house to watch film. "Fitch was a young coach who had enough confidence in himself to bring a veteran player into his home and pick his brain," Wilkens wrote. "He didn't get upset or insecure when I said something that wasn't exactly what he wanted to hear." As the season progressed, Fitch continued to lean on Wilkens, sitting next to him on team planes and collaborating with him on play design, scouting reports, and team dynamics.

Fitch was willing to admit that he did not have all the answers. His hours in the film room dissecting tape earned him the nickname "Captain Video." All that hard work paid dividends when the Cavaliers made the Eastern Conference Finals in just their sixth year of existence. He lasted three more seasons before players started bristling at his gruffness. His eye began to wander, and other franchises, impressed with the successful makeover in Cleveland, beckoned.

In 1979, the Boston Celtics named Fitch, 20 years removed from coaching Coe, their new head coach. Since stepping down from coaching Boston, general manager Red Auerbach had only hired former Celtics players. Fresh off of two consecutive losing seasons, he decided to look outside the organization's alumni network for the very first time. "Fitch is a disciplinarian," Auerbach said. "That's his biggest asset."

Fitch had the good fortune to arrive in Boston at the same time as a rookie forward named Larry Bird. The 1979 NCAA title game, pitting Bird's Indiana State club against Magic Johnson's Michigan State, was the most-watched NCAA basketball game in history. The general public could easily identify Bird, who had also graced the cover of *Sports Illustrated*. Bird, on the other hand, couldn't pick his new coach out of a lineup. Prior to his introductory press conference, a man approached Bird to discuss personnel. The lingering, nosey stranger even followed Bird up to the dais. "Larry," the stranger said, "I'm your coach, Bill Fitch."

With Bird and Fitch aboard, the Celtics improved from 29 to 61 wins. That offseason, they managed to acquire two future Hall of Famers in one transaction, trading the first and 13th picks in the 1980 NBA Draft to the Golden State Warriors for center Robert Parish and a pick used to select Kevin McHale. A 1990 NBA general managers poll called the trade "the most lopsided in history." At the time, however, the deal was no sure thing. Parish had been mostly mediocre in his first four seasons, but Fitch couldn't get the image of him gracefully running the floor during the 1975 Pan-Am Games out of his head. And McHale's lanky build scared off some NBA scouts, but not Fitch, who had heard rave reviews from his ties at the University of Minnesota. Fitch helped convince Auerbach to swing the deal, and McHale and Parish paired with Bird to revive the Celtics dynasty. In 1981, Fitch won his first and only NBA championship.

It took just four seasons for the Celtics players to turn on their rigid disciplinarian coach. "Our goal in 1983 wasn't to win a championship," said Celtics forward M.L. Carr. "It was to get rid of Fitch."

Carr's stated mission was a success, but not all of the players were happy to see Fitch go. Bird, who later described Fitch as "by far the best [coach] I've ever seen," told his teammates they would rue the day they ran him out of town. Rick Carlisle, who the Celtics drafted shortly after Fitch left Boston, said that his teammates remembered Fitch fondly. "The stories about Coach Fitch in Boston were reverential in that player after player would talk about the fact that he was tough and demanding, but that he, to a man, raised the level of virtually everybody he ever coached," Carlisle said. "They were very appreciative."

Throughout his nearly 30 years in the NBA, there was always at least one franchise looking for a drill sergeant to repair a dilapidated culture. "Captain Video" went on to coach Hakeem Olajuwon and the Houston Rockets to an NBA Finals appearance in 1986, and then had stops with the New Jersey Nets and Los Angeles Clippers before finally retiring in 1998. He coached more 2,000 games and lost 1,106 of them, second most in league history. Any old coach can lose a game or two. It takes a special one to lose more than a thousand.

"He took five different franchises from either expansion or the lottery to the playoffs, conference finals, Finals, or an NBA championship," said Carlisle, who became a successful NBA head coach after getting his start as Fitch's assistant in New Jersey. "He never failed to rebuild and lift a franchise out of the lottery."

Fitch's success occurred in spite of, not because of his small-college pedigree. But once he reached the NBA, he helped grow the profile of college strategists, a lane through which future D3 players would travel into the league. At the same time, another, larger avenue for small-college players opened. The American Basketball Association (ABA) came after the NBA's players and territory, forever altering the pro hoops landscape and creating a few front office jobs along the way.

CHAPTER 3

MERGERS AND EXPANSION

How the ABA opened the door for former small-college players who couldn't shake their love of the game and how NBA expansion propped that entryway ajar

For the first 17 years of Andrew Olson's life, Amherst College might as well have not existed. He never planned to travel along that long diagonal line from San Diego to the Western half of Massachusetts, a bishop in search of its endgame. Very few kids dream of playing basketball at Amherst College. No NBA public-address announcers bellow to a packed arena, "At guaaaard, from AMHERST COOOOLLLLLEGE." No casual eateries throw the Amherst College game on one of their many TVs on a Saturday afternoon. Dick Vitale doesn't rave about any "diaper dandies" from Amherst College. But for the small sliver of teenagers for whom collegiate basketball is even a possibility, reality often forces them to recalibrate. Olson was one of those kids.

A maxim floats around in the ether of Division III: "They don't recruit you; you recruit them." It's only partly true. For the top prospects, Division III recruiting resembles its Division I cousin, and coaches pursue players with all of the aggression and subtlety of a hopelessly romantic teen. However, the scope of a Division III recruiting operation can and often does lend itself to the merits of a solid inbound lead.

Amherst's wooing of Olson began at an AAU tournament the summer before his senior year. A Colorado College assistant coach, impressed by Olson's play, jotted down his name. Division III recruiting budgets are more gas money than plane tickets, so coaches sometimes swap lists with their cross-country counterparts. In this particular instance, the Colorado College coach's list ended up in the hands of an Amherst assistant. Seeing an email from the Amherst coaching staff didn't elicit too much excitement out of Olson, but his family, none of whom had a college degree, encouraged him to reconsider. They pushed him to think beyond his four years of collegiate basketball and consider what a degree from a place like Amherst, one of the top liberal arts colleges in the country, could mean for his future.

Olson made his official visit to Amherst on an unseasonably warm March weekend in 2004. He met with head coach David Hixon, who, with his piercing blue eyes, square jaw, and side-parted brown hair, didn't look anything like Olson's mental image of the man with the thick New England accent on the other side of those recruiting calls. Hixon introduced Olson to members of the basketball team who would graciously guide him through a day in the life of an Amherst student.

Given the sheer number of athletes on campus, as well as the academic rigor of the typical course load, the social life at Amherst ebbed and flowed with the calendar. But on that first sunny and warm spring weekend, seemingly the entire school would decide to cut loose. Olson's visit just so happened to coincide with that very weekend. He went to one class, then spent the rest of the day playing drinking games and Wiffle Ball with the guys on the team.

Olson had all sorts of preconceived notions about the nerds or snooty rich kids he might encounter, but the guys reminded him of the basketball players around whom he'd spent his entire life. They came from all over the country—New York, New England, Minnesota, even California. During a pick-up game the next day, the team exceeded Olson's expectations. The 6'5" and 6'6" forwards stepped out and stroked threes with ease. They pushed the ball, made the extra pass, and thought one step ahead.

Before heading home, Olson and his dad watched an Elite Eight game—it was March, after all—where undefeated St. Joseph's fell to Oklahoma State. Olson studied the play of Jameer Nelson and John Lucas III, two sub-six-foot point guards who controlled the game and picked their spots perfectly. It reinforced the bittersweetness of the weekend. One of the very best academic schools in the country wanted him to enroll. They even had a good basketball program, one just weeks removed from their first Division III Final Four. But saying yes would mean waving good-bye to ever playing in the real Final Four, to advancing in the only bracket that mattered to 99.99 percent of basketball fans. As difficult as it was to swallow leaving San Diego *and* opting out of his scholarship dreams, Olson knew Amherst was his best bet to further his basketball career and invest in his future. After returning home, he called Hixon and told him that he planned to accept one of the 1,600 spots in the Class of 2008.

From his very first high school game, Carl Scheer was hooked. "I've got no idea what marijuana is like, but I got a real high on basketball that night," he later said about his 39-point debut. His immediate success on the court expanded his mind, and inspired a lifetime of chasing competition's intoxicating buzz.

Scheer rode his basketball abilities to Colgate University, where he also pitched for the baseball team. The Colgate athletic department pushed Scheer to major in physical education, fearing a more rigorous course of study would distract from his pursuits on the court and field. Scheer, beginning to grasp that he would not be a pro athlete, knew he needed to position himself for life after college.

In 1956, he transferred to Middlebury College in Vermont, where he could still play intercollegiate sports while also freely pursuing his academic interests. After graduating with a history degree, Scheer attended law school and then settled in Greensboro, North Carolina, to raise a family. He loathed being a lawyer. For kicks, he announced basketball games at nearby Guilford College. Guilford, like Middlebury, would eventually join NCAA's Division III.

During Scheer's stint as announcer, Guilford had a forward named Bob Kauffman, who was a special small-college talent. The Seattle Supersonics drafted him third overall in the 1968 NBA Draft, right behind Elvin Hayes and Wes Unseld. Agents were basically unheard of at the time, so when Kauffman wanted assistance navigating his contract negotiations, he remembered that the play-by-play guy was a lawyer by trade. He asked Scheer for help.

NBA executives were not accustomed to an intelligent, well-spoken lawyer representing their players. "We had some negotiations and conversations about [Kauffman]," said Jerry Colangelo, who at the time was the general manager of the Phoenix Suns. "We were impressed with Carl and actually recommended him to the commissioner of the NBA for future reference."

Not long after, NBA commissioner Walter Kennedy heeded the advice of Colangelo and others. He hired the 32-year-old Scheer as an administrative assistant. Scheer was thrilled to leave his law practice and reenter the world of sports. One of his primary responsibilities was to apply his legal knowhow to merger conversations with the upstart American Basketball Association. The ABA tipped off in 1967 with a simple goal: force the NBA to merge or buy them out before the checks started bouncing higher than their signature red, white, and blue balls. If all went according to plan, the ABA owners would then possess an NBA franchise for a fraction of the NBA expansion price tag.

Between the upstart league and the expanding NBA, the number of professional basketball teams doubled. That meant double the coaches, double the owners, and double the general managers. ABA teams, which pooled their resources and offered lavish-seeming contracts to any NBA player who would listen, also looked to poach other talent as well, like, in the case of Scheer, budding executives. In 1970, the Carolina Cougars named Scheer president and general manager. "We wanted to get the best man in America for this job," said owner Jim Gardner, "and we did."

Scheer oversaw both the business and basketball sides of the franchise. A typical day involved shuttling around North Carolina selling advertisements and sponsorships, then returning to the office to discuss trade ideas with the coach. After a rocky beginning, he hired future Hall of Famer Larry Brown to his first pro coaching job. The team improved, and Scheer took home the 1973 Executive of the Year award.

When winning couldn't clot the Cougars' financial bleeding, the package deal of Scheer and Brown fled west for a fresh start with the ABA's struggling Denver Rockets. Scheer fronted a local effort to buy out the team's previous owners, then led a complete makeover of the franchise, changing the team colors, moving into a new arena, and adopting a new name—the Nuggets.

Prior to the 1975–76 season, the ABA had plenty of talented players, but there were barely enough solvent teams to field a league. Scheer spearheaded an effort to finally force the NBA into a merger. He convinced the other owners to pitch in so he could sign David Thompson, the top overall pick in the latest NBA draft. Then, while planning an extravagant ABA All-Star Game in Denver, Scheer and a few staffers concocted a unique halftime show—the first-ever dunk contest. Julius Erving bested Thompson thanks to an iconic dunk from the free throw line, which became the league's trademark moment. Those twin orbs—the tri-colored ball and the large afro atop Dr. J's head—represented everything wonderful, unique, and threatening about the upstart ABA.

Scheer's plan succeeded in bringing the NBA back to the negotiating table. "They had to merge," said Hubie Brown, who coached the ABA's Kentucky Colonels, "because [the ABA] had so many great young players. [The NBA was] losing them to the ABA."

With Scheer as one of the key negotiators, the ABA and NBA finally reached an agreement during the 1976 offseason. The four most stable ABA franchises—the Nuggets, New York Nets, San Antonio Spurs, and Indiana Pacers—each paid a $3.2 million entry fee to join the NBA as expansion teams. Many men contributed to pushing the agreement between leagues across the finish line. Few, if any, were as integral as Scheer. "Carl Scheer was, in my opinion, the single guy most responsible for elevating the ABA to a level where a merger was possible," Alan Rothenberg, vice president and general counsel for the Los Angeles Lakers, told the *Los Angeles Times*.

Fittingly, Scheer and the Nuggets were the first of the four ex-ABA teams to wire the NBA and officially join their ranks.

DESPITE HAVING JUST a few years of pro basketball experience on his resume, Scheer was actually one of the more qualified ABA team presidents. Harry Weltman, for instance, who played small-college ball at current Division III member Baldwin Wallace University, was a sports marketing and advertising professional when he took over as president of The Spirits of

St. Louis. Businessman Norm Sonju, another small-college hooper, actually passed up the opportunity to run an ABA team. "The league looked so tenuous," he said. It was still a crucial moment in his unlikely path to the NBA.

In 1977, just after the ABA merger, Sonju lay in bed with his wife, Carole, in their home just outside of Chicago. "Honey," Sonju said. "I'm looking at the possibility of going to run an NBA team."

Carole, though not much of a sports fan herself, was well aware of her husband's love of basketball. Norm played at Grinnell College and even tried to chase a pro career after his time with the Air National Guard. Every summer, he ran a basketball clinic at a Christian resort in the Adirondacks. He even served as a volunteer head coach at a local college for two seasons. His desire to work in pro basketball wasn't exactly a surprise, but the timing was curious. Norm was a successful businessman near the top of the corporate ladder, and Carole was pregnant with their third child. "Well," she replied, "which cities have NBA teams?"

Norm grabbed a pad and jotted down the 22 cities. Their conversation took place just a few months after the Blizzard of '77, a historic storm that dumped more than eight feet of snow on Buffalo, New York. Carole assessed the list, took the pen, and, remembering that blizzard, drew a line through "Buffalo."

There was just one problem: Norm wasn't looking at the possibility of going to run *any* NBA team. He had been offered a job to run one team in particular. The Braves. The *Buffalo* Braves.

Sonju, who had never worked in professional basketball, might've seemed like a peculiar choice to run an NBA team. But he possessed a gravitational pull that brought a handful of past, present, and future basketball icons into his orbit. The first future Hall of Famer Sonju befriended was Don Nelson. The pair met in the summer of 1957, when Sonju and a high school aged "Nellie" played in the same nightly pick-up games in Williams Bay, Wisconsin. They forged a friendship that stretched beyond that initial summer and well into Nelson's NBA career.

While Nelson was winning championships with the Boston Celtics, Sonju was busy rededicating himself to Christianity, earning his MBA at the University of Chicago, and marrying Carole (Nelson was a groomsman).

Along with Nelson, Sonju founded a faith-based summer basketball clinic, which eventually ran for 33 summers. Through the camp, Sonju started collecting influential basketball friends like a kid at the beach gathering sea glass. "All of my relationships were with a certain kind of person who was very interested in the Christian causes that I was involved in," said Sonju.

Like many of the small-college basketball players who reached the NBA, Sonju did so thanks to his connections. None was more important than his friendship with Jerry Colangelo. "He's a very strong Christian in terms of his faith," said Colangelo, a dear friend of Sonju's. "That was an entree for him with certain individuals who were of a like mind, including myself."

Sonju and Colangelo first met thanks to an introduction by Colangelo's wife, Joan, who Sonju had known since high school. As a teenager, Joan had graciously welcomed Sonju and his friend into a Christian youth group and, according to Sonju, made them feel "like a million bucks." Sonju and Joan reconnected after a Chicago Bulls preseason game against the Celtics, while Sonju was waiting in the gym to greet Nelson. Joan saw Sonju, said hello, and then introduced him to her husband, a young Bulls executive. Not long after, at a Fellowship of Christian Athletes luncheon in Chicago, Sonju saw Colangelo again. From there, the friendship between the Colangelos and the Sonjus grew. When John Y. Brown, the owner of the ABA's Kentucky Colonels, asked Colangelo to recommend someone to run the team, Colangelo thought of Sonju, who loved basketball and was a successful vice president at a management services company.

Even though Sonju declined the offer, it still put him firmly on Brown's radar. When the former Colonels owner then bought a controlling stake of the Braves, he made a second overture toward Sonju, offering him a job as president of the team. Sonju took days to reply, frozen in his tracks by his wife's frigid response. Brown, starting to get nervous that Sonju would spurn him again, flew out to Chicago to make his pitch in person. Brown invited Carole into the kitchen for a private chat. When they re-emerged into the living room, Carole addressed her husband. "Honey," she said, "I think we ought to go to Buffalo."

Carole only had to endure one Buffalo winter before the cash-strapped Braves moved to San Diego. Sonju helped the team set up shop in their new city (even running a "name the team" contest that landed on "Clippers") before he became a free agent. Rather than returning to corporate America, Sonju decided to give the NBA another shot. He was not one to concede easily.

Decades earlier, during his first semester at Grinnell, Sonju realized that his Chicago public school education had not adequately prepared him for a rigorous liberal arts curriculum. "I don't think I read a book in my years of high school," he said. He worked hard to adequately complete his assignments, and the teaching faculty helped him until he was up to speed. "If I didn't go to a small college with small classes where I could get help," he said, "it might've been tough."

He eventually settled in academically, which gave him enough comfort and confidence to thrive socially. He was president of his house and a multisport athlete, competing in basketball and track. Sonju, like many of the small-college men who reached the NBA, didn't take long to establish himself as a leader. "People who have an impact have something going for themselves regardless of where they come from," said Colangelo in reference to his pal, Sonju. "There are doers, and there are not."

Sonju was a doer. Many in the league respected him, understanding the less-than-stellar results in Buffalo were largely out of his control. "In league operations, he was thought very highly of," Colangelo said. "All the virtues he had that made him successful in his business career, he just put into the new position he had."

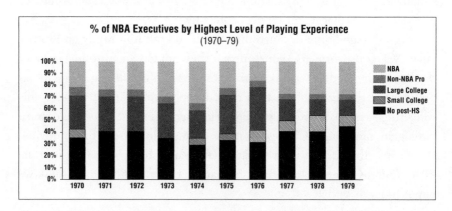

Sonju joined the NBA at a time when more teams were hiring basketball men as lead executives. Throughout the 1970s, a majority of top basketball decision makers had played at least at a major college, if not in the pros. It created an environment in which someone like Sonju or Scheer, businessmen first and basketball men second, could thrive. "Candidly, it was an edge," Sonju said. "I came with an MBA. I came knowing how to run a business, how to run a company, how to look at financial statements, how to understand things. I knew how to work with people and with a business plan to make it a reality."

One might get the impression that these business-types might not have lived and died with their team's performance as much as a GM who once played in the league. Scheer was definitive proof that that was not the case.

When the Nuggets traveled, his family forbade him from listening to games on the radio. They made him too emotional. Banished outside, Scheer would pace around his swimming pool, waiting for his wife to yell out the score every few minutes. If the Nuggets were losing, he would kick a lounge chair and then resume his pacing. At home games, he stood in the corner by the visiting team's tunnel. He leaned so hard on the arena's orange banisters that they started dying his shirts. Nuggets employees eventually learned to put towels over the railings. He'd yell and gesticulate at every missed opportunity and unfavorable whistle. If a soda sat on the ground within his pacing radius, it was a good bet that by game's end he'd kick it. After a loss, Scheer's family would leave a tub of rocky road and a spoon out waiting for him on the kitchen table. Those cartons left the freezer never to return; Scheer always ate the whole gallon, sometimes so quickly he'd start to shiver.

Scheer's competitive spirit extended to the boardroom, where he fought like mad to convince the NBA's old heads to adopt two of the ABA's most successful gimmicks—the three-point line and the dunk contest. Red Auerbach led the fight against the three-pointer. During a heated debate, he told Scheer, "Next time, you guys will come to me and want to give one point for a layup." The vote passed by a slim margin, and the three-pointer was added in the 1979–1980 season, forever changing the game.

The dunk contest came four seasons later. With the success of the 1976 ABA All-Star Game still fresh in Scheer's memory, he pitched a similar format to NBA executives just two months before Denver hosted the 1984 All-Star Game. Several league power brokers, including future commissioner David Stern, liked the idea so much that they found enough corporate underwriting to establish an entire second night of events. All-Star Saturday featured a dunk contest and an Old-Timers' Game. The demand for hotel rooms doubled, and the event was an instant success.

While Scheer was busy pitching new ideas and kicking soda cans in Denver, the cooler-headed Sonju moved to Texas to kickstart an NBA franchise with hundreds of thousands of dollars out of his own pocket. While helping the Buffalo Braves plan for relocation, Sonju studied the Dallas/Fort Worth area with great interest. He felt confident that, under the right guidance, a franchise would flourish there.

On his hunt for financial backing, more than 125 investors turned him down. Don Carter, a man who made his fortune co-running his mother's multi-level marketing company and wore a cowboy hat so frequently it might as well have been sewn to his scalp, finally agreed to back the venture. The NBA's expansion committee—led by Sonju's buddy, Colangelo—voted to admit Dallas as the league's 23rd franchise. Sonju named the new team the Mavericks. Their logo, fittingly, was the letter "M" wearing a giant Stetson.

Sonju instilled the Mavericks with organizational discipline. Not a single detail was left to chance. He requested shorter broom handles for the maintenance staff to ensure they never accidentally clipped a fan while sweeping up a mess. He walked the stadium at halftime to monitor the pace at which lines moved. The lettering on the uniforms, the upkeep of the floor, the number of lights in the scoreboard—he made sure all of it was just so.

Sonju even had the stadium staff practice "shot clock malfunction drills" just in case the new clocks mounted on top of the backboards failed. "Sure enough," said Keith Grant, the team's equipment manager, "the first month of the season, it happened. And we got them on the floor in place with minimal time wasted so they could play the game."

Sonju managed to walk the tightrope between monitoring all of the details and trusting his basketball staff to make decisions. His job was to lead, to provide quality control, and to close all sales and negotiations. Unlike many other basketball operations leaders, especially the former NBA players, Sonju did not travel the country to scout prospects. He left many final decisions on personnel matters up to Rick Sund, his trusted "basketball man."

Under Sonju's steady guidance, the Mavericks became the model expansion franchise. For the first seven years of their existence, they won at least as many games as the prior season. In 1988, they reached the Western

Conference Finals with a roster almost entirely composed of players the team had drafted and developed. Even when the Mavericks were inexperienced and overmatched, Sonju somehow maintained profitability. By keeping a careful eye on costs, they cash flowed positive in an era when nearly half of NBA teams were losing money. The team finished in the black during each of Sonju's 16 seasons in Dallas. "We did everything we could to run it like a business," Sonju said.

In addition to his success on the business side, and despite his hands-off approach to scouting, Sonju oversaw an innovative basketball operation. He and Sund employed the very first "pick protection" in league history in 1984. To help get the Pacers comfortable with trading away their first-rounder, Dallas wrote in language that the pick would not convey if it landed in the top seven. Indiana agreed to the deal, and a mechanism that is now applied to most traded draft picks was born.

Sonju and Sund were also indirectly responsible for the so-called "Stepien Rule"—named after Ted Stepien, the Cleveland Cavaliers owner whose win-now mandate pushed the team to trade four first rounders to Dallas in 1980 and 1981. The rule, which prevents NBA teams from trading first-round picks in consecutive seasons, is an appropriate legacy for Stepien, who had a lot of bold and terrible ideas as a sports executive. As a promotional stunt, he once threw softballs from the top of a 52-story building, denting a car and breaking a bystander's wrist. In the early 1980s, keen on vertical integration, he decided to start his very own regional sports network called The Sports Exchange. He bought all the necessary equipment and even hired some talent before realizing he needed someone with cable experience to actually run the business. That particular gaffe was the one that brought Harry Weltman, the small-college alum who briefly ran the ABA's Spirits of St. Louis, back to pro basketball.

Weltman agreed to help Stepien with his cable network under the condition that he would also run the team's basketball operation. His friends thought he was crazy to basically run into a burning kitchen and start casually chopping onions. Weltman figured partnering with Stepien was worth the risk. Weltman served as the Cavs' (a "punchy and strong" nickname Weltman helped popularize) lead basketball executive from 1982 until his firing in 1986. He got one more shot in the NBA, a subpar three-year stint with the woebegone Nets. When he resigned, he told *The New*

York Times, "I would now prefer doing something else somewhere else." He never worked in the NBA again.

Scheer, who was relieved of his duties in Denver in 1984, also felt the pain of working with a subpar owner. He spent a few seasons in the mid-1980s as general manager of the newly relocated Los Angeles Clippers and their infamous owner, Donald Sterling. "Dealing with Donald was impossible," Scheer said. "He could not make up his mind. If he took an elevator down, he'd ask the operator what he thought and by the time he reached the lobby he'd changed his mind."

In 1986, frustrated with the lack of progress and unwilling to look in the mirror, Sterling replaced Scheer with Elgin Baylor, L.A.'s first basketball superstar. The move was a sign of the times. In the 1980s, former players took up nearly a third of the league's GM posts.

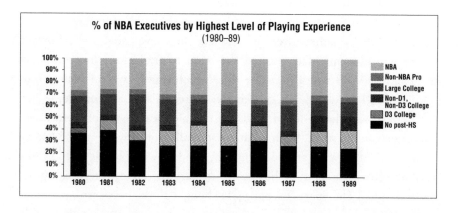

When the NBA announced four new expansion teams in 1987, the league's doors reopened for Scheer. The owners behind the Charlotte Hornets' bid needed help navigating the unfamiliar world of the NBA. In their search for an experienced lead executive, primary owner George Shinn heeded the advice of many, including Stern, Colangelo, and Sonju. "[Shinn] knew nothing about basketball, per se," said Sonju, who was on the expansion committee. "I felt he had to have an experienced guy, and Carl was so respected."

Scheer joined the Charlotte franchise as general manager in 1987. By leaning into their unique teal uniforms and fan-friendly mascot, Scheer and team, according to *The New York Times*, executed "careful marketing" and "visible team involvement in the community" to build their base. They then patiently acquired talent through the draft. More than 300 straight sellouts later, the Hornets were a new, shining example of expansion success, one that helped Charlotte eventually attract NFL and NHL franchises. "A lot of the things that were done right, I got credit for them," Shinn later told *The Observer*. "But I'll admit most of them weren't my idea…Once I got the team, it was all Carl."

Scheer eventually lost his life to Alzheimer's complications, a cruel end for a man who possessed such a sharp mind. The nurses who cared for Scheer knew they could keep him happy by pulling old NBA games up on YouTube. At the funeral, his son, Bob, paid homage to his dad's tendency to fudge attendance totals. During the third quarter of Nuggets games, an employee would bring Scheer a piece of paper with the actual attendance. He would cross out that number and write the total he wanted announced. "When my dad passed away," Bob told the full room of mourners, "we really had no idea how many people would show up. My mom said about 50. They told me this room sat about 600. My dad would want to announce an attendance of 17,432."

Many NBA luminaries attended Scheer's funeral or sent the family messages. It was a testament to a remarkable basketball life, one that stretched back to a small-college gym. His time at Middlebury, like Sonju's at Grinnell, fanned the flames of love they had for the game. It provided them with an education that would set them up for the challenges that lie ahead. It taught them that, even though others might be better, there was still a place for them to compete and to win. Scheer captured the spirit well when he told Jim Fair of the *Spartanburg Herald Journal*, "I have always been an overachiever and have always had to fight insurmountable odds. I have a great thirst to be successful and I have a great inner strength and self-discipline. It's because I haven't been blessed with great talent."

While Scheer and Sonju provided a successful alternative to the former pro players who led most front offices in the 1980s and '90s, they did not help create any sort of small-college network. They may have thought fondly of their college experiences, but those warm feelings never inspired them to seek out others with similar backgrounds. In fact, Sonju had no idea that Scheer, his friend and colleague, had also played basketball at a small college.

"I don't remember ever thinking about what school he went to," Sonju said. "It's just one of those things that never occurred to us."

The ABA was a wormhole, a temporary rip in pro basketball spacetime. For those few years, there existed a path for these small-college grads from their normal, workaday lives into the basketball career of their dreams. When the NBA absorbed the ABA, the wormhole began to seal up, and the improbable direct route from outsider to the top of an NBA front office closed for good. Expansion was oxygen. Each new or relocated franchise breathed life into these outsiders' basketball careers, keeping them wanted and relevant. Nothing on a resume was as powerful as previous NBA experience. "If they had a position [in the league]," said Colangelo, "they had an opportunity to establish themselves in their jobs."

Colangelo's words rang true—the NBA careers of Sonju, Scheer, and Weltman all stretched into the 1990s, an unexpected continuation of Lou Mohs' legacy in the front office. Meanwhile, a contingent of coaches from New Jersey was doing their best to make sure Bill Fitch wasn't the only former small-college player patrolling the league's sidelines.

CHAPTER 4

Jersey Guys

*How two former small-college players found
a coaching community that sharpened their
teaching skills and lifted them into the NBA*

The year 2004 was a unique time—an incoming college freshman
could look up their roommate via Google or Yahoo, but couldn't
friend them on Facebook, which had yet to expand beyond a handful
of colleges and universities. When Andrew Olson typed in the name
of the stranger who would soon sleep no more than a yard away from
him, he found an article in a local Ohio paper. Apparently, his future
roommate had created some sort of rocket. *Oh great,* Olson thought to
himself, *my roommate is literally a rocket scientist.*

On Freshman Move-In Day, these two completely different people
from completely different worlds that the universe paired together
unpacked and crammed their belongings into a tiny dorm room. Like
the majority of Amherst students, they lived on a coed floor. Their
room sat across the hall from the women's restroom. A steady stream of
18-year-old girls wearing nothing but a towel would soon parade daily
right across from his usually open door. Olson's mom wondered why
she approved—nay, encouraged!—her son to travel across the country
for *this.*

Over the first few days on campus, it seemed as though most of
the new classmates he met played a sport. Amherst offered more than
two dozen varsity sports. It took more than one-third of the student
population to fill the rosters. Differences in personalities, priorities, and

interests could drive a wedge between the athletes and the non-athletes. But there wasn't the luxury of a large enough student body for one camp to completely isolate themselves from the other.

On his recruiting trip, some of his future teammates told him that the hardest part about Amherst was getting in. Once he was in, they said, the schoolwork would be doable. They assured him that enough of the people were cool and normal, whatever that meant. Initially, he did not feel that was the case. Of course, there were other students like him—first-generation college students whose idea of long-term plans consisted of what time they would head to the dining hall for dinner. But the vast majority brimmed with an intimidating confidence. They moved about the campus as if the spaces they inhabited were built specifically for them.

Fortunately, Andrew and the other freshmen on the basketball team had common interests and personalities. There were five of them—two from New Jersey, one from upstate New York, one from Michigan, and Olson from San Diego. Of the five rookies, only Olson seemed destined for an immediate spot in the rotation. Amherst drew talented kids from all over the country, so players generally paid their dues. There were too many seasoned upperclassmen for anyone to expect to waltz on to campus and into meaningful minutes.

Afternoons in the fall alternated between pick-up games and weight training. A strength coach sometimes guided the lifts, but the pick-up games were, per NCAA regulations, player led. Amherst's campus only had two indoor basketball courts. The afternoon runs, referred to as "captain's practices," were mostly held in the upper auxiliary gym— women's volleyball was in season and therefore had dibs on the main gym. The team had to skip a captain's practice here or there to cede the space to the fencing or ultimate frisbee clubs.

Across the country and across divisions, NCAA winter sports can first practice on October 15. Many Division I schools have built a Midnight Madness tradition, where fans pack the gym and players take the court when the clock strikes 12:00 AM, the very first possible moment of sanctioned practice time. To the New England Small College Athletic Conference—a conglomerate of high-academic liberal arts colleges stretching from Connecticut to Maine—October 15 was unreasonable. The serious students at their serious institutions could not be expected to juggle their rigorous academic coursework for two superfluous weeks of in-season activity. So NESCAC winter sports officially started no earlier than November 1. While the rest of campus celebrated Halloween, the winter athletes ignored the noise and turned in early before their first day of practice.

It didn't take long for Olson to understand that David Hixon's practices were as precise as the side part in the coach's straight brown hair. Each session had the same familiar beats—the pre–practice chat at halfcourt, the multiple variations of three-man weave to warm up, the dedicated shooting time, the scrimmage. During the season's first week, Hixon, an Amherst College graduate, ran the team through the four-out offense and the principles of their switching man-to-man defense with a command rivaling any of Olson's professors. Hixon had been teaching offense and defense at his alma mater for more than 30 years. When he and his buddies sat around discussing their ambitious plans for the future, he told the group that he hoped to coach the Amherst College men's basketball team. Less than five years after graduating, his dream came true.

Hixon coached his first team to the NCAA Division III Tournament in 1994, the first year the NESCAC allowed their members to participate in national tournaments. Five NCAA appearances later, Amherst advanced to the national semifinals for the first time in 2003. It marked the coach's transformation of his alma mater into a national small-college powerhouse. Hixon's success led to other coaching offers—bigger and better jobs. Outsiders and casual acquaintances wondered why he kept turning down what they saw as no-brainer opportunities. Whenever anyone questioned his decision to stay at Amherst, Hixon would think, *If ya have to ask, ya just don't get it.*

Three games into Olson's freshman season, Amherst's senior starting point guard tore his Achilles, thrusting Olson into the otherwise-veteran starting lineup. Opportunities don't always come at the perfect time or in the perfect way. Maybe Olson would've been more comfortable taking the reins after having a chance to better learn the offense. Then again, maybe Hixon would've preferred to get his dream job at Amherst when he was a little older and a little wiser.

Like any incredibly successful career, Hixon's time at Amherst was full of good fortune. It only took a few games with Olson in the starting lineup for Hixon to realize he was experiencing another major stroke of luck, perhaps the most fortunate in his career. The California kid who responded to one of his assistant's emails and happened to visit on an unseasonably warm March weekend was special. Special enough to lift his program to new heights.

It might surprise NBA fans that broadcaster and former head coach Mike Fratello was once a fierce athlete. At Hackensack High in New Jersey, he captained the football, basketball, and baseball teams. His short stature (5'7" and around 150 pounds) and cherubic face made for deceptive packaging—he was the toughest kid in the school. "Pound for pound, he was the finest athlete I ever coached," Hackensack football coach Tom DellaTorre told *The Atlanta Constitution*. "He had such a big heart. And he always wanted to play the roughest position on the team."

Hubie Brown, who, before his time in the ABA and NBA, coached multiple high school sports in Jersey, always left his games against Hackensack impressed with Fratello. "Here is this kid who is a leader in all three sports," Brown said. "That doesn't happen, okay? Michael had the total picture, even at that time."

From a young age, Fratello knew he would go into coaching. He was a natural leader, even outside of sports. When Hackensack High students took over City Hall on "Youth Day," Fratello played the role of mayor at the mock council meeting.

He attended Montclair State, a small public university in New Jersey that specialized in education. "Montclair State made so much sense at the time," Fratello later told the school's magazine, "because it had a great physical education program, and my mom and dad could see my games. It was the perfect place."

Montclair State provided Fratello the opportunity to prepare for a coaching career both in the classroom and on the court or field. He attempted to play three sports, but his busy schedule left little time for schoolwork. At the end of his freshman year, he was at risk of academic ineligibility. To keep his grades up, he would need to drop his weakest sport—basketball.

The end of his competitive playing career did nothing to dampen Fratello's enthusiasm for the sport. Between summer school courses, he drove down to Duke, up to Niagara, or anywhere else where they were willing to pay him to coach basketball. "I was a basketball fanatic the whole time," he said.

To make extra cash, Fratello also worked as a lifeguard at a pool run by Hubie Brown. Brown also invited Fratello to play in the summer basketball league he oversaw. During a game, Fratello tore some cartilage in his knee and couldn't walk. Brown drove him home and physically carried him into the house. It was the beginning of a lifelong and life-changing friendship.

Fratello's eventual rise to the NBA began in the Poconos, at a summer basketball camp called Five-Star. By the early 1980s, Five-Star was the premiere summer destination for top preps players. But in the mid-1960s, high costs and low enrollment had the camp trapped in a corner. By signing up dozens of Jersey high school kids, Brown single-handedly saved it from shuttering. To camp founder Howard "Garf" Garfinkel, Brown was now a made man.

The camp's director, Army coach Bobby Knight, instilled West Point structure and a culture of education. In lieu of playing games all day, campers spent the morning rotating between 13 stations. Each had a dedicated coach who taught shooting, passing, ball handling, or defense. After lunch, the campers sat around the three-point arc and listened to a coach's lecture while digesting their food. For coaches, these lectures became the equivalent of delivering a speech at the Democratic or Republican National Convention. It was their chance to announce themselves as one of the up-and-coming stars in their field. Some even used the talks to catapult themselves out of the high school ranks. "I became an assistant at William and Mary for one year," Brown said, "because the head coach at that time saw me do a lecture at the Five-Star Basketball Camp."

Five-Star helped players announce their presence, too. Multiple campers from the first summer went on to have successful college careers and were later drafted into the NBA. As Five-Star's reputation grew, more and more of the nation's best high schoolers flocked to the Poconos each summer. For players, the camp provided the opportunity to compete against elite talent. For coaches, it was a basketball salon, where ideas were shared and connections made.

Garf created a flywheel, a one-stop shop for college coaches to locate not only their next recruit, but also their next assistant coach. College coaches quickly realized that having an assistant at Five-Star was a slick way to get close to the most talented prepsters. So, with an added nudge from Garf, many college head coaches hired Garf's counselors as assistants. "Garf is the one that opened the door," said Ron Rothstein, who worked at Five-Star on his way to becoming an NBA head coach, "and I think the coaches, No. 1 being Hubie, kicked that door wide open. Everybody followed on through."

One of those coaches who marched through the open door was a young high school assistant coach named Mike Fratello. Even though Garf had a rule against hiring high school assistants, Brown lobbied on Fratello's behalf. Garf refused. Hubie kept insisting, and Garf finally relented. Immediately, Fratello impressed his fellow coaches. "Michael could teach right out of college," Brown said. "He was the total package as a young kid."

Garf tasked Fratello with running the coaches' 6:30 AM exercise program before breakfast. Then, after a day of stations and games and lectures, the coaches all convened at the restaurant down at the bottom of the hill for dinner and drinks. "That's where you would get your doctorate degree," Brown said.

From the time they arrived until the bar closed at 2:00 AM, conversation zinged. The coaches argued about everything from specific teaching techniques to the portability of college out-of-bounds plays to the high school level. Tables were their whiteboard, pepper shakers and glasses their X's and O's. "Being the competitive people that we were, we were determined to show the other guys we were smarter than them," said Rothstein. "We picked up so much knowledge of the game because everybody was willing to share or everybody was willing to challenge the next guy. There were great arguments and back and forth and camaraderie. It was special."

The arguments didn't stop at Five-Star. In the late 1960s, a crew of Bergen County high school head and assistant coaches regularly met at a burger joint after games to sip beers and discuss the evening's results. Fratello was awestruck at the knowledge surrounding him. His mother always told him, "Be a good listener." So he shut his mouth and opened his ears. The other coaches spent the night drawing up plays and press breakers on napkins and placemats. When they got up to leave, Fratello would gather the papers up and take them home. Then, he'd transcribe them and store them in a three-ring notebook, which he still has to this day.

One night, Long Beach State coach Jerry Tarkanian was in town to recruit Les Cason, the top player in Jersey. Cason played at East Rutherford High for a passionate young coach named Dick Vitale. A group of the self-dubbed "Jersey Guys" accompanied Tarkanian to dinner, where he peppered the eager young coaches with questions. Later in the evening, they decided moving around sugar packets and saltshakers in a cramped restaurant was insufficient. They took the debate to the alley outside, replacing the saltshakers with garbage cans. The coaches were so caught up, they didn't even notice the police had arrived. The cops suggested the coaches call it a night. "Maybe we got a little too loud, a little too excited, and the neighbors didn't like it," Fratello said. "They wanted to sleep. We wanted to teach pick-and-roll defense."

One of the Jersey Guys X'ing and O'ing that night was Richie Adubato. In many ways Adubato's background mirrored Fratello's—he grew up in Jersey and played multiple sports at a small, public in-state college that specialized in education. Adubato's alma mater—Paterson State College—was another trade school for coaches. In the mid-1960s, more than a dozen young Paterson grads went on to run varsity or JV basketball teams in New Jersey. The 5'11" Adubato, known as "Hercules" to his teammates, was a consistent outside shooter on the hardwood and an ace baseball pitcher. After an unsuccessful tryout with the Philadelphia Phillies ended his pro dreams, he taught and coached multiple sports, supplementing his income by calling bingo and bartending. In 1972, Adubato took over the head coaching job at Upsala College, a now-defunct liberal arts college in New Jersey, where he experienced first-hand a major overhaul in college athletics.

THE NATIONAL COLLEGIATE Athletic Association plays a seemingly contradictory role. It is both promoter and police. The rules it enforces help keep the playing field level, but sometimes doling out punishments can be bad for business. The NCAA originally built its rules and regulations to govern all of its nearly-700 member schools—from the biggest public universities to the smallest private colleges. The cash cows—the name brand football and basketball programs—contributed a majority of the revenue to the NCAA's tournaments and television contracts, yet made up a minority of the voting members.

At the NCAA's 1972 annual convention, leadership addressed the two issues most salient to its largest member schools: rising costs and rampant cheating. Recruiting was evolving from a mostly regional pursuit into a more national one. With more schools in pursuit of talent, the courtship process grew more competitive. Not all schools, especially those that helped fatten those national television deals, felt it necessary to abide by every rule. The 1972 convention focused primarily on building more specific and more enforceable recruiting guardrails.

The debate around, say, off-campus entertainment for recruits, didn't really apply to most of the small schools. It was not the first time an item raised at these conventions was crucial to one subset of NCAA members and almost irrelevant to another. The role of athletics at big and small schools was diverging exponentially. It made no sense to govern one—with its recruiting wars and packed stadiums—with the same rules as the other, where athletics were just another part of extracurricular student life. As a result, another conversation at that 1972 convention built momentum and quickly moved to the meeting agenda's foreground—the reorganization of the NCAA.

"We see the NCAA as an umbrella over all college programs," said Stanley Marshall, a small-college athletic director and chairman of the NCAA's college committee. "But under the umbrella, there would be a university division and a college division, the latter in all likelihood with two subdivisions and each division with its own bylaws."

The smaller schools, which wanted influence over a more bespoke set of rules and regulations, were overwhelmingly in favor. So too were the larger schools, those that appeared on national television and drew big crowds to tournament championships. It would be easier to grow their business and police cheating without constantly having to worry about little brother. "Why should Michigan with its 101,000-seat stadium dictate policies to MIT, which to my knowledge has no seating capacity?" asked Wayne Duke, commissioner of the Big Ten. "And I don't think it's right that MIT should dictate policies to Michigan."

In August of 1973, the NCAA held its first ever special convention to vote on the proposal. It passed nearly unanimously, with 366 "ayes" to only 13 "nays." The Michigans of the world—all large universities with major football programs—would fall under Division I. Then the smaller schools, which had previously fallen under the catch-all "College Division," would be split into two groups: Division II and Division III. Each division would decide their own rules and crown their own champions. Member institutions would still settle many matters collectively, but they were now free to draft their own agendas regarding recruitment and scholarships. Division III's largest differentiator, one that remains in place to this day, was the complete banishment of athletic scholarships.

UNDER RICHIE ADUBATO, Upsala College transformed into one of the better basketball teams in the nascent Division III. Cross-divisional games were allowed, so Adubato would schedule schools like Georgetown and Army to sharpen his team for the postseason. When Upsala first qualified for the 30-team Division III Tournament field in 1978, Adubato was well on his way to attracting the attention of a Division I school like Fordham or Seton Hall. At least that was the next step he had mapped out. Instead, he went straight to the NBA.

Both Mike Fratello and Adubato reached the NBA in 1978, a journey made possible by the relationships forged over late-night beers and saltshaker pick-and-rolls. Hubie Brown was the first of the Five-Star coaches to make it to the pros. Riding the attention he received from those camp lectures, as well as some key connections, Brown landed a job with the Milwaukee Bucks in 1972. As the lone coaching staffer, he served as both lead assistant coach and advance scout. He would help with practice, catch a flight to an NBA game, work on his scouting report on the red-eye home, and then present it to the team the next morning.

Brown's first pro head coaching role was in the ABA, the gift to outsiders that kept on giving. He led the Kentucky Colonels to the 1975 league championship, further cementing himself as an up-and-coming coach to watch. When the Colonels folded in 1976, the NBA's Atlanta Hawks swooped in and hired Brown. The Hawks' new owner, Ted Turner, also owned baseball's Atlanta Braves and a fledgling television network called

TBS. Turner's time and money were spread thin, so Brown had to make lemonade out of a not-so-sweet and very cheap roster of players. "Money was very important to [Turner]," Fratello said, "and how much he could spend on the teams was important to him because he was trying to get TBS off the ground."

Brown managed to guide the Hawks to the playoffs in just his second season. When a spot on his bench opened up that offseason, he had unilateral control over the hiring process—standard practice at the time. He offered the job to Fratello without interviewing or considering anyone else. "I didn't want anyone else," Brown said. "I wanted a guy that could teach."

Every summer at Five-Star, Brown witnessed Fratello coach the nation's top high school talent, some of whom would later play in the NBA. It gave Brown confidence that Fratello could effectively teach the very best. In Atlanta, Brown oversaw the final seminar in Fratello's coaching education, a course that would prepare the pupil to run an NBA team of his own.

Fratello spent his first day of Hawks training camp mostly observing, jotting down notes on index cards. At the end of practice, while Brown, Fratello, and the team's third assistant, Frank Layden, dried off in the coach's locker room, Brown nonchalantly said, "Oh, I just want to tell you, I'm not going to be here tomorrow for practice."

Once he hit the NBA, not only did Brown remain an active guest lecturer at basketball camps, but he also became an in-demand motivational speaker for corporate crowds. He planned to fulfill a longstanding speaking obligation that conflicted with the second day of training camp. Brown turned to face Fratello. "You run practice tomorrow."

Fratello couldn't believe it. His mentor, the man he had known since high school, was marching him directly in front of the firing squad. "Hubie, what do I do?" he asked, hoping for an itinerary, something, anything to help him get through the day.

"I saw you writing down all those notes in practice," Brown said. "Do the same thing tomorrow that we did today. But do it better."

Fratello managed to get through the Brown-less practice without incident. It helped that not one player on the stingy Turner's Hawks roster had more than four years of NBA experience. They were all still learning the game, and Fratello had the teaching chops to help them. "Teachers can coach at any level," Brown said.

That opinion, a tenet of Brown's, was not shared by many of the league's coaches and general managers, especially those with NBA playing experience. But Brown, thanks to his unilateral control over hiring, was free to ignore those naysayers. "People used to laugh when I brought these guys into the NBA," he said. "Why are you bringing [them]? Because I know they can teach. People underestimate that the player at the NBA level knows everything coming from college."

During the late '70s and '80s, the size of an NBA playbook was more *War and Peace* than *The Great Gatsby*. Teams had eight or more offenses, each with multiple options, plus a litany of out-of-bounds plays from both sideline and baseline. "You had to come in there and be able to grasp all of the continuities and the teaching that goes with all of that," Brown said. "A lot of guys actually hired ex-players. That's fine, but our thing was to bring in guys that could teach and get respect."

Fellow Jersey Guy and Five-Star celebrity Dick Vitale shared Brown's belief that skilled teachers could effectively jump a level or two. Immediately after the Detroit Pistons lifted Vitale up from the college ranks and named him head coach, he called Adubato. "I've known Richie all my life and knew how unbelievably knowledgeable he was," Vitale said. "He was outstanding at the scholastic level, the collegiate level, and the small level…He's a tremendous teacher."

Adubato, who had turned down previous opportunities to work with Vitale, couldn't pass up a job in the NBA. "It's the chance of a lifetime," he told *The Herald-News*. "Imagine going from a college division basketball school to the pros."

Best-case scenario, Adubato figured, he'd parlay a successful run as an NBA assistant into a big-time job, somewhere like Ohio State. Vitale, a born hypeman who became a living legend as ESPN's enthusiastic lead college basketball announcer, had higher hopes for his pal. "He'll be an NBA [head] coach in three years," he said.

Adubato, ever the overachiever, fulfilled Vitale's prophecy just a year later.

FRATELLO AND ADUBATO joined the NBA as assistant coaches in 1978, right in the midst of that first major slide along the X's & O's/Jimmys and Joes coaching spectrum. The teams that hired Bill Fitch and his preliminary wave of college coaches were early adopters of a growing trend. Owners and general managers were more frequently pursuing coaching talent in the same collegiate gyms in which they hunted for draft prospects. As a result, the share of former NBA players in the head coaching ranks dropped from nearly 80 percent in 1970 to less than half by 1980.

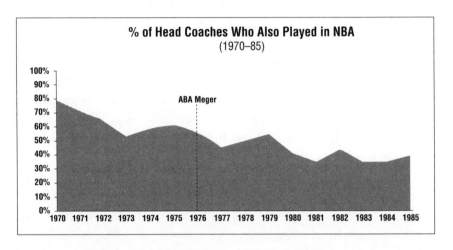

Coaching used to not matter. Suddenly, these dictatorial former amateur players pacing the sideline in fancy suits were of utmost importance. What changed? One place to start is with the dramatic shift in the NBA's racial demographics. In 1970, 55 percent of the league's players were Black. In 1977, the first season after merging with the more Black ABA, that number popped to 70 percent. It continued climbing year after year. By the early 1980s, three out of every four players were Black.

In the 1950s and 1960s, the prevailing notion that pro players didn't need coaching took hold when an unspoken quota system kept the league mostly White. Perhaps the all-White owners and overwhelmingly White general managers, having witnessed the change in demographics, started to believe a firm-handed coach might be exactly what their team needed. "A lot of people use the word 'undisciplined' to describe the NBA," Al Attles, a former NBA player and one of the league's few Black coaches in the late '70s and early '80s, told *Sports Illustrated*'s John Papanek in 1979. "I think that word is pointed at a group more than at a sport."

In the second-to-last NBA Finals before the merger, the Golden State Warriors, coached by Attles, played against the Washington Bullets, coached by K.C. Jones. It marked the first time in pro sports history that two Black coaches faced off for a league championship. Rather than marking the beginning of a new era, where Black representation in coaching started to resemble the racial makeup of the players on the floor, it was more of a brief blip.

The blip peaked in 1977-78, two seasons after the merger. That season, three of the five Black coaches—Lenny Wilkens, Elgin Baylor, and Willis Reed—were Hall of Fame players who eventually landed on the 1996 NBA's 50 Greatest Players list. The other two, Satch Sanders and Attles, had enjoyed long NBA playing careers. Meanwhile, 11 of the league's 17 White coaches had never played in the NBA. Of the six who did make it to the league as players, only two—Jerry West and Billy Cunningham—were named one of the 50 Greatest Players.

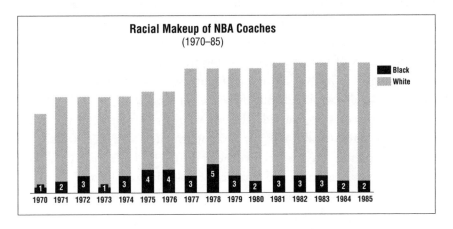

Until the mid-1980s, for a Black man to become an NBA head coach, he unequivocally had to have played in the league. In most cases, it was a prerequisite for him to have been a star. Meanwhile, NBA executives and owners plucked more and more skippers from the college ranks, creating opportunities for White coaches who never played at the highest level. Prejudices against former Black players left NBA head and assistant coaching roles open, cracking the door ever so slightly for a lucky few former small-college players.

"I hate to say it, but there still are some people in the game who think Blacks can't coach, or they think Blacks aren't as honest or as intelligent as the Whites who coach," Wilkens, one of the few Black coaches from the 1970s who managed to forge out a lengthy and successful career, said in Bob Ryan and Terry Pluto's seminal book, *Forty-Eight Minutes*. "I've been astonished by some of the remarks I've overheard that have been made by NBA people."

As the racial makeup of the league's rosters shifted, a coaching persona was born: the "system coach." The faces of the new movement? Brown and his Five-Star guys. "For technocrats like Hubie Brown and his slew of proteges, including [Rick] Pitino, Richie Adubato, and Ron Rothstein, the 'system' was built-in protection against personal failure," wrote Harvey Araton and Filip Bondy in *The Selling of the Green: The Financial Rise and Moral Decline of the Boston Celtics*. "If the team won, the system was brilliant. If it lost, the players didn't fit the system."

Even today, the term "system coach" elicits visceral reactions from that era's coaches. When asked if he was the first "system coach," Brown responded, "No, no, don't ever say that kind of stuff about anybody." Rothstein also took umbrage with the "system coach" label that got slapped onto the trunk of the Five-Star coaching tree. "I reject the term," he said with a laugh. "What we did is we taught the game the way we thought the game should be played. But there was a lot of leeway in that 'system.' It wasn't that we were married. The guy who is the most dogmatic in his system was Hubie. And it was just amazing to watch his system work."

When pressed on the fact that he and Fratello both structured their teams around certain rules and a particular style of play, Brown clarified, "It doesn't matter how you coach as long as you win. As long as you take over a bad situation and win."

During Fratello's first season as a Hawks assistant, Brown was quoted in a profile in *The Atlanta Journal-Constitution Magazine* as saying that his job was to "strain [the players'] talent until they cry out for mercy." He also shared his belief that the players "have to be completely subservient to my goals." In that same piece, Brown goes on to lament the fact that "these urban kids who come off the streets think the sport is just run-and-gun and dunk-and-shoot and they're so damn cocky. They just won't fit in."

The hard feelings between Brown and the Hawks' less subservient-minded players were mutual. "I wouldn't conform totally to what Hubie

Brown wanted," former Hawks player Terry Furlow told *The Philadelphia Inquirer*. "When you play for the Atlanta Hawks, Hubie Brown is in control of your life." The Hawks subsequently traded Furlow a quarter of the way through the 1979–80 season.

While Brown was lauded for transforming the Hawks into a well-oiled machine that could win without stars, Vitale struggled with the Pistons. A dozen games into his second season, the team fired him, leaving his assistant, Adubato, to take over as interim head coach. That offseason, the team cut ties with Adubato as well. He went back to teaching in New Jersey, believing his time in the NBA was done for good. "I hate to go out a loser," Adubato told the *Detroit Free Press*, "and I feel I am going out a loser for the first time in my life."

AFTER FIVE SEASONS in Atlanta, Brown took the head coaching job with the Knicks. He once again built out his bench from his network of teachers. In fact, eight of Brown's nine assistant coaches during his NBA career were once counselors at Five-Star. Both Adubato and Fratello joined the Knicks staff. Adubato lasted long enough this go-round to build a reputation as a defensive savant. He became an in-demand lead assistant. Over the next 15 years, Adubato took over teams as interim head coach twice—once with the Dallas Mavericks and again with the Orlando Magic.

Fratello, another one of the so-called "Hubie clones," became a hot coaching candidate in his own right. For Fratello, the elephant in the room was ironically his short stature. Many around the league believed owners were convinced that the 5'7" Fratello was, as Knicks business manager Frankie Blauschild put it, "too short to win the respect of the players." When a coach's eyeline barely reaches the lettering on his players' jerseys, it becomes a constant reminder of the fact that he never played pro ball.

Some of the former NBA players who then became head coaches saw interlopers like Fratello more as a threat than a member of their fraternity. "Believe me," Brown said. "There was a division in coaches' meetings and everything at that time. The pro player didn't think that the college coach knew what it takes to play in the league, never mind coach in the league."

Owners and GMs thought differently. In 1983, the Hawks brought the 36-year-old Fratello back—this time as head coach. It was Fratello's first head coaching job since his days as the 23-year-old coach of the Hackensack High freshman team. When he was Brown's assistant, Hawks brass witnessed how effective Fratello was as a teacher and leader. In their eyes, Fratello's huge basketball IQ dwarfed his short stature. Plus, he was willing to take a smaller contract than a more established coach might've requested, which went over well with Turner.

Fratello believed, even though many of the players were holdovers from his days as an assistant, that he would have to rebuild trust with the team. "You have to earn the respect of the players," Fratello said. "They're very smart and they judge you. They'll judge you in practice, and then when you move over 18 inches and you're the head coach, then they'll judge you in games."

Initially, Hawks players generally thought highly of Fratello. "He knows the system. He knows everything about us," Hawks guard Wes Matthews told *The Atlanta Journal-Constitution*.

Even the new players, whom Fratello had not coached, became believers. When the Hawks retired Dominique Wilkins' jersey in 2001, the Hall of Famer went out of his way to praise his former coach. "Mike is probably the most underrated NBA coach of all time," he said.

When it came to forming a relationship with Wilkins, Fratello didn't need to start from scratch. Wilkins was one of the many future NBA stars who attended Five-Star, where Fratello, and coaches like Fratello, were held in such high esteem. The Jersey Guys, according to Vitale, had a "big-time reputation" around the league because so many great players, including Moses Malone, Michael Jordan, Isiah Thomas, and Patrick Ewing, attended the camp.

Without Five-Star and without Brown, it's hard to imagine a couple of small-college players like Fratello and Adubato would've ever been NBA head coaches. Their careers are case studies in how one person's success can serve as the rising tide that lifts all of a network's ships. The Jersey Guys attended the right camps and met the right coaches. The hard-working bunch was then well-positioned to step into jobs that, due in part to the league's changing demographics, were less dominated by former NBA players. They were a crucial chapter in the history of the "pro coach," a story whose echoes still reverberate across the D3 pipeline today.

CHAPTER 5

LIFER VS. CONVERT

*How two small-college players took diverging paths
to NBA general manager jobs in the 1990s*

Andrew Olson's first three seasons at Amherst lifted the program into another stratosphere. He acclimated quickly to the college game, winning conference Co-Rookie of the Year. As a sophomore, he earned second-team all-conference honors and helped lead Amherst to the Division III Final Four for the second time in school history.

Junior year, the arrow kept going up and to the right, both for Olson individually and for the team as a whole. He was a Division III facsimile of Steve Nash, a blurred eddy of flopping brown locks, baggy purple shorts, spin moves, and behind-the-back passes. He had an innate understanding of when his teammate needed an easy bucket and just what play to call to achieve that. Not only did Olson have the pulse of his team, but he also knew exactly when the crowd was ready to explode. And, yes, there was a crowd. By the end of the regular season and into the postseason, Amherst students marched across the frozen campus and squished into their designated quarter of the bleachers. They cheered enthusiastically and chanted "Safe-ty School, Safe-ty School" at the opposing students and fans, even though they, too, attended an elite liberal arts college with a single-digit acceptance rate. Olson's on-court genius appealed to the basketball junkie and the casual fan alike. He could feel the crowd's growing frenzy and, like any experienced showman, always delivered at the perfect moment. A deep pull-up three or a no-look pass could damn near blow the roof off of Amherst's gym.

Olson led Amherst to their second straight Final Four appearance, where they took care of business and won the national title. After the final buzzer sounded, Olson and his teammates threw on championship hats and hugged each other as confetti rained down on them. They squished together to pose with the trophy, all of them holding up an index finger to indicate that they were, undisputedly, No. 1. Olson swept all of the postseason awards—NESCAC Player of the Year, D3Hoops.com first-team All-American, NCAA Tournament Most Outstanding Player, and National Association of Basketball Coaches (NABC) Division III Player of the Year.

Off the court, he was soft-spoken and thoughtful, eager to cede the spotlight to his more rambunctious teammates. He was the basketball equivalent of the comedian who would ham it up during their set and then barely speak above a whisper offstage. The night of the National Association of Basketball Coaches banquet, an event held annually at the Division I Final Four, Olson had to make an acceptance speech. He timed out his carefully prepared remarks to just shy of two minutes, the time allotted to each winning player. Shortly before his award was announced, the Division I Defensive Player of the Year, Ohio State freshman center Greg Oden, delivered an acceptance speech lasting no more than 15 seconds. In Olson's mind there was no way that the Division III POY could go longer than Oden, the presumed No. 1 pick in the upcoming NBA draft.

Unfortunately, Olson's improvisational abilities didn't extend past the hardwood. From the dais, he looked out at the who's who of college basketball staring back at him—coaches and players he recognized in an instant. Up until that moment, those familiar faces had never heard of him. After that night his name would probably slip out of their memories like air from a loosely tied balloon. He managed to stammer out a few "thank yous" before shuffling back to his seat. After his flubbed speech, he craved a big game, some way to prove to the crowd just how capable he truly was.

A few weeks later, Oden officially ended his very short college career by declaring for the NBA draft. The Portland Trail Blazers selected him first overall. Meanwhile, not a single agent or pro scout whispered tantalizing promises of fame and fortune in Olson's ears.

Even after his remarkable season, the undersized Division III point guard wasn't exactly popping up on any NBA team's draft boards.

Senior year would be the encore to near-perfection, a season that could only match and never top its predecessor. Olson's career kept moving right along the x-axis of time; only there was no room on the y-axis of achievement to slope any higher. The best he could do was repeat. Repeat as champion, repeat as Conference Player of the Year, and repeat as National Player of the Year. Anything less would be a step back, a negative slope, an utter failure.

It took some time to get used to the fact that, at captain's practices, *he* was now the captain. The class a year above him had been there throughout his entire Amherst journey, from the recruiting trip to the national title. Suddenly they were gone, blasted off into the real world.

The previous season's two young assistant coaches had also moved on to bigger and better jobs. Koby Altman, the new graduate assistant (a part-time coaching role earmarked for a student pursuing an advanced degree), was a few years removed from his own days as a NESCAC point guard. Three years after graduating from Middlebury College, Altman decided to trade his burgeoning New York City real estate career for a ticket back into the world of basketball. For Altman, the job's allure was certainly not the $7,000 stipend. He was drawn to the hours spent in the office with a living legend in Coach Hixon, the chance to potentially put a national championship on his coaching resume, and the free tuition to one of the best sports management programs in the country.

UMass-Amherst, a large state school that shares a downtown with Amherst College, is one of 200 colleges that offer master's degrees geared toward aspiring sports professionals. Thousands of prospective marketers, promoters, administrators, event managers, and coaches enroll in sports management programs every year. Like many graduate programs, the real magic is less in the coursework and more in the network. As one of the nation's oldest sports management programs, UMass had alumni in enviable positions across college and pro athletics.

On the coaching front, Altman found himself in a unique situation, one where the regular season felt more like a preamble than a culmination. All of Amherst's wins were expected, a checkmark on top of an existing checkmark in an already completed box. Each regular-season loss (all two of them) prompted alums to email Hixon, asking what was wrong with the team. Along the way Olson scored his 1,000th career point and added to his school-record number of career assists.

Olson and Hixon could only exhale once they made it back to the Final Four, their third straight. In a semifinal win, Olson notched his first career triple-double. The championship game took place the very next day. Amherst suffered a wire-to-wire loss. In the locker room, Olson wiped the tears from his eyes, thanked his teammates with a short speech, and slipped off his Amherst jersey for the last time.

Despite failing to replicate the magic of his junior season, both the NESCAC and NABC once again named him Player of the Year. Given another chance at nailing the acceptance speech, Olson redeemed himself at the award dinner dais. To even have the chance at a mulligan for the speech was unprecedented—he was the second D3 player in the 25-year history of the award to win it twice. On the D1 side, only Virginia's Ralph Sampson and Duke's Jay Williams had achieved such an honor. That weekend, Altman and Olson spent time together, not as player and coach, but as peers. They toasted the culmination of Olson's exemplary D3 playing career, and the next steps in Altman's basketball journey.

By the late 1990s, Bob Whitsitt was without a doubt one of the most powerful sports executives in America. He ran both of Microsoft co-founder Paul Allen's pro franchises—the NBA's Portland Trail Blazers and the NFL's Seattle Seahawks—scooping deeply from his owner's overflowing coffers to turn the teams into winners.

In 1999, Whitsitt's Blazers had the NBA's highest payroll: $74 million in contracts doled out for an impressive collection of aging former stars and volatile-but-promising youngsters. Opposing coaches likened his team-building strategies to that of a fantasy basketball manager, someone who collected all the talent he could with little regard for how those players might gel. When asked how his roster might cope with the fact that there were only so many minutes and one ball to go around, Whitsitt would pull out his usual refrain: "I wasn't a chemistry major in college. I was a sports major."

Whitsitt's alma mater, the University of Wisconsin-Stevens Point, did not in fact offer a major in "sports." His go-to quote, however, doesn't stray from the truth. During college, Whitsitt dedicated a lot of time and energy to athletics (and he never did enroll in a chem course).

Whitsitt's athletic education began well before his time at Stevens Point. On summer days in his native Madison, Wisconsin, he biked to the sandlot for baseball or the playground for pick-up hoops. He wouldn't pick his bike out of the dirt and pedal home until long after everyone else left. When the temperature dropped below freezing, his friends played hockey on the iced-over baseball field. Sports and competition nourished him. "Some people like to eat," Whitsitt said. "I like to play sports."

By high school, Whitsitt developed into a 6'2" three-sport athlete. When it came time for college, he knew he could only afford to attend one of Wisconsin's public schools. He wasn't a Big Ten talent, so if he wanted to continue playing sports, he'd have to leave Madison. Whitsitt wound up committing to play football at Stevens Point, one of nine UW schools that made up the Wisconsin State University Athletic Conference. When he attended Stevens Point in the mid-1970s, the conference, which would eventually join NCAA's Division III, still competed in the NAIA, a rival governing body dedicated to smaller colleges and universities. Like many small schools in that era, Stevens Point's athletic programs had open doors and fluid rosters. Whitsitt quit football prior to his freshman season, but ended up playing basketball for one season and baseball for four.

While waiting in the athletic director's office to pick up another letter for his letterman's jacket, Whitsitt saw a brochure tossed in with a pile of papers. He picked it up and brought it back to his dorm, where he read about Ohio University's one-of-a-kind master's degree in sports business administration. Whitsitt figured, *Hey, all I do is play sports. I'm a junior, I have no connections, no mentors, and my playing days are coming to an end. Maybe a master's from Ohio could get me a job with a pro team.* He applied for one of the few dozen spots in the program and eagerly awaited the admissions letter. When it came, he opened the envelope, only to find out that he didn't get in.

One measly rejection letter wasn't going to deter him. He opted to return to school for one more semester and try to play football. Maybe adding another letter to his letterman's jacket would help when he reapplied to Ohio the following year.

Between Whitsitt's fourth and fifth years of college, his brother got engaged. The October wedding date presented Whitsitt with quite the conundrum: if he did end up making the football team, he'd either have to abandon his teammates on a gameday, or miss standing by his brother and new sister-in-law as they said "I do."

At the time, the potential conflict seemed far less likely than any other wedding day snafu, like rain or an overserved groomsman. Stevens Point had a winning football program and only a few open roster spots, and Whitsitt hadn't played in four years. That summer, he came down with mono. Rather than spending his days lifting weights, he slept. When he discussed the wedding dilemma with his family, Whitsitt's brother started laughing. "You've got no chance of making the team," he said.

Whitsitt and his brother eventually made a deal. If he made the team but wasn't a starter, Whitsitt would tell the coach he needed to skip the game. Maybe the coach would excuse him or maybe he would just cut him outright, but at least Whitsitt would be forthcoming. However, if Whitsitt somehow not only made the team, but also earned a starting spot, he would play the game. Afterward, he'd quickly get cleaned up and drive down to Madison for the ceremony, hopefully arriving on time.

On the first day of practice, Whitsitt sat 10th or 11th on the 1977 Stevens Point tight end depth chart. That all changed during a preseason scrimmage. After some of the other tight ends dropped a few passes, the team's star quarterback, who knew Whitsitt from the athletic social circles on campus, ordered him onto the field. Before the coaches could even respond, Whitsitt huddled up with the starters. He caught a few passes and, in one day, leapfrogged nearly a dozen guys. On Opening Day, he started at tight end.

Per the terms of the agreement, Whitsitt suited up for Stevens Point on the Saturday of his brother's wedding. The decision has caused Whitsitt many-a-sleepless night—not because he regrets his decision, but because he hurt his shoulder going up for a pass in the fourth quarter. Prior to the game, Whitsitt figured that he'd have time to quickly shower, get dressed, and arrive at the church in Madison with about 15 minutes to spare. He didn't account for an injury that would require an hour of attention from the training staff after the final whistle. An usher had to stand in for him during the ceremony. At the reception, his conversations fell into two camps. There were those who said, "Good game!" and congratulated him on the win. Then, there were those who said, "How the hell could you miss your brother's wedding?" Both groups, seemingly without fail, gave Whitsitt a whack on his bad shoulder.

IF WHITSITT REALLY wanted to know what it would've been like to major in sports in undergrad, he could've asked Garry St. Jean about Springfield College. For an aspiring basketball coach, attending Springfield College was sort of like taking coding classes in Bill Gates' old garage. The school where Dr. James Naismith invented basketball had churned out physical education teachers for decades, spraying graduates near and far to spread the gospel of fitness. St. Jean grew up in Chicopee, Massachusetts, less than five miles from Springfield's campus. Many of his teachers and coaches were proud Springfield alums.

As a senior at Chicopee High, St. Jean earned All-Western Massachusetts honors in both basketball and soccer. On the court, the 6'5" forward prided himself on his rebounding and passing, a bulldog who mucked it up and did what it took to win. His name popped up on a few top prospect lists, leading to recruiting letters from several larger schools, including Army and Navy. He wrote them back, confessing that he didn't believe he was smart enough for the service academies. St. Jean, the first in his family to pursue higher education, only seriously considered one option. If Springfield was good enough for his local coaching role models, it was good enough for him. "You just loved your coaches," said St. Jean, remembering his high school days. "You loved the game. You loved to practice. You loved to play. I was just like, 'This is what I want.'"

At Springfield, St. Jean roomed with another Western Mass kid named Gene DeFilippo. The pair became best buds, drawn together by a love of sports and a desire to coach. While college athletes at bigger schools might sit around and talk about playing in the pros, St. Jean and DeFilippo dreamed about the day they'd be head coaches—St. Jean with a college basketball or

NBA team, DeFilippo with the University of Texas football program. "We certainly weren't headed to the NBA or the NFL [as players]," DeFilippo said. "So we thought, *You know what? We better get ready to hit the road and land on our feet coaching.*"

A knee injury ended St. Jean's promising small-college basketball career after just one season. Rather than mope around feeling sorry for himself, St. Jean continued to light up the campus with his big belly laughs and magnetic personality. "It was one of the unwritten rules: you didn't walk around the campus with your head down," St. Jean said. "You said hello to people."

Springfield College was more than just a friendly place full of friendly faces. It was the ideal environment for an injured young man to maintain and reframe his relationship with athletics. As a physical education major, St. Jean took courses in both basketball skills and basketball coaching. Rather than doodling out-of-bounds plays during a math class, he could earn credits toward his degree by learning how to implement an offense and teach a 2-3 zone. Even after his injury, St. Jean still made frequent stops into the head basketball coach's office to talk hoops—a luxury he likely would not have had a bigger school. "[Garry] was the best student of the game," DeFilippo said. "He would ask questions: 'How do you handle this as a coach?' 'How do you handle that?' He was always asking everybody questions, wanting to learn as much as he could. Not just the X's and O's of it, but how to be a leader, how to coach it, how to explain it."

St. Jean secured his first head coaching job before even finishing his undergrad work. Three years after suiting up for Chicopee High, he took over as his alma mater's varsity coach. Once the players, many of whom knew St. Jean well, got used to calling him "Coach" instead of "Garry," they realized he was as prepared as a first-time coach could be. St. Jean was another Springfield College apostle, preaching the school's gospel of "spirit, mind, body."

ALTHOUGH IT'S UNCLEAR whether or not his foray into football had anything to do with it, Ohio University accepted Whitsitt's second application into their sports management program. As a fallback plan, Whitsitt had also applied to Ohio State University, which had just started a similar program of their own. Figuring he had already experienced a smaller school, and perhaps holding a bit of a grudge against Ohio University for denying him the first time, Whitsitt decided to attend Ohio State.

To Whitsitt's physician father, sports management school was a bridge to uncertainty. Medical school trained young men and women to work in hospitals or start a private practice. Sports management programs readied students for a business that, in 1977, was barely even a business. This was especially true in pro basketball.

The NBA, licking its wounds from its battle with the ABA, was dealing with the realities of a post-merger world. Nearly a decade of bidding wars and antitrust lawsuits meant higher salaries, no-cut contracts, and free agency. With the players now empowered to claim more of the pie, the league office and team owners—many of whom were new to the sport— were left to figure out how to make the pie bigger.

For Whitsitt, the allure of working for a bigtime ballclub was far more immediate than any worries about one day supporting a family. After growing up in a town without professional sports and attending a small college, the NBA and NHL and NFL still inspired a childlike sense of awe and wonder in him. When it came to the next step after grad school, the job description, the city, the league—none of it mattered, as long as it was in sports. He wrote letters to every single team in all of the major leagues, the largest stadiums and arenas, and even a few college programs. The hundreds of copies of his resume, hundreds of envelopes, and hundreds of stamps yielded exactly zero job offers. Team staffs were small, internships were rare, and the few that did exist tended to go to the well-heeled and well-connected.

Whitsitt expanded his limited network by volunteering at events alongside students and faculty from Ohio University, which led to an interview with the Indiana Pacers. The one-time model ABA franchise was teetering, knocked off-kilter by the NBA's unfriendly absorption terms. The front office was understaffed and overworked, each employee brimming with unwanted tasks. It was, in other words, an organization in desperate need of an intern.

Whitsitt beat out two Ohio University students for the job and got to work, happily situated underneath the lowest rung on the team's corporate ladder. He supported the business side, helping out with whatever the half dozen or so full-timers couldn't wait to delegate. It didn't bother Whitsitt one bit. *Shit, I'm still at Market Square Arena,* he would think.

He stayed on with the team after graduation. With such a flat and small corporate structure, he quickly learned every aspect of the business. After just three years, Pacers general manager Bob Salyers elevated the 24-year-old Whitsitt to assistant general manager. Salyers tasked Whitsitt with overseeing the team's entire business operation—ticket sales; media relations; budgets; and negotiations around radio rights, advertising, and sponsorship. Since the team was on the verge of bankruptcy or relocation, Whitsitt's first mistake could very well be his—and the franchise's—last. "I really got a lot of opportunities when I was young because of the tough circumstances," Whitsitt said. "The Pacers barely got into the NBA. They were financially struggling to survive. You really had to be sharp and frugal and aggressive and innovative."

With limited resources at his disposal, Whitsitt did his best to not only tread water, but also swim upstream. He took a fresh-out-of-college media relations intern named Greg McCollam and appointed him director of a brand-new promotions department. McCollam found sponsors for giveaway items like hats or T-shirts, creating a previously untapped revenue source. "Back in the '80s, [promotional sponsorship] was a new thing that was just starting to bubble up," McCollam said. "Bob had the foresight to say, 'Hey! Let's jump on this!'"

It's difficult to comprehend a 22-year-old department head and his 24-year-old supervisor wheeling and dealing on behalf of an NBA team, but that was the reality in Indianapolis. At no point did McCollam ever feel like Whitsitt was a child executive stomping around in his daddy's wingtips. "At that time, it never crossed my mind how old or young he was," McCollam said. "He was just my boss. You always got the feeling that he knew what he was doing."

Whitsitt started dabbling in the basketball side as well. "I was so impressed with his energy and dedication to learning the business," Salyers, the team GM, later said. "You could see what was happening to him. He never stopped working, and his knowledge of the entire basketball operation grew day to day."

One of his first orders of business was to negotiate contract terms with the team's 1982 first-round pick, Clark Kellogg. Kellogg's agent believed his client, the eighth overall pick in the draft, deserved a $2 million contract. Pacers leadership told Whitsitt the team absolutely could not go above

$1 million. At the first meeting, Kellogg's agent turned apoplectic at the very notion of negotiating against the assistant GM, who was just a few years older than his client. After a few weeks of shouting and posturing in the newspaper, the Kellogg camp accepted that Whitsitt, who had never once negotiated a player contract, was the only one who would be sitting across that table. With the ABA no longer in existence, options, even for a coveted player like Kellogg, were limited. Kellogg's camp eventually blinked first and agreed to Whitsitt's terms. "It wasn't because I was overly skilled, because I wasn't," Whitsitt admitted. "I literally gave him every dollar we had available. The owner told me, 'I don't care if we sign the guy. Tell him to go back in the draft. We're out of money.' So I got credit for signing a guy for way, way, way under his market value."

Whitsitt's time with the Pacers not only allowed for an accelerated acquisition of skills, it also put him in close proximity to pro basketball's power players. Frequent calls with the league office introduced him to Joe Axelson, the NBA's vice president of operations. When Axelson took over as GM of the Kansas City Kings, Whitsitt was one of the nine candidates he interviewed for a top marketing role. "Bob was by far the best one," Axelson said. "He has great business and marketing sense and knows basketball. It's a rare combination, and I think he's an example of the type of people you will start seeing more of in the NBA front offices."

While Whitsitt spent his 20s mastering the inner workings of NBA front offices, Garry St. Jean spent *his* entire 20s teaching physical education and coaching basketball at Chicopee High. "I thought I had the greatest job in the United States of America," St. Jean said. "I loved it. I didn't like it; I loved it."

Early in his tenure, the local state representative took St. Jean and his team to the statehouse as a reward for a winning season. While there they met some Boston Celtics players. The ever-gregarious St. Jean struck up a conversation with the pros, and when they mentioned a summer camp they ran, St. Jean said his ears perked up like a German Shepherd's. By the end of the chat, he had agreed to work the camp as a way to help pay for some of his players to attend.

At the Celtics camp, St. Jean found his own New England version of Five-Star. At night, counselors would drink beers and gather around the chalkboard while Don Nelson and Satch Sanders drew up plays. *Holy moly,*

St. Jean would think to himself, *this is like a dream*. The counselors—mostly other high school coaches—would ask the pros questions, transforming the lectures into an open forum that would last late into the night. The lessons learned during his summers at Celtics camp helped St. Jean build on his strong coaching foundation. But it was the relationships he formed at the camp—one relationship in particular—that changed his life.

For a former NBA player who attended a big state university, Don Nelson is an integral part of the small-college pipeline. He directly or indirectly helped several former small-college players—including his own son—find a home in the league. Chalk up part of his ubiquitousness to sheer longevity. As a player and a coach, Nelson worked in the NBA for just shy of 50 years, giving him ample opportunity to cross paths with other coaches and general managers. There's more to it, though. Nelson was an innovator—one of the few coaches who saw the future of the game and pushed his teams to actualize it. Rick Carlisle, a longtime NBA head coach and current head of the NBA coach's union, called Nelson "one of the most creative men in the history of NBA basketball." Nelson is exactly the type of open-minded, curious thinker who would seek out and gravitate toward those in his field with non-traditional backgrounds.

One season after hanging up his sneakers, Nelson took over as the Milwaukee Bucks head coach and general manager. In 1980, he wanted to hire a college scout, preferably someone who knew the game and would make for good company. He offered the job to that friendly fella from the Celtics camps—St. Jean, who remembered Nelson telling him, "I want you to be three things: I want you to be honest, I want you to be loyal, and I want you to work hard."

St. Jean thought to himself, *Jeez, that's pretty easy!*

Nelson helped immerse St. Jean in the pro game, involving him in coaches' meetings, practices, and the installation of offenses and defenses. It was a crucial time to cram. Once the season began, St. Jean would spend most of his time away from the team scouting college games. Every so often he would meet the Bucks on the road and sit on the sideline for a game or two. On one of those rare dalliances on the bench, veteran NBA referee Earl Strom noticed St. Jean. Strom asked Nelson, "Who's your new guy?" Nelson told him it was their college scout.

"He can't sit there if he's a scout," Strom replied, citing a rule that only coaches could sit on the bench. So what did Nelson do? He elevated St. Jean to assistant coach.

For nine seasons, St. Jean played good cop to Nelson's bad, first in Milwaukee and then with the Golden State Warriors. At the beginning of his tenure, most teams still only had two assistant coaches and a trainer, so St. Jean spent a lot of quality time with Nelson. "They formed a bond," said Garry's son, Greg, now an NBA assistant coach. "What was so great for my dad was he had a crash course in learning a different way of thinking about basketball." Nelson taught St. Jean the method behind the Celtics' success in the '60s and early '70s, converting him from a basketball fundamentalist into someone more accepting of different styles of play.

Nelson won three Coach of the Year awards during his partnership with St. Jean. Naturally, the top assistant for one of the league's best coaches began to garner head coaching buzz of his own. That fortuitous proximity to a well-regarded coach—the same phenomenon that transformed an outsider like Mike Fratello into a viable candidate—presented St. Jean with the opportunity to interview with several clubs, including the Sacramento Kings in 1992. Their owners, a group of commercial real estate guys, wanted to meet in their Los Angeles offices. St. Jean flew down toting thick binders filled with offensive and defensive strategies. The notes proved less important than his personality and ability to connect with the owners. "In an interview, there's X's and O's, but it's really about relationships with people, earning the respect and trust," St. Jean said. "It starts with ownership groups and management."

The Kings hired St. Jean, even though he wasn't GM Jerry Reynolds' first choice. "I thought Fratello and [Del] Harris were the best-prepared candidates," Reynolds wrote in his autobiography, *Reynolds Remembers*. "However, [new owner] Jim Thomas thought Garry St. Jean was more optimistic and positive."

St. Jean's tenure in Sacramento serves as an important lesson into where power lies in the NBA—with ownership. It takes strong relationships to propel one of the hundreds of qualified coaches into the few dozen NBA head coaching jobs. St. Jean aced his interactions, first with Nelson and later with the Kings' ownership group. After the Kings dismissed St. Jean following five losing seasons, his relationships helped him to very quickly regain his footing—this time in the front office.

IN 1986, AT just 30 years old, Bob Whitsitt became the Seattle SuperSonics' new team president. He was the youngest lead executive in the NBA. "The only thing I was lacking was gray hair and name, stature, and age," he said. "I probably had as much or more experience than quite a few other people doing similar jobs around the league because I had actually done the work. I'd actually been in the trenches. I'd actually done each job and then got promoted up, as opposed to just landing on top and trying to bullshit my way like I know what I'm doing."

His motto that first offseason was "Maximize your opportunity." He made six major trades, acquiring a handful of new players and four additional first-round picks. The local radio shows started referring to him as "Trader Bob." The players called him "The Liquidator." To some around the NBA, Whitsitt came off as a young, arrogant hot shot, someone moving too recklessly and aggressively not to eventually crash. Internally, however, he made sure to always ask for help and solicit opinions. "If you stop learning," Whitsitt said, "I think you're dead."

Before his first season in Seattle, the Sonics were Vegas' biggest longshot to win a championship. But behind their revamped lineup, they unexpectedly advanced to the Western Conference Finals. During the playoff run, Sonics coach Bernie Bickerstaff praised Whitsitt for how he approached his first season as a lead executive. "Bob walked in here very organized and, more than anything else he did that impressed me, he listened to what everybody had to say," Bickerstaff said. "So many guys want to run basketball teams their way and don't care what anybody else has to say. He made this rebuilding process a collective effort."

The Sonics continued their winning ways throughout the latter half of the 1980s, thanks in part to Whitsitt, the young dog learning new tricks. The salary cap, a series of league-mandated spending rules instituted in 1983, was still relatively novel when Whitsitt joined Seattle. Teams and executives had to adapt to a world governed by a series of complicated payroll criteria. Whitsitt quickly became an expert, and the Sonics became known league-wide for their tidy payroll, which gave Whitsitt the flexibility to wheel and deal.

In the early 1990s, Whitsitt's risky, out-of-the-box bets elevated the Sonics into one of the top teams in the Western Conference. He knew that in order to win big, he needed to swing big. With the 17th pick in the 1989 draft, he chose Shawn Kemp, a dominant high school player who hadn't played college basketball. NBA scouting guru Marty Blake called the odds against Kemp "astronomical." Kemp developed into a dunking double-double machine and a perennial All-Star, helping to lift the Sonics to perennial title contention and solidify Whitsitt's reputation as a top general manager.

Whitsitt entered the NBA as a relative rarity in the late 1970s—a talented young professional who dedicated himself to the business of sports. Behind the same stubborn perseverance that fueled his successful foray into small-college football, Whitsitt cobbled together valuable experience. He became one of the first front-office lifers to master the inner workings of an NBA franchise, doing so at a time when business-minded GMs like Carl Scheer and Norm Sonju were a dying breed.

By 1995 more than half of the league's teams had a former NBA player running their front office. The number of general managers with no collegiate playing experience, a group that, from the NBA's inception until 1988, oversaw at least a quarter of all teams, had basically gone extinct. As the decade came to a close, Whitsitt was one of just three general managers who attended a current Division III school. One of the others was Garry St. Jean.

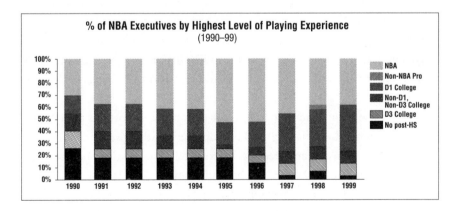

So how exactly did St. Jean, a lifelong coach with a losing record and a year of small-college playing experience, land an NBA general manager job? For one, NBA front offices were riddled with unsuccessful coaches. Throughout the NBA's first three decades, franchises preferred to kick losing coaches upstairs rather than fire them outright and eat the remaining years on their contract. St. Jean, however, was a unique case—a fired coach who moved directly from one team's bench to the top of another team's basketball operation. Once again, he had his affability to thank. "The reason that we ended up with Sainty was that he had been so well-liked and so respected when he was [coaching in Golden State]," said P.J. Carlesimo, who was the Warriors head coach when they hired St. Jean in 1997. "It was really the Golden State people [owner Chris Cohan and team counsel Robin Baggett] who had brought Sainty's name to the front. And then it struck a chord because it was somebody that I knew from the league and that I knew was a great person."

Behind the same charisma that won over the Springfield College campus, St. Jean landed some of the league's top posts. Once the Warriors made the move official, Jorge Ortiz of the *San Francisco Examiner* intuited that St. Jean got the job in large part due to his magnetic persona. "In the sometimes cutthroat business of the NBA, a pleasant personality is sometimes perceived as a weakness," Ortiz wrote. "[St. Jean] had done it without compromising his nature. In fact it worked to his advantage."

He and Whitsitt took different paths and amassed a wildly different set of skills, only to land in the exact same role. A career coach like St. Jean might not have known the intricacies of the salary cap, or how to sell sponsorships. But that mattered less in the 1990s, when the GM role became more basketball-focused. As the business of basketball grew, so too did the size of a team's front office, leading to a further bifurcation of the basketball and business sides. Whitsitt, unlike his many peers who played in the league, was the rare lead basketball executive also tasked with optimizing the business.

St. Jean, on the other hand, was not the academic sort. As an assistant coach, he remembers having to look up the word *segue* after a general manager used it in a team meeting. Fortunately, by the time he became a general manager in 1997, he had helpful resources at his disposal. When asked about how he approached salary cap strategy, he said, chuckling, "When you get in these positions, either a head coach or a GM's position, it's good to do a little self-evaluation and figure out where your strengths are and where you need to grow and improve. I knew I struggled at Chicopee High in a lot of math classes. I knew I had to have people with me that knew that inside and out. I thought my strengths were relationships with people. You delegate when you get in those positions."

He also kept the NBA's league office on speed dial. Whenever a general manager was wondering whether or not a particular deal would work under the cap, they could call the league office and speak to a lawyer. "They probably thought they were dealing with a first grader," St. Jean said. "They were so patient with me. I think about it today and I sit back and I chuckle."

St. Jean's self-deprecation undersells the pertinent skills he did bring to the job. He saw the game through the eyes of a coach. Eric Musselman, who St. Jean hired as the Warriors head coach in 2002, couldn't believe the depth of St. Jean's interview process. "It was the most detailed interview I've ever had in my life," Musselman said. "He gave me a pen. 'Get up on the board. Three seconds to go. Diagram the play you're running against the Milwaukee Bucks. And put the Bucks roster up there.'"

More than 20 years later, Musselman, now a successful head coach at the University of Arkansas, still remembered the high bar set by that interview. "I literally laugh at how comical and unprepared interviews are," he said, "compared to what Garry St. Jean put me through."

Even while grilling him, St. Jean managed to win Musselman over. "Garry's the greatest people person that I've ever been around," Musselman said. "No enemies. Everybody loves him."

Whitsitt, on the other hand, did not have a 100 percent approval rating. In 1998, after he had moved from Seattle to run the Portland Trail Blazers, *Sports Illustrated* asked 25 agents to cast votes for the best, worst, and toughest front-office heads. Whitsitt was the only one who received votes in all three categories. Ten of the 25 agents called him the toughest. The one who voted him for worst said, "I've found him to be neither straightforward nor truthful."

By the time his stint in Portland came to an end, thanks to a dysfunctional and underperforming team branded the "Jail Blazers," Whitsitt had his fair share of naysayers. He also had plenty of fans around the league. "People knew he was brilliant and very creative and unafraid," said Rick Carlisle, a Blazers assistant coach during Whitsitt's reign.

The Jail Blazers roster experiment that defined Whitsitt's tenure in Portland should not undermine his unlikely and unparalleled rise. For a small-college alum, Whitsitt came to the GM job in a novel way, climbing up through the front office without coaching professionally at any level. He managed to transform himself from a novice to an expert in countless disciplines—everything from sponsorship deals to contract negotiations to the salary cap. He thought about risk differently than his peers and took big swings, some of which paid off handsomely. He built himself into a front-office unicorn with a uniquely broad skill set that appealed to league owners.

Both Whitsitt and St. Jean spent their small-college days staying deeply involved in sports and preparing for their dream careers. The paths they walked—front-office lifer and converted coach—were then hiked again by many a former Division III player.

While they set the tone for the future boom of D3 players in the NBA, their role in helping build the pipeline was an indirect one. Like Norm Sonju, Whitsitt wasn't exactly seeking out other small school alums to groom. In lieu of academic or athletic pedigree, he was far more concerned with the more recent bullets on a candidate's resume. "At some point, where you're from is just nice to chat about if you have nothing to chat about," Whitsitt said. Despite his indifference, he still managed to help a generation of D3 alums. The league was ready for more front-office lifers, and Whitsitt blazed the trail.

CHAPTER 6

OPEN BORDERS

*How former small-college players broke down barriers
and accelerated the NBA's international reach*

Not long after his first foray into competitive hoops at the YMCA, Andrew Olson's first-grade teacher asked the class to draw a picture of what they wanted to be when they grew up. Olson drew a stick figure with an orange basketball attached to the right stick arm. Underneath it he wrote "I will play pro basketball." Like a misguided wish to a monkey's paw, Olson's drawing technically came true, just not the way he wanted. If only he had been more specific.

Most college basketball players, especially those at the Division III level, understand that their playing careers will end with the final buzzer of their senior year. When Amherst lost in the national championship game, Olson strongly suspected that was not the final curtain. Throughout the year, notes from agents offering to help him find a team overseas occasionally popped up in his Amherst email inbox.

Olson's soft-spoken manner masked a confidence that bordered on irrational, an unwavering belief in self that powered him to D3 stardom. He knew that in early June the NBA would hold its annual draft combine, a chance for top college players to showcase their abilities in front of league executives. He waited for an invite that never came, an invite that, deep down, he knew would never come. All he wanted was a chance to compete with the best, even if it meant taking a beating.

Nine point guards were selected in the 2008 NBA Draft. Olson, of course, wasn't one of them. Following the draft, NBA teams built out their Summer League rosters. New draft picks and second-year players suited up alongside guys either competing for the last roster spot or hoping to impress European scouts. Olson held onto that one last sliver of hope that maybe one of those agents who emailed him would call with a Summer League opportunity. That call, like the draft combine invite, also never came.

Olson accepted reality and hastily figured out a plan to play overseas. Maybe if he had some other passions, he would have pursued a career outside of basketball. But he didn't, and he knew that he would regret passing up an opportunity to continue playing. The whole process of finding an agent and a team overseas was daunting and confusing. He was unsure of what questions to ask or where to direct them. Compared to all that went into his college decision, he barely did any research. From the few options the agents presented him, Olson opted to sign with a mid-level professional club in Germany.

In the span of three months, he became the first in his family to graduate from college and then the first in his family to cross the Atlantic. Olson played well in his first season—well enough, he thought, to warrant a spot in a higher division. It was another in a series of calls that never came. When his agent told him that there were no opportunities in Europe's higher leagues, he reluctantly began plotting for life after basketball. While playing a second and final season in Germany, he spent his free time studying for and earning personal training certifications. When the season ended, he returned home to San Diego, retired from basketball at age 24. Up until that point, life revolved around the game. He was left to wonder what he would do without it.

In the summer of 1988, Mike Fratello found himself in Moscow in desperate need of some contraband. He placed an order with Bob Wussler, a Turner executive with strong contracts in the former Soviet Union, who was flying in to meet Fratello and the rest of the Atlanta Hawks. When

Wussler arrived at the Cosmos Hotel, he delivered each item on the coach's detailed list.

Fratello then threw on a big Soviet chef's hat and, along with his wife, commandeered the hotel's kitchen. Thanks to the ingredients Wussler smuggled in, Fratello had everything he needed to cook a traditional Italian pasta dinner for the Hawks and their hosts, the Soviet National Team. He gathered the Soviets around the saucepans, working through the language barrier to teach them the proper way to stir and simmer the gravy. By the end of the evening, the two parties had emptied their plates, filled their bellies, and taken another step toward bridging the cultural divide.

When Hubie Brown invited Fratello to join the Hawks coaching staff in 1978, he unwittingly set into motion a chain of events that would put the Montclair State grad at the forefront of the NBA's international expansion. Hawks owner Ted Turner, who brought Fratello back as the team's head coach in 1983, was beginning to forge business and diplomatic relationships within the Soviet Union. The United States had boycotted the 1980 Moscow Olympics, and the Soviets responded in kind by sitting out the '84 Los Angeles Games. Turner stepped into that void, creating the Goodwill Games, an every-four-year multisport multinational athletic extravaganza. It would, of course, air on Turner's television networks.

The first Goodwill Games took place in Moscow in 1986. The schedule coincided with a completely unaffiliated event, the FIBA World Championships in Spain. Turner cleverly scooped up the television rights to the global basketball tournament and shoehorned it into the Goodwill production, even though more than 4,000 kilometers separated the competitions. Turner asked Fratello, who had never worked in television, to announce the games.

At the World Championships, Fratello watched the Soviet National team with great interest. A few of their star players appeared talented enough to compete at the NBA level. The Soviets blocked their players from signing with Western leagues, but the Hawks, unlike any other NBA team, had an owner with a direct line to the Soviet Olympic Committee and Soviet Basketball Federation. So the team began working on a player pipeline from Moscow to Atlanta. The Hawks were heavy in their pursuit of two players in particular—a lefty wing with the strength of a charging bull named Sarunas Marciulionis and a nimble big man named Sasha Volkov.

In 1988, the Hawks requested the NBA's permission to tour the Soviet Union. NBA commissioner David Stern, who was keen on growing the league's international audience, not only approved the trip, but he and his wife also joined the traveling party. Fratello was willing to do whatever it took, even cooking the Soviets an Italian pasta dinner, if it meant signing a few of their players. "He saw the talent on that team," said Kim Bohuny, who worked on Turner's Goodwill Games efforts before joining the NBA as senior vice president of international basketball operations. "If he had the ability to get these players before any other NBA team, obviously he was going to take advantage of that."

The Hawks fought a war on two fronts—the first to convince the Soviets to allow their players to join the NBA, and the second to ensure that, when that day came, their team would be the main beneficiary. Along with general manager Stan Kasten, Fratello chased the Soviet National Team across Europe, catching them at as many Olympic warmup games as possible with the hopes of stealing a minute or two of conversation with Marciulionis and Volkov.

During a 1988 meeting in Vilnius, Lithuania, to discuss Marciuliunas' future, representatives from the Hawks met with the Soviet Olympic Committee, Lithuanian Olympic Committee, Lithuanian Sports Ministry, and Marciuliunas' club team. Bohuny, who was there as part of the Hawks contingent, could see how stressed Marciuliunas was as he watched 30 people decide his fate. She went to speak with him after the meeting, and Marciuliunas graciously invited her over to his house to join him and his wife for dinner. When Bohuny walked into Marciuliunas' kitchen, she saw an unexpected, but familiar, face—Golden State Warriors assistant coach Donnie Nelson. "What are you doing?" she asked the 26-year-old Nelson, not to be confused with his father, NBA player-turned-coach Don Nelson.

"Oh," said Nelson, "I've been living here for a few months." He told Bohuny he was crashing at the house while running camps and clinics around Lithuania.

Bohuny knew the Warriors, who had also been tailing the Soviet National Team, would not let Marciulionas go without a fight. "Almost everywhere Mike [Fratello] would be," Bohuny said, "Donnie would be also." When she saw Nelson literally making himself at home in the Marciulionis' kitchen, she began to first entertain the idea that the Hawks might lose the pursuit.

THAT MARCIULIONAS KITCHEN dweller, Donn Nelson, was born in September of 1962, about a month before his father scored six points in his NBA debut. Baby Donn spent his first summer in the Adirondacks, toted around in his father's arms as Nellie waited tables and helped Norm Sonju launch his basketball clinic. At around six years old, Donn won the Quad Cities Fourth of July raffle. His friends urged him to pick the fishing pole as his prize, but he skipped over it in favor of the backboard-less basketball rim. When the family returned to Boston, where his dad was playing for the Celtics, they hung the rim on a telephone pole.

The younger Nelson claims his parents never pushed him into basketball. Still, he found his way to the game. He quickly learned that an accomplished father can cast a large shadow, especially when said father stands six-and-a-half feet tall. As a high schooler, Donn caught Iowa University coach Lute Olson's eye at a summer basketball camp. "He's not blessed with his dad's size, at least not yet, but he's probably a better shooter and he plays very aggressively," Olson told the *Quad-City Times*. "He's a lot like I remember his dad."

Nelson passed up opportunities to play collegiately at big Division I programs, preferring to stay close to the Brookfield, Wisconsin, home of his mom and three younger sisters. He enrolled at Wheaton College in Illinois, a small liberal arts school with a strong Evangelical Christian backbone, where he majored in physical education. As a four-year starter, he scored a lot of points, mostly in vain. Wheaton struggled to compete in the College Conference of Illinois and Wisconsin (CCIW), one of Division III's toughest leagues. Nelson's talent shone through. He made all-league three times, including as a sophomore, when he was the only underclassman on the all-CCIW teams. Nearly every local newspaper article about Nelson during his college career mentioned his famous father. One would think his full legal name included the appendage "son of Milwaukee Bucks coach Don Nelson."

At his mother's urging, Nelson spent several college summers with Athletes in Action, a Christian international touring team that played hoops and spread the gospel. "I had the chance to see how basketball was played in different countries and different cultures," Nelson said. "It was just an incredible mix of experiences that cannot be replicated." The trips would change the course of Nelson's professional life. An Athletes in Action tour brought him to Lithuania for the first time, where he found himself helpless to defend Marciulionis. He filed away the memory.

Nelson, who had grown up in NBA locker rooms and had also done some scouting for his dad's Milwaukee Bucks teams during college, knew he was too small and slow to play in the league. He aspired to continue playing, potentially in Europe. "I also really want to coach, probably at the high school level," Nelson told *The Rock Island Argus* during his final college season, "or be involved as a youth pastor at a church."

Instead, the fresh-out-of-college Nelson joined the Warriors as a part-time staffer. It was unheard of for a small-college player to jump directly to a job in the NBA, but not all small-college players shared a name with one of the best coaches in the league. The next season, Nelson Sr. joined the Warriors as head coach and vice president. The younger Nelson had a good sense of humor about it, telling the *Oakland Tribune*, "I had to pull a lot of strings to get him in. It was tough."

Donn did a lot of scouting, often making the trips that the more experienced members of the Warriors staff opted to skip. They went to the tournaments in Hawaii; he attended the tournaments in Alaska. Having grown up around the NBA, he possessed a sixth sense for which prospects would or would not cut it in the league. And thanks to his time with Athletes in Action, he was comfortable traveling to the far corners of the world and forging relationships through basketball. Many of the stamps on his passport were mementos from his pursuit of Marciulionis. Nelson visited Lithuania often, usually staying at Marciulionis' home. While following the Soviet National team around Europe, Nelson began building out what would become basketball's most comprehensive global rolodex. That network ultimately defined his career.

Around the same time, Lithuania began their bloody and arduous path toward independence from the Soviets, clearing the way for Marciulionis to sign with the Warriors. In 1989, he became the first player from the former Soviet Union to join the NBA, a milestone that was nearly waylaid at JFK Airport. Nelson planned to meet the Marciulionis family in New York and help them through customs, but his plane arrived at the opposite end of the airport from Marciulionis' gate. Customs agents refused to let Nelson through until he mentioned that he knew Warriors star Chris Mullin, whose dad used to work in customs at JFK. Once those agents heard the name "Mullin," they escorted Nelson to the Marciulionis family, whose paperwork was not completely in order. "I firmly believe that if I hadn't ever mentioned Mullin's name, Sarunas would have been detained," Nelson told Jeff Chapman of the *Oakland Tribune*, "possibly even returned to Moscow if the right people couldn't be reached."

With Marciulionis finally in Warriors blue and gold, Nelson dedicated much of his time to the Lithuanian, assisting him with on-the-court skillwork, helping him acclimate to American life, and venturing over to his house every other night to watch film. The younger Nelson, straddling the coaching and scouting worlds, notched a historic victory. The next challenge would be to prove he wasn't a one-hit wonder.

DESPITE MISSING OUT on Marciulionis, Fratello and the Hawks did not leave their dalliance with the Soviets empty-handed. Days after Marciulionis signed with the Warriors, Sasha Volkov joined the Hawks. Fratello did everything in his power to position his new big man for success.

It helped that the relationship between Fratello and Volkov got off to such a cordial start during the Hawks' summer tours with the Soviets. "When Sasha came in 1989," Bohuny said, "he knew Mike, he knew his family, and I think he felt very comfortable playing with him because he felt he knew his game and he understood where he came from." Fratello made a point to communicate clearly, so that Volkov could grasp his directions. He also took care of Volkov and his family off the court as well. "He invited me to Christmas at his house," Volkov told Pete Croatto, author of *From Hang Time to Prime Time*. "If I had some problem not in basketball but in life, he always came to my house to help me. His wife took care of my wife. And I became part of his family."

Volkov's first season in the NBA coincided with Fratello's final campaign as head coach of the Hawks. Much of the roster did not share the Ukrainian big man's warm, fuzzy feelings toward their skipper. Sam Smith of the *Chicago Tribune* reported that it was "a near-mutiny that got Fratello run out of Atlanta in 1990 after seven seasons there. Like another emperor, this 5'6" czar has a little Napoleon in him, often seeing players as battlefield objects to be moved around much like those garbage cans that late night in New Jersey."

Thanks to the positive experience Fratello had announcing the Goodwill Games, the recently fired coach joined Marv Albert on NBC's national broadcast team. Ever the teacher, Fratello thrived when given the opportunity to mark up plays for the audience. Albert repurposed the "czar" nickname appointed to Fratello during his coaching days, calling him the "Czar of the Telestrator." It was a fitting moniker for someone so influential in opening up the NBA to Russia and Eastern Europe.

Fratello announced nationally televised games for three seasons, staying top of mind to both fans and team executives. His telestrator drawings acted to apply a shiny new coat of wax, transforming him from retread to top coaching free agent. The experience helped inspire agents like Fratello representative Lonnie Cooper to push their out-of-work clients into broadcasting. Owners liked hiring big names, and nothing helped a fired coach stay relevant like a job in TV. Unlike many coaches who use broadcasting as a bridge to their next job, Fratello didn't stick to inoffensive and uninteresting sound bites. "When he was a color man with Marv," said NBA on NBC colleague Bob Costas, "he was, without being obnoxious or ripping anybody, still willing to offer a critique of a situation."

In 1993, the Cavaliers hired Fratello as their new head coach. Five-Star Basketball guys Ron Rothstein and Richie Adubato, who had both recently been relieved of head coaching jobs themselves, joined his staff. The Jersey Guy bond was so well understood that, when Larry Bird coached against Fratello, he refused to do the traditional pregame interview with announcer Hubie Brown for fear that Brown would just regurgitate the conversation back to Fratello.

After six seasons in Cleveland, Fratello returned to the Turner umbrella—this time as an announcer for games on TNT and TBS. He had one more stint as an NBA head coach, spending two-and-a-half seasons with the Memphis Grizzlies, taking over for—who else—the man who did so much to empower him and elevate him throughout his career, Hubie Brown.

Following Brown one last time was a poetic ending to Fratello's NBA coaching career, but the truly beautiful culmination of the czar's life as a teacher and a coach came in 2014, when he became the head coach of the Ukrainian National Team. Volkov, who was then president of the Ukrainian Basketball Federation, personally invited Fratello to lead his nation's team.

Their partnership helped yield Ukraine's first-ever appearance in the FIBA World Cup in 2014. It had been nearly 30 years since Fratello first set eyes on Volkov and his talented Soviet teammates. Through the decades of war, independence, peace, and, sadly, war again, there was always the love and respect between Fratello and Volkov, a relationship rooted in the game of basketball.

IN MARCH OF 1992, the Palace at Auburn Hills presented three consecutive nights of entertainment, graciously provided by the Bay Area's finest. The first two evenings, the suburban Detroit arena hosted the Grateful Dead. On the second night, somewhere amidst the tie-dyed and swaying wookies, stood Donnie Nelson and Sarunas Marciulionas. The following night, the Warriors would take on the Pistons in the very same arena. Marciulionas, no stranger to playing in games underneath a cigarette haze in Europe's gyms, wasn't quite accustomed to *that* type of smoke. He wondered how they were going to play with that smell in the air.

Following the show, which the Dead closed with "Not Fade Away," Nelson and Marciulionas met with the band and asked them if they'd help finance Lithuania's Olympic efforts. Thanks in part to the band's generosity, the newly independent nation's basketball team qualified for the Olympics. After defeating the former Soviet Unified Team in an emotional bronze medal match, Marciulionas and the Lithuanians proudly waved from the medal stand while clad in their now-iconic tie-dye outfits. Nelson, who served as an assistant coach, had a front-row seat for their historic achievement.

Nelson remained with the Warriors for a few more seasons, content to continue his coaching curriculum. "Right now I'm going through an educational process," he told the *Oakland Tribune* in 1993. "I'm learning as much as I can from one of the best teachers in the game [his father, Don]. Eventually I'm going to want to take that education and do something with it on my own."

Garry St. Jean, who was the elder Nelson's top assistant at the time, admired Donnie's approach. "The thing I loved about Donnie, he was really inquisitive," St. Jean said. "He was always dreaming." St. Jean felt a kinship with Donnie, the son of his mentor and a fellow small-college grad.

Surprisingly, Donnie was not the first Wheaton grad to reach the NBA. Both Les Habegger (Sonics GM from '83-'85) and Randy Pfund (Lakers head coach from '92-'93 and Heat GM from '96-'08) spent years coaching at small colleges before fortuitous connections elevated them to NBA staffs and eventual leadership roles.

Thanks to some good old-fashioned nepotism, Nelson didn't have to do his time wandering in the coaching desert like Pfund and Habegger. His last name provided a shortcut to the Promised Land. Nelson's impressive achievement was not that he made it to the league in the first place, but what he did when he got there. "Every son of an established person has to prove themselves," said longtime Suns executive Jerry Colangelo, who hired Nelson as an assistant coach in Phoenix. "Donnie went about his business. He was personable, he worked hard, and he gained the respect on his own."

Following three seasons on the Suns' staff, Nelson reunited with his father, who had taken over as coach and lead basketball executive of the Dallas Mavericks shortly after Norm Sonju's retirement. In Dallas, Donnie decided to travel the Garry St. Jean path—he gave up coaching and fully dedicated himself to the front office. "The coaching profession lost a superstar when he decided to go to the management side," said Rick Carlisle, who as a rival assistant coach, witnessed Nelson's strength as a strategist.

As an executive, Nelson proved he was not a one-trick pony when it came to international scouting. Matching up with Marciulionis in a scrimmage was a stroke of luck, but the skills he acquired in pursuing and signing the Lithuanian lefty were portable. After more than a decade in the league, he had shaken hands, taken in games, and shared meals with basketball bigwigs from all over the world.

Keith Grant, the former Mavericks equipment manager who later rose as high as assistant general manager in Dallas, occasionally accompanied Nelson overseas. He watched in awe as Nelson, who he refers to as "the mayor of Europe," expanded his international network. "We were all trying to find that extra edge, and Donnie beat everybody to it," Grant said. "You don't know how far that goes when somebody from the NBA brings you into their circle."

Americans can be spoiled by their country's healthy financial and legal systems. In other corners of the world, contracts carry little weight unless they're underwritten by a strong personal relationship, like those Nelson had been building over the course of decades. By traveling from country to country, sitting on the same bleachers and sharing meals with everyone from high-ranking basketball officials to juniors coaches, Nelson was perpetually prepared to pounce on the next global prospect. "He developed a vast network of friends in the basketball world," Kim Bohuny said. "Not just in Europe, but in each continent, and he figured out how to do business in each of those systems."

Through backchannel communications and reams of paperwork, Nelson signed the NBA's first Chinese player, Wang Zhizhi, in 2001. "That's Donnie working the relationships to help get something done," Grant said. "There's no question about that."

As if successfully importing the first NBA players from China and the former Soviet Union wasn't enough to prove his international bona fides, Nelson also helped orchestrate a 1998 draft night trade that brought two foreign-born future MVPs to Dallas—Steve Nash and Dirk Nowitzki. The Mavericks coveted Nowitzki for months leading up to the draft, ever since a meet-cute that was textbook Donnie.

During the Nike Hoop Summit in Dallas, Nelson noticed that event organizers had turned away the man accompanying the teenaged Nowitzki. Nelson introduced himself to the man and bought him dinner and a beer. The companion turned out to be Nowitzki's guru, Holger Geschwindner, the quirky coach who oversaw the young German's training and managed his career. That dinner, according to Thomas Pletzinger's biography *The Great Nowitzki*, was "more important to Dirk's future than any team meeting at the top of the tower." (To take the small school connection a step further, Geschwindner learned the game from a boarding school headmaster named Theo Clausen, who in turn learned the game during his time at Springfield College.) After successfully trading for Nowitzki's draft rights, Nelson booked a flight to Wurzburg, Germany, where he, Geschwindner, and the Nowitzki family got drunk and pledged "eternal friendship."

In 2002, Nelson took over for his father as the Mavericks lead basketball executive. He oversaw the construction of the 2011 team that won the franchise's first NBA title. As Nowitzki's stellar career wound down in the late 2010s, Nelson again identified and acquired a franchise anchor from overseas. He began scouting Luka Doncic when the Slovenian prospect was just 14 years old, working off of a recommendation from some of his international contacts. Despite Doncic's unprecedented success in the top European leagues, not all NBA scouts viewed him as a can't-miss prospect. Carlisle, the Mavericks coach at the time, remembers Nelson as the only person in the league who knew how good Doncic would be. When Nelson declared that Doncic would be the best player in the 2018 draft, Carlisle asked if he was as good as Argentinian Hall of Famer Manu Ginobili. Nelson replied, "Maybe better."

Leading up to the draft, Nelson worked the phones, eager to find a way to turn the Mavericks' No. 5 draft pick into Doncic. He eventually found a trade partner in the Atlanta Hawks, owners of the third pick. "Make no mistake, they were targeted," said Rick Sund, who was working as an adviser for the Hawks at the time. "They were taking him one. There are a lot of teams that wouldn't have taken Doncic first. They would've."

When asked about Dallas' decision to pursue Doncic so aggressively, Grant gave Nelson full credit. "It was all him," Grant said. "There was no question."

In a business not known for its job security, Nelson spent more than two decades with the Mavericks before an ugly divorce in 2021. Even though he spent much of his career working with his father, Nelson's long list of accomplishments as a talent evaluator and team builder helped him emerge from out of his dad's shadow. He will go down in NBA history as an innovator and a builder of international basketball bridges, a legacy that stands on its own. "He knew the importance of developing relationships— be it domestically or internationally—and he did a terrific job in doing that," Colangelo said. "Therefore, he developed his own reputation in terms of who he was. Not the son of Don Nelson—but Donnie Nelson himself."

Bohuny, who has had a front-row seat since the very beginning of the league's globalization efforts, said that Nelson is "regarded as the greatest international scout ever." She's not alone in that opinion. "I'll make this statement categorically and really unapologetically," Carlisle said. "Without Donnie Nelson, the impact of the international game on the NBA would be nothing like what it is today."

It's a legacy that traces back to Nelson's summers as a Wheaton College student spent traveling with Athletes in Action. By playing such a vital role in globalizing the game, Nelson became yet another small-college alum who unwittingly prepared the league for what would soon be a steady stream of leaders with D3 backgrounds.

Bill Fitch and Mike Fratello helped legitimize the notion that coaches who never played professionally could impact winning. Carl Scheer, Norm Sonju, and Bob Whitsitt proved that executives with a head for business and a love of basketball could lead to organizational success on and off the court. And Donnie Nelson showed that open borders could provide a competitive advantage for those with an open mind. With Division III's founding in 1973, more and more small-college guys working in basketball were now collectively bonded together under the Division III banner. The conditions were finally right for the formation of the D3 pipeline's two largest branches.

PART II:
Main Branches

CHAPTER 7

A COACHING FAMILY

*How Jeff Van Gundy's unexpected position in the NBA
provided opportunities for other "D3 schleps" to shine*

Basketball brought Andrew Olson across the country and then across the world. But when his playing days ended, he was finally free to return home to San Diego. That first post-retirement summer, he worked as a personal trainer and dabbled in commercial real estate. His life without basketball made for an unnatural fit—like a suit and tie on a gym teacher.

His break from the game didn't stem from a lack of opportunities. Had he wanted to, a few phone calls would've undoubtedly unleashed a flood of coaching jobs. Those same characteristics that pigeonholed him as a Division III prospect—short, White, unathletic point guard—made him the prototypical coach in the eyes of many.

Administrators at a local private high school cold-contacted him with a head coaching job offer. Olson's ego prevented him from taking it. College classmates of his were bankers and consultants earning six figures and already celebrating their first promotions. Others were well on their way to MBAs, JDs, or MDs. Compared to them, he felt he would've been a failure to "just" coach high school ball.

The college assistant route was also mostly a non-starter. Schools generally compensated graduate assistants with a few thousand dollars, a meal plan, and a free master's degree. Going down that path meant he'd have to chase the best jobs across the country and hope for some luck along the way. Olson was the type who saw the tried-and-true path as a failure of creativity. It was a sentiment innate in his style of play. Why set up a teammate with a two-handed bounce pass when you could achieve the same result with a no-look behind-the-back dime?

In 2010, the lure of entrepreneurship was strong. To paraphrase *The Social Network*, which hit theaters that same year, Olson looked at his options and said, "A high school or small-college coaching job isn't cool. You know what is cool? Starting a vertically integrated basketball skills and personal training business."

An Amherst degree gave him more confidence to explore, to do things his own way. He was no stranger to big dreams. Even though he fell short of his Division I goals, that ambition carried him to two Player of the Year awards, a national championship, and a few years of playing overseas. A coaching job would've locked him into a path. With the training business, his future still seemed limitless. He started plotting out a career—build a booming business, maybe create an app, maybe even write a book.

Thanks to his summers spent coaching school-aged kids, he had a built-in clientele and some positive word-of-mouth buzz. Once every few weeks, a former teammate or the parent of a client would introduce him to someone else, resulting in more business and more possibilities. The success stemmed from following his passion, sure, but it was more a function of following his network. And his network was basketball.

Stan Van Gundy remembers receiving the phone call from Orlando Magic general manager Otis Smith that fateful morning in the summer of 2011. "You're on *SportsCenter*," Smith told Van Gundy, the Magic head coach. "I don't know how the hell they got it."

In the video, the mustachioed Van Gundy, wearing glasses, a long-sleeved gray shirt, and some striped blue shorts, calls for a ball. While encouraging campers to experiment with different dribbling combinations, he walks on to the empty court and unleashes a through-the-legs-behind-the-back combo followed by a crisp spin move and between the legs crossover. People in the audience gasp.

Bloggers and the nascent NBA Twitter community swarmed to the 15-second clip like ants on a dropped lollipop. The spirit behind the video's viral popularity made it abundantly clear: nobody expected the

50-some-odd-year-old coach to have handles like *that*. "People look at me: short, fat guy coaching, and just assume I could never do anything," Van Gundy said. "The bar was low. So the fact that you can get the ball from one hand to the other, people were even surprised by that."

Stan's younger brother, Jeff, also a former NBA coach, claims to have shared his brother's ability to dazzle on the court—as long as nobody was actually guarding him. "When I was doing individual workouts, I could beat the cones on the court off the dribble every time," Jeff told Dan Patrick for a 2015 column in *Sports Illustrated*. "It was those darn other players that got in the way of my greatness."

Self-deprecating comments aside, the Van Gundy brothers were once accomplished collegiate players. Stan, who originally committed to Division II UC-Davis, had a change of heart when his dad took the head coaching job at Brockport State, a Division III public college just outside of Rochester, New York. With his parents and brother set to move from their Bay Area home, Stan decided at the last minute to tag along and enroll at Brockport State. Since his dad was the coach, he knew two things—he would have a spot on the team, and the coach would be really tough on him.

Standing just 5'7" and rail thin, Stan never missed a single game in his four years at Brockport St. He didn't shoot much, but when he did, he made a high percentage. Over the course of his sophomore and junior seasons, he sank a school-record 53 consecutive free throws. Stan was also an excellent student—a double-major in physical education and English who graduated *summa cum laude* with a 3.83 GPA. Thanks to his combined excellence on the court and in the classroom, Stan won his school's and his conference's outstanding student-athlete awards.

Even though Stan was a solid player in his own right, his younger brother was the more accomplished on the court. Jeff originally enrolled at Yale University, but the assistant coach who recruited him left the school. After fall pickup games, the coaches informed Jeff he would be playing JV. "Getting cut, just like getting fired later in life, it's a body blow whenever anyone tells you they're better off without you," Jeff said.

During his freshman year at Yale, Jeff wrestled with a decision— should he sacrifice an Ivy League education so he could transfer and play varsity college ball, or should he stay and effectively give up on hoops? He ultimately opted to leave Yale.

Had he transferred directly to a D3 school, he would have had to sit out a year. So Jeff Van Gundy became the first and (probably) only person to ever transfer from Yale University to Menlo Junior College. Then, after a year at Menlo, it was off to Brockport to play for his father. That arrangement also lasted just one season. His dad was fired, so Jeff, who was voted team MVP and named captain for the upcoming season, refused to stay. He transferred to Nazareth College, his fourth school in four years. "He kind of was before his time," said Bill Nelson, the coach who recruited Jeff to Nazareth. "He was his own transfer portal."

The match between Van Gundy and Nazareth turned out idyllic, a marriage well worth the three divorces preceding it. "It was one of the best decisions of his life," said Bill Van Gundy, Jeff's dad.

In Jeff's first season at Nazareth, the team won their NCAA Regional and earned a trip to the Division III quarterfinals. Nazareth played Clark University with a trip to the Final Four on the line. Clark's coach, Wally Halas, remembers focusing his pregame scouting efforts on Van Gundy. "He was a tough, small point guard," Halas said. "Knew how to play, could score a little bit, dogged defender, just a really solid, good Division III guard." Van Gundy went toe to toe with Clark's star guard, Dan Trant, who the Boston Celtics drafted later that year, but Clark outlasted Nazareth for the win.

That spring, Nazareth graduated four of their starters. Coach Nelson prepared Jeff, the lone remaining starter, for a rebuilding season. Nelson remembered his point guard growing furious, telling him, "Rebuilding's for losers." Jeff set a high bar in offseason workouts, which bled into the regular season. The "rebuilding" team went 20–6. Jeff set a single-season school assist record and was named to the All-East Region team. Nelson calls Jeff the best defensive player he ever coached, one who always matched up with the opposing team's top guard. When asked to recall a quintessential Van Gundy play, Nelson describes Jeff's unique ability to scramble from the top of the key down to the baseline as a help defender to take a charge. "He would go flying into the wall," Nelson said, "whether he should or shouldn't have." The robust Rochester D3 community knew him as "All-Out Jeff."

"He must have a heart like Secretariat," said Nelson, who sat "All-Out Jeff" on the bench only two minutes per game. "He was just relentless out there."

As a high school senior, Rochester area resident Kevin Broderick attended a Nazareth game to get a feel for the Division III level. He was blown away by Van Gundy, who hounded the ball on defense and played so precisely and efficiently on offense. *If that's what Division III point guards look like, I'm done here*, Broderick thought.

Even opposing coaches left a game against Nazareth in awe. "Jeff is the biggest over-achiever *[sic]* I have seen in basketball," Geneseo St. coach Tom Pope told Nazareth's student paper, *The Gleaner*. "He's not big, he's not fast, he's not quick. He just beats you with enthusiasm, hustle, poise, and tremendous knowledge of the game. He's a genuine coach on the floor."

Jeff acted like a coach off the floor as well. When Nelson would scout local teams, sometimes he'd look across the stands and, to his surprise, see Jeff sitting there, taking in the action. During one Nazareth game, an opponent busted out an exotic defense—an inverted triangle and two. Nelson called timeout. Before he could speak, Jeff took charge of the huddle and broke down exactly how to attack the defense. Sure enough, his strategy worked to perfection.

The most ludicrous chapter in Jeff's Nazareth lore took place at Roanoke College. The game was heading for a second overtime when one of the referees called a technical foul on the Nazareth assistant coach for arguing. With no time on the clock, Roanoke made both technical free throws. The referees waved their arms, signaling the end of the game. Rather than accept the loss, Jeff gathered the refs together. "Listen!" he said. "My father's a coach, and I've been in this situation before. These points should go into the second overtime." Convinced by Jeff's confidence, the refs reversed their decision. They applied the two free throws to the beginning of the second overtime and called the teams back to the floor.

A few years later, one of the referees from that game ran into Nelson. "You son of a bitch!" the ref said. "You don't know how much trouble we got in by making that mistake." Turns out, Jeff was wrong. Those free throws at the end of the first overtime should've ended the game. And they would have, had he not sprung to action.

When asked to provide a scouting report on his kids, the elder Coach Van Gundy said that his boys were "as good as players as their abilities would take them. Stan was very unathletic. Stan lacked quickness, of course. Size definitely was not there. But he was a very skilled ballhandler. He didn't turn the ball over. He was a very good shooter. Let's say this: his performance went beyond his ability. Jeff was a better athlete, though not a great one by any means. But he saw playing differently than Stan. Stan shot the ball, and I'm going to tell you the term 'shot selection' during his high school years was not a major term at all. Jeff worked and became a good shooter, but he had to really work at that. He actually saw the role that he was playing as he was running an offense. The combination of the two would've really been a good player."

As Stan and Jeff Van Gundy's playing careers wound down, they immediately transitioned into coaching. Their dreams never revolved around riches or notoriety, only teaching the game they loved. They hoped to one day run their own program, preferably at the small-college level. The brothers Van Gundy grew up surrounded by coaches, revering coaches, and aspiring to be coaches. Many credit the patriarch, Bill, with creating the Van Gundy ethos, the rich soil that sprouted what has become a mighty coaching tree. Bill, however, rejected that premise and then deflected much of the praise toward his wife, Cindy. According to Bill, the boys learned their trademark tireless work ethic from their mother. Plus, she hailed from Indiana, the basketball capital of the Midwest, and knew a thing or two about the game herself.

Bill, of course, also knew his way around a basketball court. His journey into coaching was, unlike his sons' straight-ahead paths, one that resulted from an abrupt left turn while in college. Bill originally enrolled at Cal-Berkeley with the expectation that he would study pharmacy and then take a job a family friend had waiting for him. Except Bill was color blind, which made subjects like organic chemistry extra challenging. As a sophomore, he acknowledged the mounting evidence that his future was not in medicine. Basketball intrigued him, so he transferred his major to physical education. "I really didn't have any idea what to do," Bill said, "but I knew that I would enjoy coaching."

In a bandbox high school gym, Bill began a coaching career that would eventually take him to the college ranks. From the time they were toddlers, Stan and Jeff rode the team bus to games and sat on the sidelines during practices. The brothers got their first taste of coaching in junior high and middle school, respectively. Bill, then the assistant varsity and head freshman coach at Cal St. Hayward, was recuperating from surgery and unable to scout a nearby game. Since his lone assistant had to run practice, a bed-ridden Bill sent 13-year-old Stan and 10-year-old Jeff on a scouting trip. Their mother chauffeured them.

The boys delivered exactly what their father asked of them. They wrote down the defense the team played, whether or not they pressed, and noted the best rebounders. Stan recalls the scouting trip as the first time he felt the excitement of coaching. From that moment forward, the boys never wavered in their career ambitions. "They were never one to be a fireman or a policeman," Bill said. "They were going to be high school coaches."

In that regard, the Van Gundy boys were not unique. According to General Social Survey data analyzed by *The New York Times*, when a father works in a particular field, their son is three times as likely to pursue that same career. Economists David Laband and Barney Lentz studied this trend of "footstep following" for decades, hoping to determine the forces behind hand-me-down careers. They found that parents, especially ones as involved as Bill and Cindy Van Gundy, don't just pass down genetic traits. They also build up a child's human capital—the knowledge and skill an employee brings to their job. Where a farmer's child might—through chores, training, and overheard conversations—learn the ins and outs of farming at a young age, Jeff and Stan grew up with access to a deep well of basketball knowledge. They willingly, gladly, and deeply drank. "It's not about the X's and O's," Jeff told Eric Gilmore of the *Contra Costa Times*, when asked about what he learned from watching his father. "It's how you go about your daily business, what loyalty you give. You don't know you're learning, but to see it firsthand every day for so long, you pick it up."

Andy Greer and Broderick, both of whom coached under Bill Van Gundy, recall him sweeping the gym floor and washing the team's uniforms. No part of the coaching job was beneath him. His humility and reverence for the position never wavered.

Of course, following in a parents' footsteps can come with other perks as well. Nepotism can and does factor in a footstep follower's career success. Although one's last name cannot perform a job in and of itself, it can open doors to exclusive rooms. Even if the child of a coach has all the tools to be successful, so too might another unconnected young coach who never gets the chance to prove themselves. Laband, the economist who studied footstep following, acknowledged that "reputational capital" can also help create a family coaching dynasty. "A successful coach reputationally can enhance a son's or daughter's chance of breaking in," Laband said. "What's happening is that the hiring staff is banking on the possibility that the second generation of coaches is going to be as good as the first generation, and that justifies taking a risk."

Despite his father's connections and a glowing recommendation from his college coach, Jeff had trouble landing a college assistant job straight out of Nazareth. He began his career as head varsity coach at McQuaid Jesuit High School, an all-boys school in the Rochester area. In the summer, Jeff met with all the players and parents to discuss roles and expectations. Once the season began, he handed out playbooks, drew up scouting reports, and delivered well-thought-out pregame and postgame speeches. Off the court, he oversaw a team study hall to help ensure the players kept up with their schoolwork. He emphasized chemistry and camaraderie, organizing outings to McQuaid football games and hosting team dinners at his apartment. "I was surprised that they were hiring somebody right out of college," said Greg Woodard, one of Jeff's players at McQuaid, "but that first impression changed very quickly. He had a very structured, disciplined program."

As a young coach, "All Out Jeff" wasn't afraid to get onto the court and demonstrate one or two of his old tricks. Late in a preseason scrimmage, a McQuaid player failed to dive for a loose ball. Jeff called a timeout. He decided the team needed a lesson. He took a short running start and slid headfirst across the floor. After brushing himself off, Jeff told the player, "I don't care what you do in the last few minutes of the game, but you better dive on the floor." Eventually, the player found an excuse and hit the deck. The bench erupted into applause, and Jeff successfully turned a teaching moment, which could have alienated a player, into one that galvanized the team.

Jeff also liked to loosen up his team with both humor and humility. Prior to McQuaid's second game of the season, Jeff walked into the locker room and delivered an unexpected pregame speech. "The other coach is going for his 300th win tonight," Jeff told the team. "I'm going for my second. Do *not* make this a coaching contest."

Jeff's time at McQuaid wasn't all jokes and motivational ploys. When his college coach, Nelson, took a night away from Nazareth to watch a McQuaid game, he remembered seeing Jeff, whose suit and tie hung off of him "like an unmade bed," ferociously argue a call with an official. The league had a rule that prevented coaches from leaving the vicinity of their spot on the bench, so Jeff opted to hook his leg around the chair and practically crawl on the gym floor to get as close to the ref as he could.

ON DECEMBER 31, 1985, Jeff Van Gundy called Greg Woodard to remind him of their New Year's Day plans. "Hey, we're on tomorrow. Ten o'clock."

"Well," Woodard replied, trying to convince his coach for a rain check. "School's closed tomorrow. And it's New Year's Day, and…um…actually, it's my birthday."

Jeff wasn't having it. He told Woodard that he needed to keep working, that he had to get better every day. So, on the very first day of 1986, Woodard spent his 16th birthday in an unheated gym, running through a workout with his 23-year-old coach.

That New Year's Day session was one of many for Woodard. During the season, Jeff carved out time to run his players through one-on-one sessions, which was borderline unheard of for a high school coach in the 1980s. At the end of the one-on-one practices, Woodard would sit in the locker room completely spent, blood dripping from his hands, an unfortunate side effect from the repeated game-speed dunks that his coach demanded. Woodard had so many individual sessions in the McQuaid gym that it's hard for him to remember *the* workout, the one that changed the trajectory of his coach's career…and his coach's *brother's* career.

During interviews or at coaching clinics, Stan expertly spins the same old yarn about how, even though he wasn't even in the same state, the Woodard Workout changed his life. "If Greg Woodard isn't at McQuaid Jesuit High School," Stan Van Gundy said, "if Jeff doesn't have a player of that caliber who brings Stu Jackson into the gym, Jeff and I are both coaching either high school or small-college basketball right now. And that's just the reality of it." The moral of Stan's story is that you cannot chart out a career path. That jobs are not steppingstones. All you can do is work tirelessly so that, should an opportunity arise, you don't squander it.

In 1985—the same year Jeff started at McQuaid—Rick Pitino, a former Five-Star counselor and Hubie Brown's assistant with the New York Knicks, took the head coaching job at Providence College. Following his first season, Pitino tasked two of his assistant coaches, Stu Jackson and Herb Sendek, with driving to upstate New York to meet some local high school coaches and watch potential recruits. Sendek, who was impressed with Woodard's play the previous summer at Five-Star, put McQuaid on the itinerary. With the Providence assistants watching from the sidelines, Van Gundy ran Woodard through one of their individual workouts, which set off a chain of events that directly led both Jeff and Stan to Division I basketball and then, eventually, the NBA.

"It would've been very apparent that this wasn't some young high school coach that was trying to cobble a player workout together," Woodard said. "It would've been very apparent that this was part of a routine, part of something that Coach Van Gundy and I had done repeatedly before that and would probably be repeating many times after."

The Providence assistants left the workout impressed with both Woodard and his young coach. Jackson knew that Pitino, an individual workout guru, would appreciate Jeff's dedication to the craft. In the car on the way back to Rhode Island, Jackson told Sendek, "This guy Van Gundy may make a great graduate assistant."

Following Jackson's recommendation, Pitino interviewed Jeff over the phone and offered him the job. "Maybe I was the last [interview], and maybe they just got tired of it," said Jeff. "There was nothing from that interview that would've given them some revelation like: this guy might be good."

Pitino welcomed him to campus with a handshake and a "Congrats, Jim." Before long, *Jeff* Van Gundy would make sure Pitino knew his name. Each morning, the coaches all arrived at the office no later than 7:00. Van Gundy beat them in every single day. Of course, it's easy to beat your coworkers to the office when you never leave. For three weeks, Jeff's unpacked car remained parked in the gym lot. He hadn't bothered finding a place to live. He showered in Alumni Hall and slept on one of the fancy couches in the recently remodeled basketball office. At the urging of his fellow coaches, Jeff finally found a place of his own and reluctantly started sleeping there instead.

As a graduate assistant, Jeff monitored study halls, checked on class attendance, and picked up lunches for the other coaches. The role was more a test of his willingness to work than a quiz on his basketball acumen. For the guy who transferred three times and poured out gallons of sweat working out in empty, small-college gyms, it was an easy one to pass. Still, he is quick to downplay his contributions at Providence. "It's not like anybody's [saying], 'Oh man, he brought me a ham and cheese today, he's got talent,'" he joked.

The job wasn't all grunt work and lunch runs. When the more tenured assistants were out recruiting, Jeff ran individual workouts, playing a small role in turning the perennial Big East doormat into a winner. "He did an amazing job, obviously along with [Pitino], in making chicken salad out of chicken you-know-what with our players," Jackson said.

At practices and in the office, Jeff had the unique opportunity to learn from Pitino, a skilled head coach who was full of innovative ideas. Jeff kept his ears and mind open. Of course, he kept his mouth open, too. The other coaches loved to kick back and watch Jeff argue, especially when he respectfully challenged the head coach. Sometimes Pitino would scream at his graduate assistant and belittle his ideas. Then, a few hours later, he would implement Jeff's proposals in practice. "You could see the potential in Jeff in practice and in games," Jackson said. "He had a really sharp mind and grasp for the game that I would attribute to his father. He just grew up a basketball person in a basketball family. His command of the game and his ability to teach, react in game situations, I thought was extraordinary."

During Jeff's first season at Providence, the team made an unlikely run to the Final Four. Pitino, one of the hottest coaching names in America, took a head coaching job with his former employer, the Knicks. "I don't think Rick would've been hired as the head coach of the Knicks had he not had experience as an assistant under Hubie Brown," said Jackson, who joined the Knicks as an assistant on Pitino's staff. Chalk up another assist to Five-Star.

Pitino only lasted two seasons in New York. His successor? Stu Jackson. To fill his last assistant slot, Jackson agonized over two candidates—Greg Graham, his college teammate and an established college coach, and Jeff Van Gundy. Jackson chose Van Gundy. "I just made the decision based on my gut because I knew Jeff was special," Jackson said. "I just knew that he was head coaching material, whether it was the NBA, college, or whatever he decided to do. I felt in my heart he would be a terrific head coach."

Jeff began his NBA career as the third assistant/scout/video coordinator. He discovered that his playing pedigree, or lack thereof, would be a moot point as long as he could help his players improve. "If you worked hard, you had their best interests at heart, and you tried to help them maximize their talents, there were very few guys who were difficult to coach," Van Gundy said. "That doesn't mean there weren't difficult days or decisions they didn't agree with, but I never thought it came down to, 'Oh, you're a Division III player.'"

Whenever a player needed him to rebound, be it morning, noon, or night, Jeff would be there. Early on in his Knicks tenure, Jeff and his parents went to visit Bill Nelson, Jeff's college coach. Nelson remembers asking Jeff if he had a favorite NBA city, to which Jeff replied, "Not really. I never leave my hotel room." He was always working, always preparing.

In a league where staffers rarely survive their head coach's dismissal, Jeff somehow managed to outlast Jackson and hang around through four separate coaching administrations. "Van Gundy became everybody's guy because they saw how hardworking, how loyal he was," said Chris Herring, author of *Blood in the Garden*, the definitive account of the 1990s Knicks.

The trajectory of Jeff's coaching career changed when the Knicks hired Pat Riley as head coach in 1991. Riley, notorious for distrusting holdovers, heeded Knicks executive Dave Checketts' advice and retained Van Gundy. "Van Gundy was the one guy that Checketts asked him to keep and he probably became his favorite assistant," Herring said.

As the Knicks coach, Riley ditched the up-tempo game he favored with the Los Angeles Lakers and embraced a physical, aggressive style of play. He built a culture of sweat equity, one perfectly suited for Jeff. Riley convinced Jeff that he could one day coach an NBA team of his own. He told Jeff that the players didn't care what he looked like or where he played. They only cared about four things—that you were competent, reliable, responsible, and sincere. After four seasons together and one trip to the NBA Finals, Riley left the Knicks for Miami. That move turned out to be another stroke of luck for the Van Gundy brothers, one that eventually led to them becoming just the second set of siblings in NBA history to face off as head coaches.

PRIOR TO RILEY'S move to Miami, when he was still coaching the Knicks, Stu Jackson took a job as head coach of the University of Wisconsin. To repair a program that hadn't made an NCAA Tournament in more than 40 years, Jackson knew he would need some outstanding assistants. He decided to run some names by one of *his* favorite assistants, Jeff Van Gundy. At the end of the conversation, Jeff said, "Listen, I know you've got a big-time job and a big-time task ahead of you trying to revive Wisconsin. You ought to just talk to my brother."

At the time, Stan was wrapping up his fourth season as head coach of UMass-Lowell. His head coaching experience was limited to Division II and NAIA, with a few low-D1 assistant jobs mixed in for good measure. Even though Stan's resume didn't necessarily warrant an interview, Jackson made the call as a courtesy to Jeff.

The elder Van Gundy brother blew Jackson away with his preparation and his character. When they met in person, Stan prepared a comprehensive binder with sample scouting reports and game prep. Here Jackson was, thinking he was doing Jeff Van Gundy a favor, only to find himself sitting across another basketball savant. If anything, Stan's mind was even quicker than Jeff's. When Jackson told basketball people he was considering hiring the other Van Gundy as his first assistant, they scoffed. Jackson was just a few years removed from being an NBA head coach; couldn't he get someone better? For the third time in his career, Jackson trusted his gut and hired a Van Gundy. And for the third time in his career, Jackson had no regrets.

While Stan didn't literally move into the Wisconsin basketball office like Jeff did at Providence, he did make himself at home. In stark contrast to the blank walls, which Stan never decorated with posters or photographs, his desk was an unkempt collection of papers, folders, and stains from some long-ago lunch. Amidst the chaos, Stan somehow created order. Whenever Jackson would walk in and ask for a scouting report, Stan would stick his hand into a seemingly random pile on the desk and pull out a bound file of top-notch work. Then he would reach back and grab a lukewarm can from the crate of Diet Cokes he kept behind him and take a swig.

In just their second season in Madison, the Badgers qualified for the NCAA Tournament. Jackson rode the success to another NBA job, leaving the Wisconsin program in Stan's hands. The D3 kid was now a D1 head coach. "I never even thought about being a Division I head coach, let alone an NBA head coach," Stan said. "I had a small-college background as a player, and my dad had coached at that level and loved it. Quite honestly, had that been where I ended up, as a Division III coach, I would've been extremely happy."

Like his brother before him, Stan's career had surpassed his wildest expectations. Rather than luxuriating in his success, he worked even harder. And then, after one underwhelming season as Wisconsin's head coach, it all came to an abrupt end. He was fired just one year into a five-year deal. So Jeff went to bat for his brother one more time.

Riley, who had just fled the Knicks and hightailed it to Miami, wanted to bring Jeff along as an assistant. The Knicks wouldn't let Jeff out of his contract, so he recommended his brother for the role. Riley interviewed Stan as a favor to Jeff and, like Jackson, left impressed. "[Riley] probably thought, or at least hoped, that I would come in and have a similar work ethic and commitment [as Jeff], so he gave me the opportunity," Stan said. "Also, it helped a great deal that I was still getting paid by the University of Wisconsin, so I saved the Miami Heat a little bit of money there."

To replace Riley, the Knicks went out and hired Don Nelson, who at this point appears to be contractually obligated to pop into each small-college-to-the-NBA guy's journey at least once. The marriage between the loosey-goosey Nelson and the gritty, disciplined Knicks was doomed from the start. Only 59 games into his first season, Nelson and the Knicks parted ways. The team gave the interim job to their longest-tenured assistant—Jeff Van Gundy.

Jeff quickly reinstalled the Riley way of doing things, which the players loved. "When Jeff took over, and we went back to the way we were used to playing," Patrick Ewing said to Adrian Wojnarowski on *The Woj Pod*, "it was like Moses parting the Red Sea or like Lincoln freeing the slaves. We were free again."

Jeff adamantly believes an NBA team would've never hired him outright as a head coach, that the only path to a team of his own was through an interim opportunity. He ended up getting that interim job with a veteran team just two seasons removed from an NBA Finals appearance. Their best player, Ewing, along with other Knicks starters, had humility and what Jeff refers to as "a natural respect for the position of coach." Andy Greer, who joined the Knicks as an assistant a few years later, called Ewing "the most humble superstar in the world." Jeff's ethos matched that of his players to perfection. "Without those types of players, it would be much more difficult to coach," Jeff said. "Whatever my shortcomings were, they would overlook them and help me get through them."

Under Jeff, the Knicks once again resembled rough-and-tumble winners. Despite the return to form, it was still a longshot that he would lock up the head coaching job the next season. Right around the time Jeff took over for Nelson, Mitch Lawrence of the *New York Daily News* wrote a column handicapping the Knicks' head coaching search. At the top were the usual big names—Larry Brown (2–1), Mike Fratello (3–1), John Calipari (10–1), Rick Pitino (15–1). All the way at the bottom—behind 71-year-old St. John's coach Lou Carnesecca (5,000–1)—sat interim coach Jeff Van Gundy. "Maybe in another lifetime," Lawrence wrote.

The odds of Jeff taking over full time, according to Lawrence, were 50,000,000–1. "I should've bet him on that," Jeff said. "I should've taken all his money."

Following Jeff's half-season as interim head coach, the Knicks announced that he would, against all odds, remain in the position on a permanent basis. The players supported Jeff, and management stood behind the stability he provided. "He is knowledgeable and passionate and a very good communicator," said Knicks president Ernie Grunfeld at the press conference announcing the hire. "And I don't think anybody will outwork him ever."

Jeff's rise from third assistant to head coach ironically occurred at a time when the head coaching ranks skewed towards former NBA players. In 1990, only one-third of head coaches had also played in the league. But by 1994, two years before Jeff took over the Knicks, former pros held 21 of the 27 slots. Phil Jackson, Rudy Tomjanovich, Riley, Lenny Wilkens, and Jerry Sloan—heady and hard-nosed former NBA players who could rein in the day's stars—represented the new coaching ideal.

In the 1990s, the NBA marketing machine shifted its focus from winning teams to individual stars. The league's television contracts grew, which led to increasingly large player salaries. Superstars, whose paychecks dwarfed those of their coaches, mostly resisted the demands of drill sergeants like Bill Fitch. "Owners and general managers now value pro playing experience more than clipboard experience, believing perhaps that former players can better relate to today's richer, bolder athlete," Jack McCallum wrote in a 1993 *Sports Illustrated* article. The longtime NBA reporter then argued that "the era of the professional coach—the clipboard-carrying, film-studying, whistle-blowing, clinic-attending, X-and-O-ing red-faced screamer—is over."

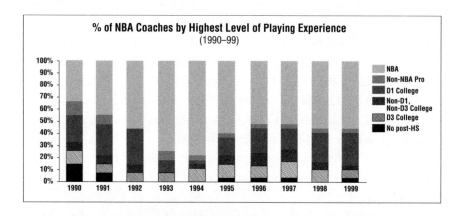

For most of the decade, McCallum's words rang true. After the "system coach" dominated the 1980s, the pendulum swung back towards the "Jimmys and Joes" end of the coaching spectrum. Jeff was the rare exception. In 2001, his final season with the Knicks, he was an endangered species—the only coach in the league with a Division III playing background.

The future of the pipeline didn't look promising, either. Even though coaching staffs grew to include as many as five assistants, just seven of the league's 100-plus assistant coaches in 2001 played D3 ball. However, of those seven D3 assistants, a remarkable number—five—eventually became an NBA head coach. And of those seven D3 assistants, four of them owed their spot in the NBA at the time to one man—Jeff Van Gundy.

There was Stan, of course, still an assistant in Miami thanks to the big assist from his little brother. Then there were three former D3 players on Jeff's Knicks staff. Jeff didn't set out to hire other coaches who had similar playing backgrounds. It just so happened, unsurprisingly, that the skills he valued and the people he knew had also played and coached D3 basketball in the Northeast. "I knew what they could do," Jeff said. "Those were the people I knew in coaching, those types of people. Not just those three, but that's what I was around my whole life. My dad, my brother, those are the people I knew and had great respect for."

As a former D3 player, as well as the brother, son, and friend of small-college coaches, Jeff knew exactly how beneficial experience at that level could be. "I do believe the humility that you gain by coaching at lower levels absolutely helps you navigate the world of professional sports," Jeff said, "knowing that you're not the most important person to the success or failure of the franchise."

He understood that winning at a small college requires work ethic, time management, and organization. It's a common misconception that a small-college coach's responsibilities begin and end with practices and games. Most outsiders aren't aware that the coach also handles recruiting, budgeting, scheduling, community outreach, floor sweeping, uniform ordering—and sometimes, hell, even washing them. "The small-college coaching experience is invaluable," Stan Van Gundy said, "because you have to do everything."

Coaching at a small college, like playing at a small college, requires sacrificing a big chunk of time for an activity that very rarely brings glory or riches. As a volunteer assistant at Division II St. Anselm College, former Division III player and future NBA head coach Steve Clifford worked nights at a boot factory. Between the hours of 3:00 AM and 7:30 AM, Clifford sat on a stool, armed with a little razor. Every 30 seconds or so, a boot piece would come across the assembly line, and Clifford would slice off the excess rubber. To pass the short intervals of time between rubber pieces, Clifford read books, mostly biographies of famous world leaders. He could've subbed at a local school and avoided third-shift work, but Clifford preferred to keep his days free so he could sit in the head coach's office, soaking up knowledge.

Like Jeff and Stan, Clifford was the son of a coach. Growing up, Clifford looked forward to the evenings when his dad hosted other coaches to talk shop. Clifford's mom would hang a white sheet on the kitchen wall, onto which his dad would project reels of game film. Young Steve was allowed to sit and listen to the discussions under one condition: he could never, ever say anything. As a good small-town, northern New England boy, he always kept his mouth shut.

When it came time for college, Clifford remained in his home state and attended D3 Maine-Farmington, where he majored in special education. Most high school coaches, his dad taught him, were PE teachers. Certification in another subject would give him flexibility to accept better coaching jobs down the line. On the court, Clifford was a pass-first point guard and the team's best defender. Like the Van Gundys, he was an excellent free throw shooter. "If you looked and I had seven points," Clifford said, "the other team probably had a couple technicals."

During summers, Clifford worked as many camps as he could. His budding coaching network, which was augmented by his dad's connections, led to jobs at Five-Star, Don Nelson's camp, and Jim Boeheim's Syracuse University camp. At Syracuse, Clifford's station was right next to the station of a rising college senior named Jeff Van Gundy. As the campers rotated between stations, the two chatted, and they continued to stay in touch after camp let out.

Unlike Clifford and the Van Gundy brothers, Tom Thibodeau did not have the benefit of soaking up human capital from a basketball coach father. Thibodeau's dad, who worked for a Central Connecticut steel company, did, however, love the game. "Basketball was his passion, and he passed that passion down to me," Thibodeau told Ian O'Connor of the *New York Post*.

Like Jeff Van Gundy, Thibodeau had a circuitous college journey, including stints at Central Connecticut State and Middlesex Community College, before settling in at D3 Salem State. Despite standing just a couple inches taller than six feet, Thibodeau, who called himself the "owner of the boards" in high school, played power forward. Opposing coach Wally Halas remembered Thibodeau as "a rough rebounder" and "tough kid."

While at Salem State, Thibodeau pursued a coaching career with the same gusto with which he chased after rebounds. His coach let him tag along to coaching clinics, at times driving up to five hours each way for the chance to learn and network. Following graduation, Thibodeau stayed at Salem State as an assistant coach. By 26, he was his alma mater's head coach, working morning, noon, and night running workouts and compiling detailed scouting reports. But Thibodeau dreamt of coaching at the D1 level. "I always got the sense from Tom that he was focused on bigger things," said K.C. Johnson, who covered Thibodeau as an NBA head coach. "Not that he would disassociate from his D3 past, he just was on to the next big thing in front of him."

The next big thing in 1985 was an assistant coaching job at Harvard. Any time he had a break, Thibodeau would travel up and down the Northeast, seeking out wisdom from the region's best coaches. In 1986, he spent an entire week at Providence studying Rick Pitino's practices. Thibodeau's work ethic and dedication impressed the Providence assistants, including Jeff Van Gundy. He was also a frequent attendee at former NBA coach Bill Musselman's minor league practices in Albany, New York. In Musselman, a small-college football and baseball player, Thibodeau found a kindred spirit and a surrogate coaching father.

When Musselman joined the expansion Minnesota Timberwolves in 1988 as the franchise's first head coach, he made Thibodeau his top assistant. Musselman's son, Eric, remembered questioning his dad's choice to hire a former D3 player and Harvard assistant as a full-blown NBA assistant coach. "Are you fucking serious?" Eric said to his dad. "All these years you've been coaching and had assistant coaches and former players and you pick *this guy?*"

"I really believe in him," said the elder Musselman. "He always asks the right questions. He wanted to watch minor league practices! He's got a great future. He's got great toughness."

That toughness came in handy during the regular Timberwolves staff pickup game, where Musselman would always team up with Thibodeau. On road trips when the team would fly out after a game, Thibodeau stayed behind with Musselman, who feared flying at night. The pair would spend the evening at bars or nightclubs and then fly out to join the team the next morning. Thibodeau joked that he was Musselman's American Express card—the coach never left home without him.

When Minnesota fired their entire coaching staff in 1991, Musselman did everything in his power to help Thibodeau stay in the NBA. San Antonio Spurs coach Jerry Tarkanian, a close friend of Musselman's, eventually hired Thibodeau. In the subsequent seasons, he bounced around but never out of the league. Whenever the head coach Thibodeau worked under was fired, a former coworker, who appreciated his diligence and expertise, would scoop him up. Prior to the 1996–97 season, Thibodeau landed with Jeff Van Gundy and the Knicks. "It wasn't like I was looking for a 6'2" Division III low-post guy," Jeff said. "I was looking for great coaches." It would be the first of nine seasons Thibodeau served as Jeff's assistant.

A few years later, during the 1998 NBA lockout, Jeff reconnected with Clifford. For a hoops junkie like Jeff, a work stoppage was torture. To cure his boredom, he popped into local gyms to watch practices and games. One of his frequent stops was Adelphi, a small school on Long Island coached by Jeff's old Syracuse camp station neighbor. The ever-respectful Jeff always called before he visited and, on occasion, asked Clifford's permission to speak to the players. Clifford always said yes. *If it's working for [former Knicks point guard] Mark Jackson, it'd probably work at Adelphi*, Clifford would think.

In 2000, Jeff hired Clifford as an advance scout. Many coaches at the time still enjoyed the same unilateral control over hiring that enabled Hubie Brown to elevate his Five-Star chums. So Jeff could offer the job to someone like Clifford without any fear of organizational pushback. Clifford was quickly initiated into the Van Gundy way. Clifford likes to tell a story, one that is only slightly exaggerated for effect: One day early in his tenure, he showed up to the office at around 5:20 in the morning. Little did he know, Jeff, Thibodeau, and the other coaches were already settled in at their desks. When Clifford walked through the door, they said, "Where have you been? Everything okay?"

One of Clifford's responsibilities was to put together the playbook. Every night he would print out the latest copy, and every morning he would come in to see that copy marked up with all of Jeff's edits. It took three all-nighters in August for Clifford to have the playbook up to Jeff's standards by training camp in September. "The thing that blew me away at the beginning was just the details and the amount of study that went into every phase of what we did," Clifford said.

After Clifford served one season as an advanced scout, Van Gundy promoted him to assistant coach. When it came to interacting with players, Clifford leaned on the wise words of Knicks president Dave Checketts. "Nobody can say for sure that I'm one of the 30 best presidents in the NBA or that I deserve this job," Checketts told Clifford. "Nobody can say that Jeff is one of the 30 best coaches in the world, or that you'll be one of the best 150 assistants. But they are the best 450 players. If you want to find a way to stick in this league, be good at helping them play better."

Jeff, like Hubie Brown, wanted teachers on his staff. Clifford fit the bill. He learned the NBA game and acclimated to the Van Gundy pace of work, spending hours behind the scenes preparing for every single question and contingency. Jeff used to tell his assistants that they weren't going to guess.

They would thoroughly study every possible solution until they came up with the best option.

To help him iterate through lineup and scheme adjustments, Jeff continued to trust and empower D3 grinders. In 2001, Andy Greer joined Thibodeau and Clifford on the Knicks staff, along with former NBA players Don Chaney and Herb Williams. Greer, Thibodeau, and Clifford formed the first D3 trio of assistant coaches in NBA history. Greer and Jeff went way back—they played together at Brockport State and formed such a close friendship that Bill Van Gundy refers to Greer as his "third son."

WHEN PAT RILEY retired (briefly) from coaching in 2003, he entrusted the Heat to his top assistant, Stan Van Gundy. That same offseason, the Houston Rockets hired Jeff Van Gundy, his first job since parting ways with the Knicks. When the Heat traveled to Houston to play the Rockets early in the season, the Van Gundys became the second set of brothers in league history to ever coach against each other, and the first set of former D3 players to face off in an NBA game.

As the national anthem played, the brothers allowed themselves the briefest of moments to soak it all in. Here they were, a couple of "schleps with a D3 background," as Jeff once so eloquently put it, about to square off in the world's premier league.

Very quickly, Stan proved that, like his kid brother, he belonged as an NBA coach. He guided the Heat to a surprising playoff appearance in his first season, and a trip to the Eastern Conference Finals in his second season. Jeff left coaching after four seasons in Houston, but his longtime assistants, Thibodeau, Clifford, and Greer, continued to work in the league, thanks to their successful track records and reputations as hard workers.

For Thibodeau it was a long and frustrating road from trusted assistant to head coaching candidate. Throughout his decades in the league, only a handful of teams interviewed him for their lead roles. It was reminiscent of Jeff, who knew it would take an interim opportunity to get a crack at head coaching. The lifelong assistant –who toiled in the shadows, never worked in television, and played his college ball at a school most NBA fans had never heard of—wasn't going to win any press conferences.

The Chicago Bulls interviewed Thibodeau for their head coaching vacancy in 2010 thanks to an unlikely assist from one of Thibodeau's former players at Harvard. Arne Duncan, who served as President Obama's Secretary of Education, also happened to be a close acquaintance of Bulls owner Jerry Reinsdorf. "Beyond the fact that [Bulls executives] John [Paxson] and Gar [Forman] saw an elite defensive mind and a workaholic," Johnson said, "Arne and Jerry were pretty friendly at the time, and Arne spoke about [Thibodeau's] character and commitment to the franchise. That played a role."

Thibodeau wowed the Bulls with his preparation and track record of success as an assistant, ultimately winning the job. "It was his basketball acumen," said former Bulls beat writer Nick Friedell. "It was his IQ. They believed in what he could do. They believed in the beginning, and even in the worst of times, frankly, how good of a basketball teacher he is because he consumed the game."

In his very first season, the Bulls compiled the league's best record and Thibodeau took home the NBA's Coach of the Year award. League insiders, according to ace NBA analyst Zach Lowe, credited Thibodeau with implementing defensive techniques that were then widely adopted across the league. He drilled his team relentlessly, doing everything he could to ensure they were never out-prepared. Even in the middle of the season on a cold January morning, with his team groggy from playing the night before, Thibodeau would end shootarounds by running through each of the upcoming opponent's inbounds plays up to 15 times. "A lot of people wait for the opportunity, and when they get it, they're not prepared," said Greer, who served as one of Thibodeau's assistants with the Bulls. "Tom was prepared and knocked it out of the ballpark."

While Thibodeau was revolutionizing NBA defense in Chicago, Stan Van Gundy was modernizing NBA offense in Orlando. Stan's success in Miami afforded him another opportunity as a head coach with the Magic, where he played a style that later became the league norm. Stan's offense, which spread the floor with four shooters, emphasized three-pointers and shots at the rim. In each of his five seasons in Orlando, the Magic led the league in share of shots taken from three and were in the bottom two in frequency of midrange shots taken, per analytics site Cleaning the Glass.

Behind these then-novel concepts and strategies, the Magic made the NBA Finals in 2009. All that winning turned Stan's top assistant, Clifford, into one of the more sought-after coaches in the league. In 2013, when the Charlotte Bobcats named Clifford their new head coach, he became the fourth member of the Van Gundy network to reach the profession's pinnacle. Together, the quartet forced the NBA to recalibrate their expectations for how a successful coach looks and acts. "It's not the regal Pat Riley on the sideline with hair slicked back and the perfect suit, or Phil Jackson sort of bemusedly looking down upon this game," said *Sports Illustrated* basketball writer Chris Ballard.

The Van Gundys, Thibodeau, and Clifford were not NBA coaches out of central casting. They were selfless scrappers who deflected praise. They were hard work personified. The bags under their eyes were a feature, not a bug. "There's a difference in how those four guys look compared to how a lot of other guys look on the sidelines," Chris Herring said.

Concepts like "image" and "Q-Ratings" were shortcuts, and shortcuts were for the unprepared. The foursome put in the necessary work, possessed the necessary experience, and benefited from the necessary lucky breaks. They paid their dues and did so with an understanding that those payments were not accompanied by any sort of quid pro quo of a promised future. Hard work was both the means and the end.

To the uninitiated, coaching is all about how one moves the pieces around on the chessboard. But, as Bill Van Gundy tells it, coaching is all about teaching. Effective teaching requires technical knowhow, sure, but, perhaps even more importantly, it requires an ability to lead and to inspire. Talk to people from Jeff Van Gundy's past, and they will tell you that he's a born leader, a raiser of bars who inspires others through his fierce loyalty. As Dr. Jon Younger, a human resources thought leader, wrote in his book *Agile Talent,* "When all is said and done, effective leadership is an act of generosity."

Jeff was just 23 years old when he coached McQuaid. His combined salary as a coach and special education assistant was less than $10,000. The study halls he oversaw, the team dinners he hosted, the outings he organized to Syracuse basketball practices—none of that was in his job description. He put in all that extra work for the kids on that team.

After the final game of his one season at McQuaid, Jeff and his now-wife, Kim, took Greg Woodard out to eat. In the car, Jeff asked Woodard if he wanted to play in the Big East. It was part question, part challenge, a way of inspiring the talented young player to reach even higher than he had previously dreamed. "That was the first time that I was really like, *Oh, wow, I could be a Division I player*," Woodard said. Later that spring, he worked out for the Providence assistants and eventually played Big East ball at Villanova.

The lessons Jeff taught in his one season at McQuaid stuck with those kids throughout their lives. Jay Gangemi, who was a stellar D3 player at Johns Hopkins following his time at McQuaid, is now a pediatric heart surgeon. "The work ethic that I've had for the last 16 years was all instilled upon me from Van Gundy from that one year," said Gangemi. "It's amazing. It really is."

Wherever he went, Jeff fostered an environment that bred and strengthened special relationships. When the mother of his friend and longtime assistant, Greer, died, it wasn't enough for Jeff to fly in for the service. He came into town several days early just to spend time and be there for Greer. "There's no better friend in the world than Jeff Van Gundy," Greer said. "None."

Jeff's generosity attracted other giving individuals like Thibodeau. When Clifford was between jobs one offseason, Thibodeau called to say that the Bulls front office wanted to fly Clifford out to Summer League and meet him. Clifford, who suspected Thibodeau was covering the trip himself, insisted on paying his own way. After bickering like two old friends fighting over the check at a diner, Clifford finally accepted Thibodeau's offer. Thibodeau never did admit to paying for the trip himself, even though Clifford has no doubt that that's the case. "That's Tom," Clifford said.

These stories of friendship and generosity are the true legacy of Jeff Van Gundy and his coaching tree. When a few fortunate connections lifted Jeff into the NBA, he held the door open for others like him—skilled coaches who otherwise would have gladly spent their entire careers at small colleges. They seized their opportunities and changed the NBA, showing owners and GMs that it was okay to entrust their teams to "D3 schleps."

But Jeff, Stan, Thibodeau, and Clifford were not enough to truly build a pipeline. For that, the D3 world needed the help of an outsider, one with a firsthand appreciation for the D3 game and a special knack for developing young talent.

CHAPTER 8

Spurs Culture

*How Gregg Popovich applied his Division III
program-building tactics in San Antonio, transforming the
franchise into the league's greatest incubator for D3 talent*

Your mid-20s are that stage in life where you're supposed to have acclimated to adulthood. Bills are supposed to be covered, health insurance is supposed to be in your name, and jobs are supposed to be *careers*.

Andrew Olson felt fortunate to wake up every day with a purpose and a means to get paid. With his clients he found a small dose of that camaraderie that eludes so many former athletes after retirement. His own journey as a player was over, but he could experience the adversity, success, smiles, and jokes with his clients. Each day might not have been perfect, but it always reminded him how basketball was so full of life.

Olson favored the sessions with the real players, the high school kids who shared his love of the game and picked up his tips quickly. But he didn't mind the more challenging hours working with his less-coordinated clients, as long as they were as committed to their goals as he was to helping them. They forced him to drill deeper into how successful athletes perform, to constantly challenge his preconceived notions.

One such client, a gawky preteen who certainly wouldn't break any of Olson's records at the local high school, had trouble jumping. As Olson explained to him the kinetic chain, it dawned on him that each jump shot has a similar series of movements, with each step contributing to how likely a shot is to be a swish or a brick. Once the idea took hold in his brain, he couldn't shake it. He kept iterating, thinking multiple steps ahead about this theory and where it could eventually lead. Not that he wasn't happy where he was, living a comfortable life in beautiful Southern California, but the prospect of a new challenge was too alluring to ignore.

Throughout NBA history, any Division III player who a) worked in the league immediately after college and then b) went on to become an NBA head coach or general manager, followed one of just two paths: 1) Their dad worked in the NBA. 2) They started their career with the San Antonio Spurs.

The first path is fairly self-explanatory. Every industry has parents who give their kids an initial leg up, either actively or passively through the power of their last name. The second path, the one through south-central Texas, is more curious. How did an organization run by a former standout player at the Air Force Academy become the top incubator for D3 coaching and management talent?

Before he was "Pop," one of the greatest NBA coaches of all time, Gregg Popovich was known as "Popo." In the 1970 Air Force yearbook, Popo's senior blurb reads, "He came to these nondescript hills from Merrillville, Indiana, with his ways and his ball. Ball has continued to capture Popo's time during his visit at the Academy. What he did while here may have been bad and it may have been good, but he learned it did not matter much either way. He has, however, learned much about life during his revealing stay, and some profess that it was due not totally to fine associations and tutelage. His future plans include happiness."

To find that happiness, a 30-year-old Popovich took his ways and his ball to Pomona College, a small, elite liberal arts school about an hour east of Los Angeles. Pomona's dean, Robert Voelkel, happened to have been an excellent small-college basketball player at Wooster College. Voelkel couldn't stand to watch Pomona's sad excuse for a team, so, with the coach set to retire, he took it upon himself to go over the heads of the department of athletics and find a new coach. His search led him to the Air Force Academy and their assistant coach, Popovich, who eagerly accepted.

"I looked for something that would involve more time on a campus, more time to be with my wife and two children," Popovich told *The Student Life*, Pomona's student newspaper, in 2020. "My interest was as much on the academic side as the basketball [side] in the sense that I wanted to be a part of a college, of a community."

In 1979, Popovich and his family moved to Southern California. As a faculty resident, the new coach, his wife, and his two young children lived amongst the students in Harwood Court. It wasn't always a harmonious arrangement. "Can you imagine Popovich in the dorms?" asked Steve Koblik, a history professor who served as the Pomona basketball team's academic advisor. "Can you imagine his response at midnight when some guys come back, having been drinking and yelling at each other? Do you think he got up, after having his family woken up, and politely said, 'Hey guys, could you cut it out?' Or do you think he grabbed them physically and threatened to do bodily harm?"

Excluding those loud, intoxicated neighbors, Popovich embraced life at the residential liberal arts college. He ran on the track, ate family meals at the dining hall, and spoke Russian with students and faculty at the school's language tables. He even joined the faculty team that competed in the college's intramural basketball league. "We were adults and we threw lots of elbows," said Lorn Foster, a politics professor and Popovich's IM teammate. "We weren't gentle and amenable."

Popovich enjoyed playing a role in the holistic education of so many bright and interesting young people. He served as chair of the student affairs committee, where he worked to eliminate single-sex Greek organizations on campus because he didn't feel they fit within the context of a residential liberal arts college. He also chaired a faculty committee, a feat that Koblik calls "unheard of" when asked how common it was for coaches to take those positions.

"Gregg was and is a teacher, and I think you have to put that in capital letters," Foster said. "Everything that he does is not so much predicated on winning or losing per se but teaching lessons that get learned to make you a better basketball player and, more importantly, make you a better person."

When it came to basketball, Popovich fostered an environment that would live up to his high standards and sustain over time. "The most valuable thing I learned from [Popovich] was the importance of building a program," said Charlie Katsiaficas, an assistant under Popovich at Pomona.

Constructing a satisfactory program required a total teardown of the old basketball culture. The previous coach hadn't recruited; he just cobbled together whatever talent materialized in the small student body. Players were free to skip out on practice to study for a big test. Before games, the team voted for who they thought should start. "When [Popovich] came here, there was not a culture of winning or success in the men's basketball program," Katsiaficas said. "The exact opposite."

Koblik, whose role as team academic advisor was born out of a close friendship with Popovich, remembered asking the coach about his ambition level. "I want to win a national championship," Popovich replied. Koblik nodded, sensing the genuineness in Popovich's answer, but the bubble over his head said, *You know, Bozo, Pomona College has been playing competitive basketball since the teens and they've never won a conference championship—let alone a national championship.*

Koblik quickly learned that Popovich was going to push himself to a degree that separated the coach from just about anyone the professor had ever met. "It's way beyond anything you can imagine," Koblik said. "If he were going to climb a brick wall, and it was 20 feet high, and there wasn't any chance he was going to get over it, he would spend a long time smashing into it before he finally gave up."

Popovich demanded the same level of commitment from his players. Given the talent level he found himself with, he didn't expect any miracles—just that the players would do everything in their power to maximize their abilities. "If you could put two feet in front of yourself, that was his ambition level," Koblik said. "But if you dragged your feet, he was on top of you. And he was nasty. Verbally nasty. It was, 'You better give your all and die on my court, or don't play for me.'"

For his first season, Popovich placed trash cans on all four corners of the court during practice so players had plenty of convenient places to puke. The demands he placed on his team were well beyond the typical expectations for Pomona student-athletes. As a result, many left the program, especially point guards, on whom Popovich was especially tough. Results did not come immediately. In January of 1980, Pomona lost to California Institute of

Technology, Cal Tech's first win in eight seasons. It was the low point in a season of nadirs, one which ended with just two wins.

To attract more talented players to the team, Popovich started targeting any and all high schools and prep schools that might have basketball players with high test scores. "Gregg understood that it's not what comes in the door, you have to find people to come in the door," Foster said.

He tapped into high schools in the Northeast, figuring at least a few kids would sacrifice a long plane ride if it meant leaving their winter coat at home. He found creative ways to work within the relatively rigid admissions process, including steering certain kids toward Pitzer College, the neighboring school with which Pomona shared athletic teams. Keeping track of his expansive recruiting operation took some serious organization. He wasn't just focused on a small, targeted list of prospects. This was an exercise in volume, involving mass mailing letters and frequent follow-ups. In the pre-computer days, Popovich relied on a system of card boxes with little pieces of paper to keep careful track of each lead's status. "His organization is off the charts," Katsiaficas said. "He's meticulous about all his prep. I learned so much about the recruiting process from him, as well as scouting and game prep."

Once the players arrived on campus, Popovich worked to connect with each and every one. Most of the kids had passions outside of basketball, and Popovich was worldly and curious enough to hold a conversation on just about anything. "Gregg has such intellectual range that he didn't need an academic advisor," Koblik said.

Popovich and family would host the players for cookies or what he called "Serbian tacos," a Popovich creation paying homage to his Serbian background. When the team traveled, he would organize team meals at destination restaurants. It was in those moments, and during the times when a player was struggling academically or socially, that he established the bonds on which his coaching style was built. "He was so intentional about connecting with people in a meaningful way," Katsiaficas said. "From the statisticians to the team manager to the second-string players to the most valuable player on the team, everybody understood that they were of significant value to the team and what they brought every day was critical to our success."

The Pomona environment enabled and even encouraged Popovich to enrich the members of his team. Along with Koblik, he applied for a chance to represent the United States in an international tournament set to take place at a new gym in Abidjan, Ivory Coast. Since Pomona would probably lose, Koblik figured that the game would help drum up some positive PR for the African teams. With the tournament scheduled for the break between semesters, Popovich and Koblik planned to take the team to Morocco for Christmas and then down to the Ivory Coast for the tournament. Koblik even ran a not-for-credit seminar on the Ivory Coast for the basketball team that fall. They made sure everyone in the traveling party was set with passports and immunizations and had arranged accommodations. "Gregg and I were rather proud of ourselves, until we had discovered that the building wasn't completed, and it was quite typical for the Ivory Coast to advertise things that didn't in fact happen," Koblik said. "The whole thing collapsed, and I had egg all over my face. So did Gregg."

The Ivory Coast trip may have been a failure, but Popovich's program building was a massive success. In 1986, Pomona-Pitzer won their first conference title in school history. Even after he started winning, Popovich didn't coach with one eye on his players and another wandering toward another, bigger job. He loved D3 basketball. "You get to really coach, not spend a lot of your time doing the other stuff the Division I coaches have to do," Popovich told Alan Drooz of the *Los Angeles Times* in 1986. "The talent level is really a lot better than people think until they see it."

Even though he was happy at Pomona, Popovich heeded the advice of his athletic director Curt Tong and opted to spend a year away from the school to avoid burnout. It wasn't standard practice for coaches to take sabbaticals, but professors did it all the time. So, Popovich figured: why not me?

He arranged to observe Dean Smith at North Carolina and Larry Brown at Kansas. When asked if they felt he was abandoning his team in any way, Popovich's Pomona coworkers all vehemently disagreed. "These are smart kids," Koblik said. "If you had a history teacher, and he was going off to the two best historians in his field, I don't think you'd be bitching about it. It reaffirmed your view that it was worthwhile spending time with this person."

The sabbatical year, most of which Popovich spent as a full-fledged assistant coach at Kansas, gave him confidence that his methods could be applied at a higher level. "The X's and O's are the same at Carolina, Kansas, and Pomona," he said. "It's [*sic*] makes you feel good about what you're doing and you realize there aren't any great secrets."

Still, he wasn't planning on making any drastic career moves. "The small-college level is the place to be if you want to coach and not have droves of people who want a piece of you," Popovich said. "That's more consistent with my personality."

Popovich returned to Pomona for the 1987–88 season. It would be his last at the college.

Several developments led to Popovich's departure. First, Voelkel, the man who brought Popovich to Pomona, died not long after Popovich's sabbatical ended. The college faculty also decided that lifetime appointments were no longer appropriate for coaches. The possibility for Popovich to earn a tenured position was no longer on the table. It rubbed Popovich, someone with a strong sense of equality, the wrong way. "I had the pleasure and responsibility of having to tell Gregg he wasn't going to get tenure," Koblik said, "which did not lead to a fistfight, but it did lead to a lot of yelling."

Then Larry Brown came calling with the opportunity of a lifetime. In 1988, the San Antonio Spurs had named Brown, whose pro coaching career began when small-college alum Carl Scheer hired him to coach the Carolina Cougars, their new head coach in 1988. To fill out his bench, Brown looked to his former assistants at Kansas, including Popovich. "My whole life, I've been taught that you hire family," Brown said. "Because you can teach family all the basketball you know, but you can't teach them to love you."

None of the new Spurs assistants had ever coached in the NBA. Popovich was right at home. Still, he understood that the jump from Pomona to the pros would make for quite the challenge. "I'm delighted," he said, "but at the same time I'm scared to death."

Meanwhile, his pals at Pomona were equal parts excited for "Popo" and appreciative of all he had contributed to their community. "A lot of people from the outside probably don't have any idea how impressive that was, to take Pomona from where they were when he arrived to the winning program he handed over to me," said Katsiaficas, who succeeded Popovich at Pomona, a job he still holds to this day.

Popovich departing for a bigger and better role was not some inevitability. It was more a series of random bounces and coincidences that pushed a comfortable-yet-driven person on to the next challenge. "It was only an accident that he left," Koblik said. "He was totally acclimated to Division III."

AFTER SIX SEASONS as an NBA assistant—four under Brown in San Antonio and two in Golden State as Garry St. Jean's replacement (working for Don Nelson, the tie that binds all D3 connections)—the Spurs brought Popovich back as their general manager in 1994. It was an outside-the-box hire spearheaded by new Spurs owner Robert McDermott. The confidence behind McDermott's recommendation stemmed from his two separate connections to Popovich—McDermott was previously a brigadier general and dean of faculty at the Air Force Academy, and his daughter was a childhood friend of Popovich's wife, Erin.

Popovich signaled the start of his new regime by trading the skilled but eccentric Dennis Rodman to the Chicago Bulls for Will Perdue. Even though the NBA of the 1990s was a players' league, Popovich refused to give Rodman the preferential treatment he demanded. The next step came 18 games into the 1996–97 season. After a loss, Popovich walked on to the Spurs' bus and informed the team that he would be taking over as head coach. The move was unexpected, both internally and externally. Bob Hill, the newly fired coach who Popovich would replace, had averaged more than 60 wins in his two seasons with the Spurs. Sure, that season they were 3–15, but the team was ravaged by injuries. To Popovich, the injuries were not a valid excuse. The team wasn't playing up to expectations, especially on the defensive end, so there needed to be consequences and accountability. "He put his reputation on the line," said Hubie Brown, who was broadcasting games on TNT at the time.

Popovich's head coaching tenure in San Antonio began about as ignominiously as it did at Pomona. With star center David Robinson lost for the season, he went 17–47. Ownership stood by Popovich, offering him a three-year contract extension as coach and GM at season's end. The public was far less supportive. In April of 1997, the time of the extension, *San Antonio Express-News* did an informal telephone survey. When asked if Popovich should be fired, 92 percent of respondents said yes.

Amidst all the losing, Popovich began implementing the same tenets that helped him turn around Pomona—accountability, humanity, and identifying previously untapped talent pools. "He was the same coach for the Division III team that he was for the Spurs," said Koblik, who regularly visited Popovich after he joined the NBA. "The Pomona alumni would come to the games and they would talk to the players who were working with

Gregg and they would discover that he was treating them the same way he had treated them when they were Division III."

While on one of his visits, Koblik was approached by Spurs forward Boris Diaw. "How long has Pop been the way he is?" Diaw asked. Koblik looked at him and said, "Boris, he came out of the womb like that." Diaw walked away, shaking his head.

During his time at Pomona, Popovich once challenged his best player to a game of one-on-one in order to demonstrate how to play with the appropriate level of toughness and determination. Despite giving up a few inches, Popovich won handily. While he couldn't deploy a similar tactic with his NBA players, Popovich was still able to prove that he was not the type to back away from a challenge. On an episode of *The Bill Simmons Podcast,* Doc Rivers relayed a story about a heated Spurs team meeting during the 1995 playoffs. Rivers, who spent his last years as a player in San Antonio, watched Popovich unflinchingly absorb Dennis Rodman's brutal personal attacks. Popovich then dished some even more vicious comments back at Rodman. As the dam burst and the players spewed insults at each other, Rivers remembered Popovich looking "like he was having the time of his life." The unburdened Spurs then went on to win their next two games to even up the series against the Rockets. "Pop's kind of like the dog who would walk up to the invisible fence and hear the beeping and say, 'Eh, I don't care' and just feel the shock," said Will Perdue, who played four seasons for Popovich in San Antonio.

Popovich was doubly blessed in that he not only had superstar players— Robinson and Tim Duncan, acquired with the No. 1 pick after his first disastrous season—but also that they were players who accepted hard coaching. "He didn't have to yell an awful lot," said P.J. Carlesimo, who served as an assistant under Popovich for five seasons. "But when somebody did something wrong, they were called on it. That was just the way it was. It's not that way in all 30 teams in the league and it's particularly not that way with some of the best players in the league."

Duncan and Robinson were different, which gave Popovich the freedom to coach the only way he knew how. "He's the boss," Hubie Brown said. "And you know he's the boss."

With his superstars in place, Popovich also benefited from his dual role as general manager. Like a college coach, he could handpick players who would fit his program. Leading up to the draft, the Spurs war room had a list of off-limit players labeled "Not a Spur." Free agency and trade conversations always included the question, "Can he be a Spur?" That meant: can he fit in without an ego and accept his role for the betterment of the team?

Building out the roster with the right kind of player and person was a little trickier in the NBA than it was at Pomona. Sending mass mailers to East Coast prep schools wouldn't cut it. Under Popovich's leadership and meticulous administrative organization, the Spurs established an expansive international scouting operation. To sustain success, winning teams need to hit on late draft picks, and the Spurs did so by repeatedly selecting under-the-radar foreign players. Between Tony Parker, Manu Ginobili, and Tiago Splitter, just to name a few, the Spurs relied on players born outside of the USA more than any other team.

Once they acquired foreign players, Popovich and the Spurs poured resources into player development and player comfort. He also possessed a genuine interest in other people and their backgrounds, which helped him to connect with new players from across the globe. "Pop is so well-traveled and he's very smart," said Kim Bohuny, the NBA's senior vice president of international basketball operations. "He studies all these cultures, he enjoys it, he enjoys learning about these different countries and cultures where his players have come from."

On road trips, especially long ones, Popovich organizes extravagant team meals. According to Bohuny, those team bonding experiences are a consistent theme among the teams who best incorporate international players into their program. Rather than sitting in their hotel rooms alone, the players strengthen relationships over Popovich's contagious passion for food and wine.

The meals served the same purpose as the Serbian tacos and road trip dinners he hosted at Pomona—to bond with the team and staff, to embrace that there is more to life than basketball, and to prove he genuinely cares for those around him. Through his relationships, Popovich sets himself apart as one of the best coaches ever. "There's that tough side of him," Hubie Brown said. "There's that discipline. There's that organization. But there's that love that he has for his players. And you can see it, and their love for him in return."

So much of the media and fan discourse about coaching focuses on halftime adjustments and substitution patterns. Those who have spent their lives coaching in the league, however, believe that basketball knowhow is table stakes. The very best coaches set themselves apart by connecting with and motivating their teams. "Everyone knows the O's and X's," Popovich said during his 2023 Hall of Fame acceptance speech. "It's not brain science…It's about relationships."

St. Jean, who coached against Popovich with both the Sacramento Kings and the Warriors, calls the Spurs' general "the master with player relationships." "He was one of those guys who truly cared about his players off the floor and how their families were doing and all that stuff," St. Jean said. "The players then trusted him and believed in him, so he could coach them hard."

Perdue, who came to the Spurs fresh off of a contentious relationship with Bulls coach Phil Jackson, marvels at how skilled Popovich was at balancing his high expectations on the court with an overarching love off of it. "I always felt like he truly cared about me as a person more so than as a player," Perdue said.

There was, however, a slight adjustment period when Popovich first landed in the pros. He could talk to Pomona players about philosophy and politics. In the NBA, he had to change his chatter. During his first season as a Spurs assistant, Popovich walked up to a player on the team and casually asked him what he thought about Iran Contra. The player told Popovich he had no idea what he was talking about.

According to Foster, Popovich's colleague and intramural teammate at Pomona, the coach realized he was dealing with a group of young men who "were smart but don't know they're smart and are really not wise to the ways of public space." So, according to Foster, Popovich took what he learned at Pomona and applied it in San Antonio. "This was a teaching job. This was not just X's and O's, but this is teaching, this is preparing these young men to be better basketball players, but also to be better in their respective communities."

Part of the education came in the form of those dinners, where Popovich might place a few different pinot noirs or cabernets in front of a player and talk to them about what they were tasting and what they preferred. "This is the level of care that he takes," Foster said. "He's teaching them that the spoon at the top—that's your dessert spoon, knucklehead."

The curriculum extended beyond the dinner table. Whether they were White or Black, had graduated or left college early—or in the case of the international guys, never attended college at all—most of the players that came through San Antonio had one thing in common: they spent their young adulthood focusing most of their time and energy on basketball. So Popovich took it upon himself to teach them what they might have missed. When the team traveled to Los Angeles, for example, he would arrange a private tour of the Huntington Library Gardens with Koblik, who left his post at Pomona to take over as president of the renowned museum and research institution. And that was just one stop in a long list of team field trips, further proof that, even though he left higher education, Popovich never stopped thinking of himself as a teacher. "I always say that I'm faking it as an NBA coach," Popovich told Pomona's *The Student Life,* "because at heart I'm a Division III coach through and through,".

THE 1999 NBA Finals, pitting Gregg Popovich's San Antonio Spurs against Jeff Van Gundy's New York Knicks, was *the* pivotal moment in the creation of the Division III pipeline. Both coaches leveraged their success to build the largest branches of the D3 tree. Even though Popovich didn't play Division III basketball, Van Gundy believes the coach's well-publicized experience at Pomona was crucial in legitimizing former D3 players at the NBA level.

"The same thing I've been impressed about with Pop is what you learn as a Division III player—the humility," Van Gundy said. "You can be hungry, you can be knowledgeable, but humility is absolutely a requirement— knowing where you fit into the big picture in professional sports."

While Van Gundy hired D3 alums who had trained as teachers at small public colleges, Popovich favored the D3 guys from private liberal arts schools like Pomona. The former D3 players were one slice of the diverse array of coaches he brought into the Spurs organization—everyone from former WNBA stars to international coaches to players from every level of college basketball. His way of hiring was an exercise in humility, a constant search for those who could provide different and better answers.

Popovich, unlike Larry Brown, didn't just hire "family," but he rarely if ever hired someone cold. They were friends of friends, or colleagues with

Before coaching five NBA teams, Bill Fitch played basketball and baseball at Coe College during the 1950s. *(Coe College)*

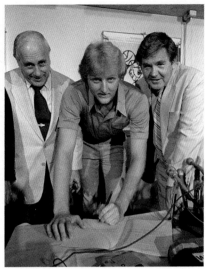

As Boston Celtics head coach, Bill Fitch teams up with president Red Auerbach and superstar Larry Bird (seen signing his rookie contract in 1979) to reinvigorate the Boston dynasty. *(AP Images)*

Norm Sonju, an original architect of the Dallas Mavericks, goes to the hoop while playing for Grinnell College. *(Norm Sonju)*

Carl Scheer suits up for Middlebury College in 1958. He later became an esteemed ABA and NBA executive. *(Middlebury College Special Collections, Middlebury, Vermont)*

Because of his hustle and work ethic, future NBA head coach Jeff Van Gundy was known as "All Out Jeff" during his D3 playing days. *(Nazareth University)*

Jeff Van Gundy picks up some valuable experience behind the mic during a postgame interview at Nazareth University. *(Nazareth University)*

Sitting between Mark Jackson and Mike Breen, Jeff Van Gundy announced 15 NBA Finals for ABC/ESPN. *(AP Images)*

Stan Van Gundy, who is pictured in 1980, could really handle the rock at the D3 level. *(SUNY Brockport)*

During his most recent head coaching stint, New Orleans Pelicans coach Stan Van Gundy barks out commands to his players during a 2021 game against the Golden State Warriors. *(AP Images)*

An opposing coach described undersized Salem State forward Tom Thibodeau as a "rough rebounder" and "tough kid." *(Salem State University)*

Head coach Tom Thibodeau and star guard Jalen Brunson were both lured to New York by Knicks president Leon Rose (not pictured), a former D3 player at Dickinson College. *(AP Images)*

As a senior, Will Hardy helped Williams College reach the 2010 Division III National Championship. *(Williams College)*

Named head coach of the Utah Jazz in 2022, Will Hardy guides his team during the second half of a 2023 preseason game. *(AP Images)*

Coach Gregg Popovich poses at the gym while coaching Pomona-Pitzer during the 1979–80 season. That D3 position was the future Hall of Famer's first head coaching job. *(Pomona College)*

Before Gregg Popovich left for the NBA, his last Pomona recruiting class included eventual NBA head coach Mike Budenholzer. *(Pomona College)*

San Antonio Spurs head coach Gregg Popovich hugs then-Atlanta Hawks head coach Mike Budenholzer after the Spurs defeated the Hawks in November of 2015. Budenholzer spent 19 seasons working for Popovich in San Antonio before embarking on his own successful head coaching career. *(AP Images)*

Brad Stevens goes to the hole while playing for DePauw University during the 1997–98 season. *(DePauw University)*

In his final season as Boston Celtics head coach before moving to the front office, Brad Stevens chats with Brooklyn Nets forward Kevin Durant during a 2021 playoff game. *(AP Images)*

Chris Finch shoots a layup for Franklin & Marshall College, where he ended up after initially having his heart set on Princeton University. *(Franklin & Marshall College)*

Minnesota Timberwolves head coach Chris Finch instructs his talented big man Rudy Gobert. (AP Images)

NBA assistant coach Greg St. Jean (middle) played basketball at Wesleyan University before joining the family business. His dad, Garry (left), attended Springfield College prior to his career as an NBA head coach and general manager. *(Garry St. Jean)*

In his one season at Williams College, future Miami Heat sharpshooter Duncan Robinson leads his team to a Division III Semifinal win against archrival Amherst College. *(Williams College)*

Koby Altman plays for Middlebury College during the 2001– 02 season. *(Middlebury College Special Collections, Middlebury, Vermont)*

Koby Altman, general manager of the Cleveland Cavaliers, speaks at a 2023 NBA Media Day press conference. *(AP Images)*

A two-time D3 Player of the Year, Andrew Olson dribbles up the floor during his days at Amherst. *(Andrew Olson)*

Now a shooting coach with the Cleveland Cavaliers, Andrew Olson works out with star Donovan Mitchell before a game. *(Andrew Olson)*

whom trusted Spurs associates had strong bonds. "It didn't matter whether you were Division I, II, III, or junior college, it was about people," P.J. Carlesimo said. "He hired good people."

People like Alex Lloyd, a former Pomona College player who worked in various departments with the Spurs between 2006 and 2012. "The Spurs organization really values people who are smart, who are hard workers that ask good questions, who have a sense of humility, and who put others ahead of themselves," Lloyd said. "A lot of those traits are found in Division III student-athletes."

Division III athletes don't receive scholarships. They occasionally play in empty gyms. Their passion for basketball is what drives them. "They don't owe anybody anything," said Charlie Katsiaficas, who recommended Lloyd to Popovich. "They're doing it for a real love that they have for the sport. Obviously, if you get into a profession or a job or a career that you really have a passion or love for, that can help you find success. It's not a guarantee of success, but it certainly puts you in position."

Looking at the Spurs' hires over the years, there seems to be a special fondness for those who cut their teeth in environments that bred humility, creativity, and an openness to hard work. One such environment was, of course, Pomona College. Popovich's first D3 hire in the NBA was also his last D3 recruit, Mike Budenholzer, the son of an accomplished Arizona high school coach. "[Budenholzer] looked and acted in every stereotypical way that a coach's son would," said Katsiaficas, who coached Budenholzer after Popovich left for San Antonio. "The guy was a dream. He didn't care about anything but the team and giving every ounce of energy that he had."

Even though Budenholzer, a 6'1" point guard who would apply full-court man-to-man pressure in pickup games, knew he wanted to be a basketball coach, he took advantage of all that Pomona had to offer. He played varsity golf and skipped a basketball season to study abroad. "You could have an experience where you were a student and still do sports," said *Sports Illustrated* writer Chris Ballard, a teammate of Budenholzer's at Pomona. "[Sports] didn't need to be your whole collegiate identity. I think that's why these guys do so well when they go on to the NBA, because they're really well-rounded."

According to Ballard, Budenholzer was the adult in a room full of the typical college schmoes still searching for a purpose. "He always seemed to see the bigger picture," Ballard said. "He had bigger goals and plans, while the rest of us were just making shit up as we went."

Budenholzer also had a grit to him that was reminiscent of Popovich. "Mike, like Gregg, was a blue-collar person," said Lorn Foster, who was Budenholzer's thesis advisor. "He was willing to work. I mean, he didn't go to a day school."

After graduating, Budenholzer played a year professionally in Denmark. When he returned, he took an unpaid four-week gig assisting the Warriors' video coordinator. The job came about thanks to an intro from Popovich, who was a Golden State assistant at the time. The next year, Popovich took helm as the Spurs' general manager. He asked Budenholzer to apply to be his video coordinator. Budeholzer told the *Pomona College Sagecast*, the university's podcast, that he got the job "mostly because of Gregg Popovich and the connection."

Sam Presti was the next former Division III player to begin an accomplished career with the Spurs. Presti attended Emerson College in Boston, whose basketball program underwent a very familiar transformation to the one Popovich orchestrated at Pomona. When Coach Hank Smith first arrived at Emerson in 1994, the team had won just 21 combined games over the previous nine seasons. It was the type of Division III program where a kid would go to the athletic department to sign up for another sport, and the athletic director would ask if they played basketball—ever, at any level—because the team needed bodies. Some of the players they rostered, according to Shawn McCullion, who was on Smith's first team at Emerson, "shot 50 percent in layup lines."

Tom Arria, a Boston kid who barely played on his high school team, ended up as one of Emerson's co-captains alongside Presti. He remembered attending a meeting between Smith and some prospective players, a group that "looked like the Island of Misfit Toys." Smith told them he didn't care how talented they were. As long as they wanted to play and they gave their all, there would be a spot for them on the team. "I'd like for all of you to come out, get to a practice, and see what you think," Smith said to the group. "And if you don't, then go fuck yourself."

Smith approached the challenge of eradicating Emerson's losing culture in much the same way Popovich did at Pomona. There was running, there was accountability, there was more running, and behind it all, there was a love and respect for the players who bought in. The Minute Drill was Smith's favorite tool for torture. Players would line up on the baseline and sprint up and back five times—10 total lengths of the floor—in under a minute. Sometimes he only required a few Minute Drills before calling it a day. Other times he unleashed an endless barrage. Coaches will often police players and punish those who don't touch the line before changing directions. Smith took a different approach. He wasn't going to babysit his players because, in the real world, there were no babysitters. There would always be an opportunity to cut corners behind someone's back. Real character was doing the right thing when nobody was looking. "That was a big thing with [Presti]," McCullion said. "It's not about the grandiose stuff. It's about the stuff that's going on behind the scenes when nobody really knows what's going on."

McCullion, now a scout for the Brooklyn Nets, also spent 10 years as Smith's assistant. "The best part about him," McCullion said, "is that he's the same person with the best player ever as he is with the player who had no business playing college basketball."

Like Popovich, Smith had a way of making everyone involved in the program feel valued. And like Popovich, he coached everyone the same— hard. Practices were tough, but they were also fun. Smith busted his assistant coach's chops and kept the team laughing. "People from the outside thought he was like General Patton," McCullion said, "but he was more like Jerry Seinfeld."

Emerson was a different school than Pomona—urban, less academic, and best known for its performing arts and communications programs. Jay Leno, Henry Winkler, and Denis Leary are among the school's many famous alums. Thanks to its reputation in those fields, the college had no problem drawing in students. Smith just had to find the ones willing to buy into his program. So he turned his biggest disadvantage into an advantage.

Until 2006, Emerson didn't have its own dedicated basketball gym. In the early 2000s, captain's practices were held at 6:30 AM on an outdoor court in Boston's brisk October chill. In a given season, they hosted games at more than a dozen different gyms around the city. Assistant coaches, who drove the team vans, had to print out MapQuest directions to home games. At the Chinatown YMCA, one of Emerson's most frequent "home gyms," the side hoops didn't crank up. If the stands were particularly full on a given night, a team parent just might have to sit at the top of the bleachers with their head in the side hoop's net.

Rather than complain, Smith reminded his team that nobody, especially not the opposing teams with their cushy home courts, felt sorry for the Emerson players. If they wanted to be a part of the program, they had to accept everything they had and, more importantly, everything they didn't. "It was a motivator and a driving factor for kids," said Arria, who, like McCullion, also spent some time after graduation as an Emerson assistant. "It garnered, more than anything, a tremendous love for the game."

"We really loved the game," Presti told Adrian Wojnarowski on *The Woj Pod*. "It was our identity, and it kind of had to be. To go through the lengths that you had to go just to get to practice, you had to really like it."

The Emerson experience taught players like Presti how to approach challenges outside of their control, avoid excuses, and view hurdles as just another way to get stronger. It was just one of many life lessons Smith instilled in his players. "He was the best professor I ever had," McCullion said. "That gym, it wasn't a gym. It was a classroom. The stuff I learned, it wasn't about basketball. It was about life."

Smith's methods worked. The team won 60 percent of its games during his tenure at Emerson, thanks in part to some of the players who bought into his program. Players like Presti, who initially played basketball at another small college, Virginia Wesleyan, before transferring back to Emerson to be closer to home and to the Boston music scene. Presti loved his drums almost as much, if not more, than he did basketball.

Like Budenholzer, Presti had an unusual maturity and level of focus for a college student. In addition to the time spent playing basketball and recording music, Presti studied hard, eventually becoming the first Rhodes Scholar finalist in Emerson history. He was laser focused in class, often hanging back after the bell to ask the professor questions. On weekend nights, his teammates would stop by his immaculately organized room and hope to convince him to drop the books and come hang out. "In his head you could tell he was like, *This would be a good team bonding experience. I guess I should put the books away*," Arria said. "He had to rationalize why he was going to do it."

Presti was serious and fastidious, but never one to put himself before the team. When some Emerson guys discussed shaving their heads for a playoff game, Presti waited until he heard the entire team had gone through with it before very reluctantly asking for the clippers. At the end of their second-to-last season at Emerson, Presti and Arria, the co-captains, wrote up a document on Emerson letterhead. It was an oath to work as hard as possible toward an NCAA Tournament berth. There were slots for each member to sign their name.

Of course, for Presti to land a job with the Spurs, it would take more than a Rhodes Scholar nomination and the experience playing for a coach with a similar approach to Popovich. Something—or someone—had to bridge the gap between Presti's and Popovich's very different networks. That magical connection arrived at Emerson in the form of a homesick kid with a well-connected dad. The kid didn't end up playing basketball, but Coach Smith was still a resource for him. As a token of appreciation, the student's dad, a school superintendent in Aspen, mentioned the fact that Gregg Popovich and Spurs executive R.C. Buford ran a summer camp at his high school. He could help an Emerson basketball player land a job as a counselor.

Smith called his two captains, Arria and Presti, into his office and presented them with the opportunity. Arria, whose mom had recently passed away, preferred not to leave Boston. Plus, he knew that the intelligent, analytical, focused Presti would make the most of it. "I knew Sam would be better at it then me," Arria said.

Presti, who spent every waking hour focused on basketball, music, and his studies, hadn't given much thought to life after college. Working the camp and having a chance to impress the Spurs brass was a godsend. At the camp, he met Buford, which led to an internship opportunity with the Spurs in the summer of 2000. Presti's internship went so well, he earned a full-time job on the front-office side

After Presti, it would take a few years for another future NBA head coach or GM to join the Spurs straight from a D3 roster. Unsurprisingly, that person also had a personality and a college experience that reflected the Popovich ethos.

In the summer of 2008, Williams College welcomed in a new coach, Mike Maker, who earned his stripes as a D1 assistant under John Beilein at Creighton and West Virginia. Maker first met his team at Logan Airport, where they exchanged how-do-you-do's and then flew to Italy for a little basketball and a lot of team bonding.

Coming to the Division III world from a D1 assistant job wasn't all that Maker had in common with Popovich. He also had ties to the service, having grown up in a military family. As such, he was always early. One morning on the Italy trip, he walked out to a prearranged meeting spot to find one player sitting there, staring out at the gorgeous vista over Lake Como. Maker silently sat next to the player, a walk-on who rarely played, for a few minutes before asking him, "What are you thinking about?"

"Coach, I'm thinking about how insignificant we are," the player said. It was at that moment that Maker realized just how different coaching at a top liberal arts college would be.

Another player Maker first met on that Italy trip was a rising junior forward with a high basketball IQ and excellent court vision named William Hardy. Hardy would go on to play a crucial role off the bench, a Swiss Army Knife who helped his team reach the D3 National Championship as a senior. Outside of basketball, Hardy possessed a quick wit and what Maker refers to as "the gift of gab." "He has a way of relating," Maker said. "The president of Williams College or the janitorial service, he wouldn't treat them any differently. That's a gift, and Will has it."

A sports hernia sidelined Hardy for most of his junior season. He stayed engaged with the team—and with Maker—by spending time in the coach's office talking hoops and life. Maker liked to kid Hardy, telling him, with his head for the game and way with people, he'd make a great coach—if only he weren't too smart for the profession.

Maker was just one of the many close bonds Hardy formed during his four years at Williams. The relationship that was most instrumental to Hardy eventually becoming an NBA coach was his friendship with some retired townies, Curt Tong and his wife, Jinx. Tong had previously served as the athletic director at Pomona College. After retiring, he relocated back to Williamstown, where he had lived while coaching the Williams College basketball team from 1973 to 1983.

Hardy first met Tong, who everyone on campus called "Coach," at a Hoop Group dinner. Williamstown is a remote small town in northwestern Massachusetts. Many of the locals take a special interest in the college—everything from the musical performances to the sports teams. The Hoop Group was a collection of folks who, like the Tongs, lived in town and supported Williams' excellent basketball program. During their initial conversation with Hardy, the Tongs mentioned they were in the process of moving some things around the house. Hardy offered to help, figuring they would appreciate the kind gesture but not actually follow up. Sure enough, the next day, they called. "It was one of those moments where you say, 'Well, dude, you kinda have to stand and deliver on this one,'" Hardy said. "You can't be the guy who offers, they call, and then you're like, 'Actually, I can't do it.'"

That first favor led to others, and eventually the Tongs became Hardy's surrogate grandparents. Before every home game, Hardy would sit in the stands and chat with the Tongs. They would ask him how his classes were going, how the team was doing, and just generally check in.

Two weeks before graduation, Hardy got a call from Jinx Tong. She said her husband wanted to meet by the tennis courts. While the Williams tennis team practiced, Curt Tong and Hardy talked about the future. Hardy told Tong that he still had no idea what he wanted to do for work. He had sent out a bunch of applications, but the 2010 job market wasn't making it easy on him. "I have a job that you'll be great for," Tong said. "I think you should work for the San Antonio Spurs."

"That's a really great idea," Hardy said, "but what makes you think I have any chance of getting a job there?"

That's when—for the first time in their thousands of conversations—Tong told Hardy that he and Gregg Popovich had been best friends for decades, dating back to their time together at Pomona. Hardy couldn't believe it. In all of their chats either about basketball or preceding basketball games, Tong failed to mention his relationship with one of the game's greatest coaches. "I guess I never thought of it" was the only excuse Tong could muster.

It turns out Popovich had called Tong to request a Williams basketball player be sent to San Antonio for an internship. "I told Curt I was looking for somebody in the film room and that I needed a smart guy and I knew there were a lot of smart guys at Williams," Popovich told *The Boston Globe*. "I asked if there were any players there that showed an affinity toward coaching or seem to have a natural ability."

Tong approached Maker with the opportunity, and when Maker refused to pick between his seven seniors, Tong made the call and chose Hardy. Williams' basketball program in 2010 was very different than Pomona's in the 1980s or Emerson's in the 1990s. They were a national title contender with high expectations both internally and externally. "You're at an elite academic school, but there are a lot of people that care about the results," Maker said. "I always called us the Duke of Division III. Will and his teammates didn't shy away from that. It wasn't 'Win at all costs,' but there was an expectation for how you perform, how you carry yourself, how you deal with success and failure and represent the brand."

Before the Spurs' interview process was complete, Hardy had actually secured a few job offers in more traditional fields. Those interviews tended to focus on his ambitions and skillset. The phone calls and in-person conversations with the Spurs were different. They wanted to get a sense of Hardy's character, and also make sure he fully understood what he was vying for—a job with long hours and low pay.

Hardy moved through the process without raising any red flags and landed the internship. "I know for a fact that Coach Tong putting his stamp on me is why I got the job," Hardy said. "I'm not going to sit here and say I was clearly the best candidate because of how smart I am. It's not that at all."

Hardy's time at Williams prepared him for the grunt work that was in store for him in San Antonio. Like all of his college teammates, Hardy didn't receive an athletic scholarship. Deciding to play D3 involved swallowing his pride and embracing humility. At a place like Williams, athletes, according to Maker, have no entitlement and are "highly intelligent, wired to do well, have an insatiable desire to succeed, and are taught to think outside the box."

When Budenholzer, Presti, and Hardy all began their careers in San Antonio, they discovered that Popovich's commitment to teaching applied to both his players and his staff. Much in the same way he prioritized player development on and off the court, Popovich built an environment geared toward coaching and front-office growth.

At first, Popovich would lay out the expectations. As Hardy learned during his interview, the beginning of a Spurs coaching or front-office career was neither glamorous nor lucrative. Budenholzer subsisted primarily on free Subway sandwich cards he collected in the office. He would also do his laundry in the facility to avoid spending time and money at a laundromat. Presti, who made $250 a month during his internship in 2000, ate fistfuls of free Power Bars and sometimes slept on training tables. "A lane opened up for Division III players who were willing to risk it, and they would show up, and [Popovich] would find a place for them and give them a chance," Steve Koblik said. "He'd pay them bupkis and he would see what they did. Would they go the extra mile? Would they be there before him? You start adding up all the shit you'd have to put up with when you were working with this guy, and if he saw you were doing the job and you were learning, then he would take interest. It's a very good way to teach as far as I'm concerned."

Popovich benefited from the fact that, given his position as both head coach and front-office leader, he had ultimate veto power over any hire. Plus, he took over an NBA team at a time when staff sizes began ballooning. He could bring in young, anonymous, and inexperienced D3 alums as interns or video coordinators. These weren't high-pressure coaching roles or scouting assignments that would send the newbies on the road. These were in-house learning opportunities. "Staffs are bigger. So there's more ways for talent to trickle up," said Seth Partnow, an NBA analytics writer and former director of basketball research for the Milwaukee Bucks. "By all accounts, Will Hardy is an absolute superstar. He wouldn't even get in the door 20 years ago. He's nobody from nowhere."

In exchange for doing all of the thankless jobs, Hardy, like Budenholzer and Presti before him, could shut his mouth, open his ears, and learn about the league. Success in that first phase required finding value in tasks like making smoothies, data entry, and picking people up from the airport. Nobody was going to shake their hand, congratulate them on a superb D3 career, and ask for them to install a new offense on Day One. "You have to separate yourself pretty quickly from identifying as a basketball *player*," Hardy said. "Now, I'm a coach. I'm somebody who used to play basketball."

When Hardy joined the Spurs in 2010—16 years after Budenholzer first started as a video coordinator—he had the benefit of walking into an established program with built-in mentors. Budenholzer taught Hardy the importance of details. If Budenholzer, then Popovich's top assistant, noticed even the tiniest of errors in Hardy's work, he let him know in a manner that wasn't always coated in sugar. "It was an unbelievable place to learn because I had a lot of people who took their time and energy to really teach me and correct me and tell me, 'That's bullshit,'" Hardy said. "You need that. I think there's a lot of people now who run from criticism or think it means it's over for them. It's not going to be perfect. I had everything to learn."

Budenholzer was the guinea pig. He had to rely more on persistence in order to learn what he needed to know. "I always felt like he was the kid who doesn't take no for an answer," said Will Perdue, the former Spurs center. "Look where it got him. I don't mean he rubbed you the wrong way; he was just constant. He was like a fly. You wave him off, and then he lands on you again."

Popovich ran his patented playbook with Budenholzer, connecting with him on a personal level while also working him hard and squeezing out every ounce of potential. "There's a real genuine care that you feel," Budenholzer said. "And when you feel that someone cares about you and wants good for you, then all the sudden that person can push you and maybe get great things out of you."

To put their younger staffers in the best positions to succeed, the Spurs refrained from pigeonholing them. It was an education style akin to that of a liberal arts college. They prioritized breadth over depth. It wasn't sufficient just to train the video guy to perform his daily tasks. Bringing him on the court to work with players or into a meeting with front-office leads may not help him do his job better today, but it would pay dividends tomorrow. "People say Bud is a great X's and O's coach," Carlesimo, who worked with Budenholzer in San Antonio, said. "Well, yes, he was, but he was also a worker. He was somebody who started in the video room and was just as good at breaking down a tape or being out there before practice or after practice or during practice with a player."

Hardy spent his internship learning both the coaching side and the front-office side. He also hopped into player workouts where, thanks to his 6'6" frame, he had a lot of value as a big-body defender. In a paper entitled "Great GMs are made, not born," executives from Korn Ferry, a leading sports staffing firm, repeatedly highlighted the Spurs for how effectively they groom future front-office leaders. "We expose our interns to every different area possible," Spurs CEO R.C. Buford, the man who has partnered with Popovich throughout their time in San Antonio, told the Korn Ferry executives. Spurs interns dabble in analytics, performance training, player development, and salary cap management.

Before embarking on a career as a general manager, former Spurs player Danny Ferry spent 2003 through 2005 learning in San Antonio's front office. "In San Antonio I was literally exposed to everything," Ferry told the

Korn Ferry executives. "It was a very collaborative environment and in the end it made me more prepared to see everything with a better understanding of what the business side goes through."

Looping newbies into high-level conversations can be risky. In an environment as competitive as the NBA, information is a valuable currency. Team employees, agencies, and journalists exchange secrets for favors or prestige. As a result, some teams limit their staffers' access to avoid leaks. The Spurs, however, chose to expand the circle of trust. "Pop and R.C., they always gave us such great access to learn," Hardy said. "You weren't hidden from what was going on. With that, you had their trust. Our job was to represent the organization in the right way and keep the things that we were privy to confidential."

Popovich and Buford, who have led the Spurs for nearly 30 years, provide lower-level staffers with stability in an unstable world. Given the volatility in the industry, many younger NBA employees are forced to move teams every few years. Spurs employees have the luxury of not always having to think about their next job. They can spend years learning from the same people under the same roof. Budenholzer worked almost 20 years in San Antonio before branching off on his own. Hardy had 11 seasons, and Presti had seven. Spending that much time in one place gave them the luxury of reaching a depth of learning that very few, if any, NBA environments could match.

That education was buoyed by a special teacher. Popovich instilled an environment where arguing was not only accepted, it was encouraged. "The one way you will not make it here," Budenholzer told *Sports Illustrated*'s Jack McCallum, "is to be a yes man."

When Hardy was elevated to head video coordinator, he would often watch film one-on-one with Popovich. During those sessions, Popovich would pick arguments, stating a questionable opinion about a counter or a wrinkle to see if Hardy would take the bait and fight back. Ettore Messina, a top European coach who worked as a Spurs assistant between 2014 and 2019, told the *Coaching U Podcast* that Popovich's talent is how he can "use the ability to argue to build a common opinion." By fostering a participatory environment, the Spurs could reap the full benefit of their diverse staff. After all, what's the point of hiring from all corners of the basketball world if those different perspectives are stifled by a dominant leader?

In his book *Think Again: The Power of Knowing What You Don't Know*, organizational psychologist and author Adam Grant relays how research studies have repeatedly proven the benefit of building a culture like the Spurs'. Conflict in a team setting can come in two flavors—relationship conflict, in which people disagree about interpersonal behaviors, and task conflict, in which people disagree about work-related decisions or procedures. A meta-analysis of more than 100 studies covering more than 8,000 teams shows that while relationship conflict usually does not bode well for team performance, task conflict is "linked to higher creativity and smarter choices."

It takes a confident leader to promote task conflict. "Pop is someone who isn't threatened by other people. So he's a guy who's always trying to find a reason," Pomona grad Chris Ballard, who covered the Spurs as a *Sports Illustrated* reporter, said.

A culture of arguing requires personnel who possess the humility that the unglamorous world of D3 sports drills into its athletes. At some point in their college playing careers, Budenholzer, Presti, and Hardy all realized that, even though they were flawed players, they could still play a role in their team's success. And they came to understand that their success mattered, whether it was at the D3 Final Four or the Chinatown YMCA. It was the same on the coaching and management side. "As a player, I was very aware of my limitations and I tried not to step out of them," Presti said to Marc Spears, then of *The Boston Globe*, in 2007. "I'm very, very aware of my limitations."

An argumentative culture is also made possible by the love and perspective that pervades the Spurs facilities. Staffers have a seat at the table for those wine-filled team meals. Like the players, they form strong relationships that can withstand the occasional work disagreement. The spirit behind those meals extends well beyond the moment Popovich picks up the check. Being a Spur means taking basketball very seriously, but understanding that people are what matter most. "All those wins and losses, they fade away," Popovich said during his 2023 Hall of Fame acceptance speech, "but those relationships stick with you forever."

BETWEEN 1980 AND 2015, large-market teams dominated the NBA. Championship parades tended to take place on the streets of big cities like Boston, Los Angeles, Chicago, or Houston. The five-time champion San Antonio Spurs were an obvious outlier. They managed to sustain success despite the inherent disadvantages of playing in a smaller city. Other small-market teams started to poach from the Spurs coaching staff and front office. And thanks to the lessons learned within the San Antonio facility, most of those ex-Spurs experienced almost immediate success, especially the former Division III players.

Sam Presti went first. The franchise formerly known as the Seattle SuperSonics snapped him up in 2007, when he was just a few months shy of his 30th birthday. A few years earlier, when Presti was in the midst of his rapid ascent from intern to assistant general manager, his hometown Boston Red Sox named 28-year-old Theo Epstein general manager. Seeing a storied organization turn to a young, analytical person without a playing pedigree was, according to Presti, "a breakthrough." He even wrote Epstein a letter to wish him well.

The *Moneyball* revolution didn't come for basketball as quickly or aggressively as it did baseball, but Presti benefited from an increased openness to this new way of thinking. He didn't need to tell the world that he majored in sports, like previous Seattle GM Bob Whitsitt did. Sonics owner Clay Bennett viewed Presti's analytical nature and youth as assets, indicators that he would be open to new ideas and approaches. "He got the job because of how he is and how he does things," Bennett said. "He is methodical. He is measured."

Presti spoke like a finance guy, not a basketball guy. He told Greg Sandoval of *The Washington Post* that he wanted to be the Warren Buffett of the NBA. He claimed he was "in a futures market" where teams tried to "predict the appreciation of an asset at the same time they identify ways to help grow that asset."

With the Sonics, Presti tried to replicate and then build on several areas where the forward-looking Spurs were hunting for an edge, including data analytics. "It wasn't that data was special to [the Spurs]. It was that they thought they might have a competitive advantage with data. So it was worth a try," said Ben Alamar, an economics PhD who Presti hired to do statistical analyses in Seattle.

Data and cold, hard financial language might seem to fly in the face of the humanism Popovich ingrained in the Spurs organization, but Presti married his analytical approach with a touchy-feely side. "Sam went out of his way to make sure people felt included and felt like part of the team," Alamar said. Alamar remembered Presti taking time to engage with interns and ask their opinions—small acts that went a long way toward building a culture.

The Seattle franchise relocated to Oklahoma City in 2008, one of the smallest markets in the NBA. Through his clear-eyed vision, attention to detail, and process-driven approach, Presti rebuilt the team into a title contender. He selected three future MVPs—Kevin Durant, Russell Westbrook, and James Harden—in consecutive drafts. "He's one of the best executives I've ever seen from a draft standpoint," said Bobby Marks, ESPN's front office insider. According to Marks, if there were a draft of executives, Presti would be the first pick, especially if the job called for building an organization from scratch. "I would give him the keys to the kingdom because I'd know there's a plan in place," Marks said.

On Adrian Wojnarowski's *The Woj Pod*, Presti named the top traits he would look for in a general manager: resiliency and adaptability. "You're going to get your ass kicked pretty much every day," Presti said. It's hard not to tie that sentiment back to everything Presti and his teammates went through at Emerson. It should come as no surprise, then, that Presti has gone out of his way to create more front-office opportunities for former D3 players than perhaps anyone else in NBA history. While he was still in San Antonio, Presti helped a younger Emerson alum named Rob Hennigan score an internship with the Spurs. Hennigan, who graduated as Emerson's all-time leading scorer, but was never above picking up a mop and dusting off the court before practice, followed Presti to Oklahoma City. Fresh off a Thunder appearance in the 2012 NBA Finals, the Orlando Magic tabbed the 30-year-old Hennigan to be their next general manager. They were impressed with his intelligence and Spurs/Thunder pedigree.

In Orlando, Hennigan built out his staff with even *more* former D3 players. One of his first front-office hires was John Halas, a prep school assistant coach who played at Trinity College in Connecticut. Hennigan also hired Shawn McCullion, his assistant coach at Emerson, as a scout.

Presti also kept going back to the D3 well. Will Dawkins, now the second-in-command for the Washington Wizards, came into the league as a Thunder intern right after graduating from Emerson. Presti was not shy about sending emails to coaches at high-academic, D3 institutions seeking out bright basketball minds. He told David Hixon, Amherst College's head coach, that he liked hiring D3 guys because they came in ready to roll up their sleeves and get to work, as opposed to immediately asking for gear or trying to get out onto the court with players. It is no coincidence that two of Hixon's former players currently work in the Thunder organization—chief of staff Glenn Wong and assistant program development coach Connor Johnson.

After Presti, the next D3 departure from San Antonio was Mike Budenholzer, who joined the Atlanta Hawks as head coach in 2013. One would think that in a copycat league like the NBA, other teams would be groveling at the feet of Gregg Popovich's lead assistant. That was not the case with Budenholzer, who, like the members of the Van Gundy tree, didn't always look the part of a polished head coach. "He's definitely not giving a ton of thought to what he's wearing on a given day," said his former college teammate Chris Ballard, "but his heart is pure."

One of the few downsides to working for the longest tenured coach in the NBA is that there is very little chance of landing an interim opportunity like Jeff Van Gundy did. Fortunately, former Spurs spread to other franchises. When Hawks general manager Danny Ferry, who played and worked for the Spurs, had a head coaching vacancy, he jumped at the chance to hire Budenholzer. Prior to the Hawks job, Budenholzer's only other time as a finalist for a head coaching position was with the Phoenix Suns, who were run by former Spur Steve Kerr.

Longtime front-office executive Rick Sund, who was an advisor with the Hawks in 2013, didn't even have Budenholzer on his long-list at the start of the interview process. Watching the very first Hawks practice with Budenholzer at the helm made Sund a believer. "It was teachable in an easy way, where even an idiot like me could understand," Sund said. Budenholzer implemented terminology like "MIG" (short for Most Important Guy), which helped the players understand how to set up defensive rotations. He excelled as both an X's and O's strategist and also as someone who could develop players and put them in the best position to succeed.

Before practices, assistant coaches ran the players through 15 to 20 minutes of player development drills they called "vitamins," a carryover from San Antonio. The emphasis on internal improvement paid off. In Budenholzer's first two seasons, three of his players made the All-Star team for the first time.

Budenholzer later moved to the Milwaukee Bucks, where he won his second Coach of the Year award and first NBA title. Like Popovich, Budenholzer was open to hiring former D3 athletes, some of whom he would go out of his way to connect with and mentor.

One such D3 alum was front-office staffer Matt Bollero, a DePauw University grad. Bollero, like Budenholzer, played both basketball and golf in college. He came to the Bucks from the Minnesota Timberwolves' front office, where he had worked for another D3 alum, Tom Thibodeau. While with the Bucks, Bollero quickly learned the difference between a job with a former Van Gundy assistant and a job with a former Popovich assistant. Right after Thibodeau got the Minnesota gig, Bollero ran into him in the team facility. The two were casually acquainted and started chatting. Thibodeau asked Bollero if he still golfed. "Not anymore," Bollero replied.

Thibodeau, in his trademark gruff voice, shot back, "Good answer!" The message was clear. In Thibodeau's world there were no hobbies. Only basketball.

When Bollero joined the Bucks, Budenholzer heard through a mutual friend that the new guy in the front office was, despite what he might've told Thibodeau, an avid golfer. Budenholzer played a round with Bollero, their first of many, just two days later.

Budenholzer taught another generation of front office and coaching assistants some of the lessons he learned from San Antonio, with his own twist. He worked to build camaraderie, not only through the traditional break bread meals, but also with other events more aligned with Budenholzer's personal affinities, like a team-wide golf tournament modeled after The Masters.

On the court, Budenholzer, like Popovich, was all business. From the coaching staff to the front office to the players to the medical staff, Budenholzer set a standard for everyone about what was expected on a day-to-day basis. "He had a well-laid out structure that was strict in some ways but also provided a lot of autonomy," said Jordan Sears, who joined the Bucks video room shortly after graduating from D3 Wesleyan University.

As an assistant video coordinator, Sears would frequently see film clips that Budenholzer angrily tagged with "Hands on knees" or "We're tired." Bad body language was a Budenholzer pet peeve, one that he tried to fight in his own quirky way. One day, when Bucks star Giannis Antetokounmpo was running through an intense individual workout, Budenholzer waddled out onto the court. He wanted to show Antetokounmpo his new shorts, which had handprints near the knees with big X's over them. The message was clear, even for the best player on the team—don't let them know you're tired!

In 2022, Will Hardy became the latest member of the special D3 offshoot of Popovich's coaching tree to land a head coaching gig. Thanks to the stability in San Antonio, he could be choosy, ensuring he left the nest for the right opportunity at the right time. After garnering some head coaching buzz that, to Hardy at least, was very unexpected, he decided to join the Boston Celtics as an assistant coach. Hardy was intentional about working with new Celtics head coach Ime Udoka, a former Spurs assistant who also played seven seasons in the NBA. Throughout his coaching career, Hardy tried to understand the emotional toll of playing in the NBA. In a very Popovichian metaphor, he said he knew all of that studying would never lead to a complete answer. "I could study wine my whole life," Hardy said. "I could read every book about wine. I could watch videos, I could read about it, I could know everything about tannins and all the other shit. But if I never drank a glass of wine, I'm not a wine expert."

Hardy thoroughly impressed folks in the Celtics organization. Their compliments sound like testimonials for an education at Spurs University. Celtics analytics staffer Drew Cannon was wowed by the thoughtful questions Hardy asked about data analyses. Celtics president of basketball operations Brad Stevens, also a former Division III player, praised Hardy's interpersonal skills and ability to communicate. "He's got a really good emotional quotient," Stevens said. "Everybody likes being around him. He's thoughtful, he's able to deliver messages in a clear, concise way, he cares about people."

In Udoka and Hardy's first season with the Celtics, they reached the NBA Finals. The success increased Hardy's desirability around the league. That offseason, the Utah Jazz named the 34-year-old their new head coach.

In his comments to the press after announcing the hire, Jazz basketball executive Danny Ainge brushed off Hardy's age, focusing instead on his maturity and preparedness for the role. "Many times in his answers," Ainge said, "he spoke my language."

Whether Ainge's "language" is that of a former player, former head coach, longtime front-office leader, or some combination of the three, the fact that a D3 guy 30 years Ainge's junior was fluent in it is a testament to the educational program in San Antonio.

In a 2022 conversation shortly after his hiring, Hardy said his goal for the first few months was to connect with his new coworkers and create the right environment. "That's really all I'm focused on—the people part. I'm focused on spending time with the staff," Hardy said. "Not just the coaching staff but the front office, the medical group, the performance team. I think that stuff's really important."

Hardy's emphasis on culture is a fitting homage to Popovich. When building the Spurs program, Popovich took some pages out of his Pomona playbook—not X's and O's, but methods to impact the Jimmys and Joes. He put a new spin on the coaching spectrum. Rather than just throw his hands up and accept that the most talented team would win, he worked to foster an environment that, through luck and skill, brought in the *right* Jimmys and Joes. Then he nurtured them as whole human beings in order to maximize their potential on and off the court.

When it came to hiring, Popovich leaned into his affinity for D3 student-athletes. He was the first NBA leader to view D3 playing experience as a qualification in and of itself. The connections he maintained to the D3 world allowed him to mine a previously untapped talent pool. Then, by bringing the same care as a teacher and mentor to his staffers as he did with his players, his organization developed the next generation of D3 alums who would lead NBA franchises. They in turn have carried his lessons with them, added their own spin, and, especially in the case of Presti, looked to empower even more former D3 players. As this crucial branch was growing, and the Van Gundy assistants spread throughout the league, other D3 alums were also breaking into the NBA. They carved out their own niches, bolstering the ranks of former small-college players in leadership roles around the league.

PART III:
SIDE DOORS

CHAPTER 9

WITH A LITTLE HELP

*How John Hammond's connections helped
lift him to the top of the NBA, even as GM's
backgrounds were changing drastically*

In the months that followed his epiphany about the kinetic chain of a jump shot, Andrew Olson's idea started to take shape. He hypothesized that tracking everything that went into a shot—preparation, balance, follow-through—would allow him to pinpoint exactly what caused makes and misses. Equipped with that answer, he could then work with players to eliminate the bugaboos that impacted their field-goal percentage. Ultimately, he hoped to compile some data for a case study that would help him determine which steps in the jump shooting process were most impactful. He even came up with a name—ASA, which stood for Accumulated Shot Analysis. He envisioned an app that could help players leverage his findings. If all went well, maybe pro teams would even engage him as a consultant.

Back when Olson first launched his training business, he insisted on doing just about everything himself. He preferred to figure out an answer on his own rather than ask for advice from someone more seasoned. He realized that his stubbornness was stunting his potential. If this ASA idea had legs, he would need help. As a political science major from a liberal arts college, Olson didn't have much experience in Excel. Luckily, his roommate did. Olson bought NBA League Pass and started tracking games, one shot at a time. He decided to focus on the Houston Rockets—an Amherst friend with connections to their front office had agreed to provide an introduction if the analysis yielded any fruit. He watched every Rockets game, manually recording more than 30 variables for each shot taken. His roommate took the data and ran some regressions. Ultimately, they homed in on six variables—half a dozen pieces of the jump shot routine that significantly impacted field-goal percentage.

Entrepreneurship appealed to Olson because he could take ownership over an idea and control his own destiny. He would have more agency, so he thought, than if he had taken the traditional coaching path. He was learning that, no matter what, having the right people in his corner was a prerequisite to success.

Since the beginning of their partnership in 2001, John Hammond, the Detroit Pistons' vice president of basketball operations, watched most practices shoulder-to-shoulder and knee-to-knee with his boss, Joe Dumars. Before one particular practice session, Hammond and Dumars sat in their usual spots as the players moseyed out onto the floor to huddle around their head coach, Larry Brown. As soon as Brown began to address the team, the locker room door burst open to reveal the team's brilliant and mercurial starting forward, Rasheed Wallace.

Both Hammond and Dumars turned their attention to Wallace, who lacked any kind of a pep in his step en route to the team huddle. After a few seconds, Dumars returned his gaze to the rest of the team. Hammond stayed locked in on Wallace, apparently trying to channel some sort of ESP that would either speed up Wallace's gait or physically toss him out of the gym. "That doesn't bother you? That he's late?" Hammond asked the seemingly unperturbed Dumars.

"No, John," Dumars calmly replied. "It would bother me if he didn't come out of that door. He's here. The fact that he walked up 45 seconds after we got started…Man, never, ever, ever sweat small details like this with guys like that."

Hammond couldn't help himself. He still thought like a coach. It made sense, seeing as though most of his career had been spent on the sidelines. Partnering with Dumars, a Hall of Famer and NBA champion, helped Hammond better understand the perspective of the NBA player. When

Hammond eventually left Detroit to go run the Milwaukee Bucks, those lessons came in handy.

The road from Hammond's hometown of Zion, Illinois, to Milwaukee is short—about 50 miles—and relatively straight. Hammond's journey to the Bucks' front office, however, was filled with detours and false starts and what appeared to be countless dead ends. Time and again, his many friends and coworkers resuscitated his life in the NBA. But to even get to the point of having a career worth saving, Hammond needed to first spend some time at Greenville College.

From a young age, Hammond only wanted to work in basketball. At 13, he aspired to coach junior high basketball and teach PE. A few years later, he changed his mind; he was clearly meant to coach *high school* basketball. Then, when Hammond sat in on a cousin's college recruiting visits, it didn't take long for him to dreamily envision his life as a college assistant. He would travel the country, convincing parents to send their sons to whatever university would hire him. Each time Hammond was exposed to a higher level, his dreams grew.

In high school, Hammond aimed to play well enough to launch himself into the exciting world of college basketball—first as a player and then, if all went according to plan, as a coach. Realistically, he knew he couldn't cut it at a big, premiere school. Still, he wouldn't have minded settling at a weaker D1 program, or even one of the Midwest's competitive smaller colleges.

One night, on the way to a Harlem Globetrotters game, the stepmom of his good friend and teammate, Scott Burgess, asked Hammond if he might consider Greenville College, a small Christian school in southern Illinois. Hammond gave a friendly response, but thought to himself, *I'm better than that.* He pushed Greenville out of his mind, never, he assumed, to return.

So much was riding on his senior high school season, one in which Hammond believed he would shine. It was a season that, ultimately, never came to pass. While out riding a friend's motorcycle, a car struck Hammond, severely injuring his right leg. The accident ended Hammond's high school basketball career. He figured his days as a competitive player were finished.

Meanwhile, Hammond's friend Scott Burgess decided to heed his stepmom's advice. He enrolled at Greenville College, where he would play on the basketball team. When Hammond learned that he, too, might be able to play at Greenville after his injuries healed, he decided to join Burgess.

The two boys arrived at their shared dorm room and unpacked. Burgess made his bed, folded up his clothes, and hung some items on hangers. Hammond did the same. They attended classes and started working with the team, which is Division III today but competed in the NAIA at the time. The lines between days started to blur together, thanks to their well-established and well-enjoyed routines.

Then everything changed. Hammond will never forget the sick, dreadful feeling of returning to his dorm room one day to see all of Burgess' stuff—the clothes, the books, the bedspread, all of it—gone. He sat in the room alone, haunted by his friend's bare bed.

The waking nightmare began a few days earlier, during a routine three-man drill. Burgess and another player collided face to face. *Boom.* It looked painful, but nothing that a college basketball player hasn't seen at least a few times. Except Burgess didn't get up. Hammond spent the night in the hospital, waiting to take his friend home.

When the doctors rushed Burgess to a bigger hospital in St. Louis, Hammond knew it was even more serious than he dared imagine. He learned that Burgess had undergone not one, but two unsuccessful emergency brain surgeries. His best friend was dead.

If Hammond and Burgess went to a larger school—a Northern or Southern or Western Illinois—the school paper would've covered the tragedy with a little article. After a week or two, most people there would've forgotten. "I would've been walking through that campus, and no one would know who I was, no one would know what had happened," Hammond said. "I would just be another student there. I couldn't have stayed. I'm sure I wouldn't have stayed."

The Greenville community was different. "That little campus took me under their wing, the entire campus," Hammond said. "It was the most unbelievable thing."

They moved Hammond into a single room down the hall, away from that bare second bed and empty second closet. When he walked through campus, professors, administrators, and upperclassmen would all say hello. When Hammond would say hi back, they'd ask how he was doing. When he'd say he was fine, they'd look him in the eyes and ask again, "John, how are things going?" They sincerely wanted to know.

As if coping with his friend's sudden death wasn't enough, Hammond's parents were both battling serious illnesses. With everything he was facing, Hammond considered dropping out. The Greenville community wouldn't let him. "You hear these stories: 'Without Greenville College, I wouldn't be where I am,'" Hammond said. "Some people use those terms very loosely. For me, it's not a loose term. It's a very deep reality."

Despite the trauma, or maybe because of it, Hammond continued playing basketball. When asked to give a scouting report on himself as a player, Hammond said he was "a guy who was happy to be a part of it." He had some highlights here and there—a 24-point half in a JV game, a few nice shots—but was never able to string together anything meaningful. "All's I had was moments," he said.

Before Hammond's junior year, budget crunches forced Greenville to eliminate the position of assistant basketball coach. The head coach, desperate for some help, approached Hammond and made his pitch: "Look, you want to coach. Start coaching with me."

In one fell swoop, the Greenville program lost John Hammond the player and gained John Hammond the coach. He spent two seasons as the head JV basketball coach and varsity assistant, launching what would be a remarkable career in basketball.

THE TIES THAT bind an individual's network are not all the same. Strong, thick strands connect family and close friends. Those bonds don't typically yield too many new second- or third-order relationships—the friends of your very best friends tend to be your pals as well. It is those looser bonds—the roommate of a one-time coworker, or the cousin of that friendly guy in the pickup game—who really help the tendrils of one person's network reach their way into other previously untapped groups.

In a landmark 1973 paper, Stanford sociologist Mark Granovetter coined the term "weak ties" to describe those looser bonds. "Those to whom we are weakly tied are more likely to move in circles different from our own and will thus have access to information different from that which we receive," Granovetter wrote.

Weak ties have been proven more effective than strong ties at helping professionals find a new job. A comprehensive LinkedIn study, which ran from 2015 through 2019, found that a connection on the LinkedIn platform with a weak tie (10 or fewer mutual connections) was twice as likely to lead to a new job than a connection with a strong tie (20 or more mutual connections).

The universe of basketball coaches is relatively small and tight-knit. When a head coach builds their staff, trust is paramount, leading many to hire only strong ties. Hubie Brown almost exclusively hired former Five-Star Basketball Camp guys as assistants. Larry Brown preferred "family." Other coaching trees, however, sampled from both strong and weak connections. Jeff Van Gundy hired former teammate and "third Van Gundy brother" Andy Greer, but he also hired looser connections like Tom Thibodeau and Steve Clifford.

Not every NBA coach or front-office employee is fortunate enough to work in a stable environment like San Antonio. Most coaches live under a constant threat of being wiped out due to poor performance. It often takes one close connection to lift an assistant coach into the league. Then it's up to the looser contacts to keep them there.

After graduating from Greenville, Hammond built a college coaching network from scratch. One relationship begat another, sparking a decade of Division I assistant jobs that culminated with a six-season stint at Southwest Missouri State. While this new network helped Hammond find his footing in college hoops, it was an old friend that elevated him into the pros. For Hammond's NBA career, Billy McKinney was the first in a series of fortuitous connections.

McKinney and Hammond first met as elementary school students in a church activity program. Throughout junior high and high school, they played basketball and socialized together. McKinney was even with Hammond just before his fateful motorcycle accident. McKinney was a transcendent basketball talent, who went on to play seven seasons in the NBA. After retirement, he hung in the league as a scout.

When Hammond was with Southwest Missouri State, he met McKinney for lunch before a game in Chicago. McKinney divulged that he was going to leave the Bulls to go run player personnel for the expansion Minnesota Timberwolves. He asked Hammond, who had made his bones in college as a recruiter, if he would join him as a scout. Hammond couldn't believe his good fortune. He and his wife moved to Minnesota, bought a house, and figured that was that. "I thought I was going to be an NBA scout for 25 years," Hammond said. "That's how naive I was."

Hammond's second fortuitous connection blossomed at the Portsmouth Invitational Tournament, an annual showcase for top college talent. Mike Schuler, a Golden State Warriors assistant coach under Don Nelson, was one of many pro scouts who flocked to the event. In his past life as a college coach, Schuler occasionally found himself scouting in the same high school gyms as Hammond. They would exchange hellos and not much more. When Hammond saw Schuler at the P.I.T., he reintroduced himself. During their conversation, Schuler asked Hammond if he wanted to go for a jog the next morning.

They both enjoyed the run and promised to do it another time. When they bumped into each other at a different scouting event shortly thereafter, Schuler once again asked Hammond to join him on a morning run. And once again, they chit-chatted like old pals.

A few weeks later, Schuler called Hammond. The Los Angeles Clippers were about to name him head coach, and he wanted his new jogging buddy to be one of his three assistants. Hammond accepted the exciting offer. After just one year as a scout, he had climbed up a rung on the NBA's version of a corporate ladder.

When asked if he felt qualified to work on an NBA bench, Hammond said, "Absolutely not." Schuler would pepper Hammond with questions during games, to which Hammond would provide the best answers he could. They weren't good enough. After the games, Schuler would tell Hammond, "I need more." *I can't give more*, Hammond would think to himself. *I don't know it.*

The Schuler Era in Los Angeles was not particularly successful, nor was it particularly long. The Clippers dismissed him in the middle of the 1991–92 season, his second with the team. At right around the same time, the San Antonio Spurs fired Larry Brown. The Clippers scooped up Brown as their new head coach, bringing him in at midseason. A new head coach could spell doom for an assistant, especially one as green as Hammond. But, of course, Hammond and Brown knew each other.

When Hammond was at Southwest Missouri State, he recruited at the same junior college gyms as Brown, then the coach at nearby Kansas. Like many young coaches at the time, Hammond admired Brown and always made a point to go say hello. Brown, who had a great deal of respect for Southwest Missouri's program and spoke at their clinics, was always gracious. Thanks in part to their shared history, Brown opted to retain Hammond on his Clippers staff.

Hammond made his own luck by prioritizing the people part of the business. "[There's] nothing more important for me professionally and even personally," he said, "than to be able to connect with people, to treat people the right way."

Following the 1992–93 season, a rare winning year for the Clippers, Larry Brown, as Larry Brown is wont to do, bolted for another job. When the Clippers hired a new head coach, they asked Hammond to move down a rung and transition from assistant coach to advanced scout. In the face of a demotion and organizational instability, Hammond found a lifeline once again in childhood friend Billy McKinney. McKinney, who had resurfaced in Detroit as their lead basketball executive, offered Hammond a college scouting role. If Hammond wasn't going to be on the bench, he preferred to at least be working for a friend. He accepted McKinney's offer.

Two seasons later, the Pistons dismissed McKinney. He was replaced by Doug Collins, who doubled as the team's new head coach. Collins couldn't cobble together his desired coaching staff in time for his first season, so he reluctantly moved Hammond, who was still under contract, back to the bench as an assistant coach. "I was retained twice," Hammond said. "I was retained by Larry [Brown] and I was retained by Doug Collins. If either one of those guys doesn't retain me, my career could be easily over. Just like that. You'd never get back in."

By not only keeping Hammond, but also moving him back to the bench, Collins breathed new life into Hammond's NBA career. And by giving him the opportunity to coach Joe Dumars—Hammond's most crucial connection—Collins unknowingly gave birth to Hammond's career as an NBA executive.

So many of Hammond's coaching relationships, those bonds that buoyed his NBA career and kept him from sinking back into the college ranks, began in the bleachers of some off-the-beaten-path gym. Usually it was Hammond, emulating the kind folks on the Greenville campus, who would make the first move with a cheerful hello and introduction. At the onset of one of his most fruitful relationships, however, Hammond found himself on the receiving end of an unprompted act of kindness and camaraderie.

Dumars, a two-time NBA champion on the back-nine of his career, but still unquestionably a team leader, asked Hammond to rebound for him after practice. The Pistons cycled through many assistant coaches and scouts during Dumars' tenure with the team. With each new staff member, Dumars, like most players, would feel them out and try to get a sense of their personality. Some coaches came on too strong, demanding the players' respect on Day One. Not Hammond. "With John, I sensed a guy who was very prepared," Dumars said, "but I also sensed a humility in him that caught my eye."

After most practices, Dumars would stay on the floor to get up some extra shots. Someone on the staff would usually rebound for him. "I want someone with me after practice that I'm comfortable with," Dumars said. "So I pulled [Hammond] aside and asked, 'Would you rebound for me?' And that turned into a 30-year friendship."

The shootarounds became a daily post-practice ritual, one that made Hammond feel at ease in his new role. While Dumars shot, the two men talked. They discussed their backgrounds, their careers, and their families. Following one of their usual post-practice sessions during the 1998–99 season, Dumars' last in the NBA, Dumars looked at Hammond and said, "You know, we're going to work together one day."

Forgive Hammond for his skepticism, but he wasn't so sure Dumars' prophecy would come true. Dumars wasn't the only one moving on. Hammond had decided to take an assistant coaching job at the University of Missouri under Quin Snyder, who worked with Hammond on the Clippers staff during the 1992–93 season. The decision confused Hammond's colleagues in the league, for whom college was viewed as a major step backward. But Hammond wanted the chance to run his own program. "The goal was leadership," Hammond said. After a decade in the NBA, he didn't believe that opportunity would ever come in the pros.

Hammond and Dumars loosely kept in touch after they parted ways in 1999. They would email here and there and maybe have the very occasional phone call. Theirs was a relationship built on those post-practice shootaround chats. "I never had a meal with Joe [when he was a player]," Hammond said. "I was never at Joe's house. We just had a good player-coach relationship."

During the heart of Mizzou's conference schedule, Hammond invited Dumars and his son to campus to watch his team play. After the game, Dumars shared that he would soon be named Pistons president of basketball operations. "I don't know if it's going to be at the end of this year or at the end of next year, but you're coming with me," Dumars said. "Will you commit?"

Hammond told him yes.

Years later, Hammond figures Dumars offered him the role because he "saw what he wanted" in his former coach. But Hammond felt he was even less qualified for a front office position than he was when his butt first touched an NBA bench with the Clippers. "I knew the big picture things, like on player acquisitions and things like that," Hammond said. "But I didn't know the intricacies of how you got those done."

For Dumars, the decision to hire Hammond went beyond just liking the cut of his jib.

"As soon as I accepted the position as president of the team, I knew that I was going to hire John," Dumars said. "It was an easy hire. No, I didn't worry about him not having any experience. Hell, *I* didn't have any experience. We knew the game, we knew people, we understood how to interact with coaches and players. I knew we'd be okay."

Hammond, even though he felt he was in over his head, brought exactly what Dumars was looking for—a basketball lifer who brought a different perspective. "I would always have the experience and the insight of a player," Dumars said. "I wanted someone who had the insight of an assistant coach. I wanted someone who had the insight of a scout."

Pedigree was also not a concern for Dumars, who played college ball at McNeese St., a small Division I school in Louisiana. "It would be a mistake for anyone to think that if you didn't go to some blue-blood school," Dumars said, "you don't really know the game."

In addition to Hammond, Dumars also hired Jeff Weltman and Jon Horst. All three played non-Division I college ball, and all three eventually went on to run an NBA team of their own.

Under Dumars' watch, the Pistons strung together seven straight 50-win seasons, six straight Eastern Conference Finals appearances, two NBA Finals appearances, and one championship. When the Pistons defeated the Los Angeles Lakers in the 2004 Finals, Dumars put his arm around Hammond.

"John," he said, "you're a world champion. And nobody will ever be able to take that away from you." It was a moment, and a feeling, that Hammond would never forget.

About halfway through the Pistons' torrid run, other NBA teams started inquiring about Dumars' right-hand man. Hammond, who wasn't even sure he'd be able to get into college coaching when he started his career, couldn't comprehend the possibility of running an NBA front office. He knew he was a product of the environment Dumars built, so he felt uneasy leaving. But with Dumars' guidance and support, Hammond carefully considered each opportunity. He started to wonder how much longer the Pistons' charmed run would last. All it takes is one injury, one bad draft pick, or one bad signing to turn a model front office into a league laughingstock. He thought to himself, *How many more chances am I going to get?*

Then the Milwaukee job opened up.

Hammond took the Bucks' reins in 2008, a time of transition for NBA front offices. In the early 2000s, NBA players ran basketball operations for the majority of teams. Some GMs were former All-Stars, like Larry Bird and Elgin Baylor. Others had been role players, like John Paxson and Danny Ainge. Some, like Bird and Mitch Kupchak, came to the job with experience either coaching or assisting with basketball operations. Others, like Dumars, stepped into the position completely fresh. The year the Bucks named Hammond their GM, former NBA players ran 18 of the league's 29 front offices.

By 2015, that number would drop to only eight of 30.

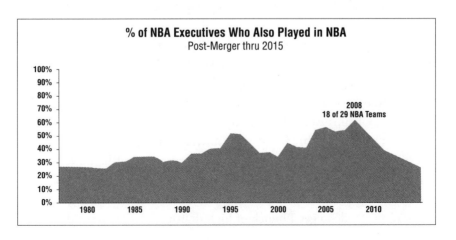

% of NBA Executives Who Also Played in NBA
Post-Merger thru 2015

2008
18 of 29 NBA Teams

According to NBA reporter Jake Fischer, the high-profile floundering of one former player in particular helped shift owners' preferences toward a different archetype. Dumars' backcourt running mate with the Pistons, Isiah Thomas, took over the New York Knicks front office in 2003. By 2008, the team, fed up with his lack of progress, dismissed him. In his book *Built to Lose,* Fischer wrote, "Thomas' failures as a front-office leader—muddying the New York Knicks' cap sheet, throwing lucrative contracts at unproven players, gambling on his basketball acumen alone—were the exact shortcomings by traditional NBA executives that encouraged owners to start entrusting the Moreys and the Prestis, the Hinkies and the McDonoughs."

The executives Fischer mentions—Daryl Morey, Sam Presti, Sam Hinkie, and Ryan McDonough—all spent their entire basketball careers in the front office. None coached in college or the NBA. Of the four, only Presti played collegiately. In his seminal 2015 *ESPN The Magazine* piece on the Philadelphia 76ers, Pablo Torre describes how the team's new ownership approached hiring a front-office lead. The group, led by private equity billionaire Josh Harris, identified two organizational models. "The first," Torre wrote, "was the approach of the Spurs and Thunder, franchises renowned for developing players and internal basketball culture. The other was the method used by the Celtics and Rockets, franchises renowned for their command of the NBA's arcane CBA and analytics." The 76ers opted for the latter, hiring Rockets executive Sam Hinkie, a data-driven Stanford MBA.

Hinkie concocted a brazen plan to aggressively lean into losing and acquire as much draft capital as possible. He signaled the beginning of the 76ers' tanking efforts by trading one of the team's brightest young players, Jrue Holiday, for the sixth pick in the 2013 draft. With their two lottery picks that evening, Philadelphia selected Nerlens Noel and Michael Carter-Williams, neither of whom panned out in the long term. In that same draft, Hammond used a pick outside of the lottery to select future MVP and NBA champion, Giannis Antetokounmpo.

Now, there's no brand of front-office analysis more cringey than leveraging years of hindsight to shout about who a team should've drafted. But what makes the 2013 draft so fascinating is the juxtaposition between the Sixers' and Bucks' approaches. The Sixers committed to tearing the team down to the studs to get a bunch of high draft picks. They wanted a bunch of bites at the apple in order to acquire a superstar who could lead them to a title. They willingly traded short-term pain for the increased probability of long-term glory.

The Bucks, on the other hand, had an annual mandate from owner Herb Kohl to be as competitive as possible. Yet they were the ones who left that 2013 draft with the guy who would eventually carry his team to a championship.

By the late 2010s, NBA fans and executives alike viewed that "treadmill of mediocrity" that Hammond and the Bucks rode as the ultimate purgatory. The way the media covered the NBA and the way fans discussed the league had changed. ESPN filled offseason airtime with the draft combine and long specials on the first day of free agency. They even hired a "front office insider"—former Nets assistant GM Bobby Marks—to enlighten a public eager to learn salary cap minutiae.

Daryl Morey, Hinkie's old boss, cocreated the Sloan Sports Analytics Conference, which, by the mid-2010s, had grown into one of the sports business' premiere networking events. Front-office executives in jeans would attend panels and exchange small-talk, while students, in full suit and tie and reeking of desperation, wandered the halls clutching resumes, hoping for their big break. More than any other event, the Sloan Conference encapsulated what former NBA blogger Nathaniel Friedman called "The Cult of the GM." Writing in *GQ*, Friedman described how GMs had become superstars in their own right. His prime example was Presti, the D3-alum turned-Theo Epstein/Warren Buffett of the NBA.

It made perfect sense that general managers would be subject to the same celebrity, praise, and scrutiny as the players they drafted and signed. ESPN helped turn the draft and free agency into tentpole events, and a growing proportion of fans viewed sports through the lens of a fantasy manager. "The emergence of a professional class," Friedman wrote, "whose skills were seemingly a reification of these expectations was all but inevitable."

Friedman painted the picture of a world into which it is hard to envision someone like Hammond fitting. As former players were shooed out of the league's front offices, they were supposed to cede the floor to front-office lifers, not to coaching grinders. Spending decades as a back-slapping coach and scout does not necessarily prepare someone to squeeze the tiniest of edges out of thousands of decisions in order to improve championship odds by a few percentage points. It does, however, prepare someone to lead.

"The most overlooked characteristic of success in the NBA at the executive level is leadership," said Rick Sund, a former NBA GM who worked with Hammond during his first tenure in Detroit.

Basketball operations departments are now massive, including scouts, video coordinators, analytics staffs, sports scientists, and more. It takes a strong leader to wrangle all of those big brains and point them toward a common goal. Fans see Presti's ability to draft superstars, but they don't get to peek behind the curtain and witness the way he organizes and empowers his staff. They don't see the humanity he imported from San Antonio. While the results flash on phones and televisions, the general public remains blind to the process. With so much of the business taking place behind closed doors, fans overlook arguably the most crucial part of the job.

In *Giannis*, a biography of the Bucks star, author Mirin Fader described Hammond as "a different kind of GM. He had empathy for players. His Midwest upbringing, his subtle humor, made him relatable. He gave interns rides home. He talked to anyone shooting late at night. He came to staffers' rec basketball league games on Sundays. If someone needed to attend a wedding, they could expect Hammond to say, without hesitation, 'Go!'"

When he heard that passage read, Hammond's voice filled with emotion. "That's exactly who I wanted to be," he said. "That makes me feel great… makes me feel like a Greenville guy."

Hammond wasn't domineering and he might not have been the most well-versed in analytics, but he knew basketball and he knew how to lead. "John's a soft-spoken guy, and there may have been some people that thought he was more destined to be just a support person for a high-level leader of an organization," said Rick Carlisle, who overlapped with Hammond in Detroit. "But I thought his wisdom of the game, I thought his ability to manage people and to put forth a vision were exceptional."

Hammond ended up leaving Milwaukee in 2017. He laid the championship groundwork, but moved on before the team won the title. He joined the Orlando Magic as general manager, partnering with Jeff Weltman, a longtime collaborator who took over as the team's president of basketball operations after the dismissal of Rob Hennigan. Weltman, an NBA front-office lifer and the son of former Cleveland Cavaliers and Nets GM Harry

Weltman, rode the pine for a few years at Oberlin College, a D3 school in Ohio. He and his dad are the first small-college father-son duo to have run NBA teams.

The fact that Hammond held a high-level executive position for an NBA franchise through the 2022–23 season is proof that the Garry St. Jean path to the front office is alive and kicking for former small-college athletes. While the Sloan Conference teems with young men and women itching to follow in Bob Whitsitt's footsteps as career front-office workers, an exit ramp still exists for coaches to transition upstairs. It's not the most well-publicized or well-worn path, but the coach-to-front-office route still supplies a steady trickle of D3 alums into NBA leadership roles.

CHAPTER 10

Hoosiers

*How big risks kicked off the careers of two
former D3 players who went on to personify
the shift in preferred coaching styles*

Comedian Gary Gulman has a bit about how one sport in particular meshed well with his sensitive personality. "Basketball," he said, "is the only sport you can practice by yourself."

The game, in a way, is the perfect team sport for introverts.

In the movie *Hoosiers*, a story about a 1950s small-town high school that wins the Indiana state championship, the team's star player is a kid named Jimmy Chitwood. He barely speaks in the film, preferring instead to express himself through jump shot after beautiful jump shot, a sweet stroke perfected on his family's little dirt patch court.

Andrew Olson was a lot like Chitwood—pensive and quiet, his immense talent built on hours of solo workouts. As a senior captain at Amherst, Olson broke with program tradition and shared pregame speech duties with his more talkative classmates. He just wasn't the rah-rah type. Olson saw the game like a coach, but he didn't have the magnetic, talkative personality that pervades the coaching ranks. With personal training he found an outlet for his basketball passion and expertise that better fit his personality. He could effectively connect with one person or a small group, and, as someone with thousands of hours of experience practicing by himself, he knew exactly how to supercharge an individual workout.

Through the training business, Olson found his coaching voice. With his ASA idea, he started to believe he had discovered a unique angle, a differentiator that also might allow him to help the very best players in the world. His physical limitations prevented him from ever playing in the NBA. But maybe, in this new world of specialized coaches, team consultants, and personal trainers, someone with his elite eye for the game and understated voice could carve out a niche in basketball's upper echelon.

"Welcome to Indiana basketball"

Whenever his schedule allowed, Frank Vogel liked to take his daughter to the little nearby park with the swing set. Most of the time, nobody bothered them, but on that particular day, Vogel noticed a man heading right toward him. He figured it was just a big Indiana Pacers fan, even though he had come to understand that sub-six foot NBA assistant coaches don't tend to attract a lot of attention in public.

Then the man introduced himself: "I'm Brad Stevens. I coach over at Butler."

The name and the face clicked into place for Vogel. A year or two prior, they had briefly met when Stevens came into the office to talk shop with Pacers head coach Jim O'Brien. Stevens' wife had recently given birth to their second child, so he was running a tried-and-true play in the new parent playbook: taking the older kid to the park to give mom and baby some peace and quiet. The two men struck up an easy conversation, mostly revolving around their favorite topic—hoops. They exchanged numbers and promised to keep in touch. In the coming months and years, Stevens would occasionally ask Vogel about the NBA and what the players were like. Mostly, though, the relationship was personal, not professional. "I don't think that either of us would consider each other a resource," Stevens said. "We're just friends."

A few years later, in July of 2013, Stevens shocked the basketball world when he left his comfortable post at Butler for a head coaching job with the Boston Celtics. For years, rumors linked Stevens to jobs at bigger, richer universities, but those reports never mentioned the NBA. Shortly after the deal went public, Stevens and Vogel ate dinner together at the Orlando

Summer League. Vogel, who had taken over as the Pacers' head coach in 2011, remembered Stevens saying something along the lines of, "Okay, here I am. NBA. Tell me about it."

"The greatest game ever invented"

The Brad Stevens story begins in Indiana. Football may have been in Stevens' blood—his dad played linebacker at Indiana University—but, c'mon, this was Indiana. Land of cornfields interrupted by monolithic basketball goals that rise from patches of chalky dirt. Birthplace of Larry Bird and Oscar Robertson. Home to Bobby Knight's fearsome IU dynasty, Stevens' favorite team as a kid. Setting for the movie *Hoosiers*.

As a high school player, Stevens was, in *Hoosiers'* terminology, more of a Jimmy Chitwood than an Ollie. The 6'1" guard set school records for career points, assists, and three-pointers made. He could shoot from outside, but he was especially adept around the hoop, where he loved to post up smaller guards. "He was pretty crafty," said University of Notre Dame head coach Micah Shrewsberry, who played against Stevens in high school. "He was just a good player."

On the other hand, Frank Vogel's hometown of Wildwood Crest, New Jersey, was known more for its beaches than its basketball. Vogel's dad, who played hoops at Temple, instilled a love of the game in Frank and his brother. They closely followed the Philly Big Five colleges and emulated the 1980s Philadelphia 76ers in their driveway.

A superhero's origin story usually involves the death of a loved one and/or a catastrophic radioactive accident. Lucky for Vogel, the career of an NBA championship-winning coach can begin somewhere far more innocent, like a basketball camp.

The proprietor of Boo's Basketball Camp, Alan "Boo" Pergament, didn't just teach kids how to dribble through their legs or make a lefty layup. Pergament preached the importance of goals, discipline, and self-improvement. "I thought I was going to be playing basketball for a week," Vogel said, "but I really got inspired to believe that anything is possible if you put your mind to it."

The counselors urged Vogel and the other campers to never, ever be satisfied with an achievement. Can you spin a ball on your finger for 10 seconds? Great. Now do it for 30. Oh, you can do 30 seconds now? Okay, how about a minute? How about five minutes? Can you spin the ball on all five fingers? Forget your hands—what about spinning the ball on an inanimate object? Spin it on your fork while you eat dinner. Spin it on a pencil and write your name.

The camp trained Vogel to set a goal, do the necessary work to achieve said goal, and then immediately get to work on a new goal. While Vogel mostly unleashed this newfound dogma on his dribbling and shooting, he also tried his hand at something else—the toothbrush trick. One of the counselors at camp could spin a ball on the handle of his toothbrush and balance it while brushing his teeth. Vogel practiced until he mastered it. In 1986, as an eighth grader, he showed off his unique dental hygiene routine as part of the "Stupid Human Tricks" segment on *Late Night with David Letterman.*

Once Vogel started reaching fame as an NBA head coach, the Letterman clip would pop up on nationally televised Pacers games. It was generally presented as a funny little human-interest moment. "Hey, look at the Pacers head coach when he was just a goofy kid spinning a ball on a toothbrush! How quaint and funny!" To Vogel, however, the experience was a powerful lesson in the magic of hard work. *An appearance on national television, a check for a few $100, and a front-page story in the local newspaper, all for spinning a basketball on the end of a toothbrush—maybe I really can achieve anything.*

Make that almost anything. To squeeze as much as he could out of himself as a player, Vogel changed his diet, started weight training, wore special shoes to improve his vertical jump, and obsessed over dribbling and shooting drills. Unfortunately, to really make a mark as a basketball player, things like "height" and "speed" also matter. Vogel's hoop dreams remained tempered. "I didn't view playing in college as a real option for me," Vogel said. "I wasn't even sure I was going to make the [high school] varsity team as a junior."

He did, in fact, make the varsity team, where he started at point guard. Vogel reckoned he was the weakest of his team's five starters. "I didn't think he was going to be anything," Joe Bimbo, Vogel's high school coach, told Mark Montieth of Pacers.com. "He had no talent whatsoever. He just worked hard."

After attending some exposure camps, Vogel's crisp fundamentals caught the eye of two or three small-college coaches. They sent recruiting letters and began a correspondence. Vogel had his mind set on becoming a doctor, so he agreed to play ball at Pennsylvania's Juniata College, which also had a solid pre-med program.

Meanwhile, Stevens, despite averaging nearly triple the number of points as Vogel in high school, wasn't exactly swimming in recruiting letters. With only one Division I offer in the bag, he started to zero in on Division III DePauw University, a liberal arts college an hour outside of Indianapolis. Stevens applied for and snagged one of the few dozen spots in DePauw's prestigious Management Fellow program. The program, which augmented the traditional liberal arts curriculum, was designed to build leadership skills. Management Fellow alums went on to Fortune 500 companies and top business schools. It would set Stevens on a trajectory toward a great job and a comfortable life—everything he thought he wanted.

"It's team, team, team"

Before Stevens' freshman year, DePauw's basketball team had strung together 13 straight winning seasons. Coach Bill Fenlon was, like Gregg Popovich, the type of D3 coach who truly embraced the liberal arts experience. His wife was a theater professor and working actress. He encouraged his team to expand their world beyond just basketball, homework, and beers in the frat house. They had a saying—"GCF," which stood for "Good Clean Fun." Fenlon would urge players to "GCF at the soccer game" or "maybe consider the opera on campus for GCF."

Fenlon was big on acronyms and sayings. Later in his run at DePauw, he would huddle the team up on the court after home wins. Following a brief pep talk, they would put their hands in the middle and say, "This ain't Duke." Then they would collectively clean up any garbage, pick up the chairs, and get the gym ready for practice the next day. It was a reminder that, no matter how well they played or how many games they won, nobody was going to dote on them.

For the usual D3 reasons, DePauw games were sparsely attended. Over a quarter of the students played a sport. Add in clubs, activities, part-time jobs, and a full academic plate, and that left the potential fanbase with a lot of competing options. Stevens remembers very little about specific games during his DePauw career, only snippets. Like the time he missed a game winner and let out a few choice words in frustration. Then he looked around at the "crowd" of a few professors and team parents and thought, *I probably should shut my mouth. I'm not in [Indiana University's] Assembly Hall. They can hear me.*

As a college player, Stevens struggled to find the right role. He averaged just eight points per game as a freshman and a sophomore. "He was used to being the man," Fenlon said. "He wasn't able to ring the bell like that as a college player, and there were just adjustments that he had to make that he struggled with at times."

Stevens didn't play like Jeff Van Gundy, who even a basketball novice could watch for five minutes and peg as a future coach. Fenlon spoke to the student paper about Stevens' maturity prior to his sophomore season, saying he "needs to keep progressing in that area." When asked to give a scouting report on himself as a player, Stevens said he "wasn't a great defender, wasn't fast enough to be a point guard, wasn't a good enough shooter to be a two-guard." There's more than a touch of false modesty in his analysis, but, regardless, his collegiate career didn't live up to his or his coach's lofty expectations.

At Juniata, Vogel encountered a very different basketball program than Stevens did at DePauw. A sub-.500 record was par for the course. Their coach, Jim Zauzig, only worked for the college part time. He held a teaching job elsewhere, then trekked over to campus for practices and games.

Vogel clocked some backup point guard minutes as a freshman and started as a sophomore. Casey Craig, who came in as a freshman during Vogel's sophomore year, remembered Vogel as a leader who seemed seasoned beyond his 19 years, someone who took charge in everything from making teams during offseason scrimmages to reviewing scouting reports. When Craig caught an errant elbow during a fall pickup run, Vogel was the one who volunteered to drive him to the hospital. Vogel kept the freshman company in the waiting room. "He was just such a great calming figure for me," Craig said.

Vogel enjoyed his teammates' company, respected his coach, and relished the opportunity to play a valuable role on a college basketball team. But for an intense and driven young man who still prayed at the goal-setting altar of Boo's Basketball Camp, the level of commitment at Juniata left a lot to be desired. A multi-week hiatus between final exams followed by just one practice before their first game in early January? Vogel found that unacceptable.

In December of 1993, Vogel's junior season, Juniata fell behind early in a game against conference foe Moravian College. They came back to force overtime before losing in the extra session. Following the game, Zauzig blamed the slow start on a beloved Juniata tradition—the Madrigal Dinner, a campus-wide party for which students would camp out in tents to stake out the best table. Zauzig lamented the fact that his team seemed more interested in the dinner than in preparing for Moravian. They had rushed out of practice and hadn't adhered to the team's 1:00 AM curfew. It was another example of how Vogel's teammates and their very normal college kid priorities didn't align with his own desire to give himself over fully to a pursuit of excellence.

It didn't help that the whole pre-med thing wasn't going so well. Vogel was barely scraping by with a GPA in the mid-2.0s. "I honestly felt like I was giving everything toward the books and I was not getting the grades to go to medical school, nor did I have an interest in it anymore," Vogel said. "To do something around the clock like you have to with medicine and medical studies, you have to really have a passion for it. And my passion, clear in my mind, was for basketball."

If he were to pursue a coaching career, Vogel figured that staying at Juniata meant a sentence of 10 years to life at the high school or D3 level. Based on his experience at a middling D3 program, that wasn't going to cut it. "My passion and commitment was far greater than that," Vogel said. "I wanted to be involved in an environment where basketball was the No. 1 thing, not the part-time thing. I just wanted a full-time job in basketball. To me, that was what Division I represented."

He had the foresight to understand that, unless he manufactured D1 connections, it would be nigh impossible to break in at that level. So he concocted a plan to leave Juniata. It wasn't an easy decision. He enjoyed his teammates and the D3 game. Sacrificing his senior season was a hefty cost, but the potential payoff was worth it.

Like Vogel, Stevens also had a change of heart. DePauw Management Fellows spent a junior year semester away from the comforts of college life, embedded in the workaday world. Stevens' internship was at Eli Lilly, a large pharmaceutical company in Indianapolis. The internship went well, and the company offered him a full-time position pending graduation. Having grown up in an area where several neighborhood dads worked at Lilly, Stevens understood how the job could set him up for life. Accepting was a no-brainer.

When Stevens returned to campus for his senior year, he had a choice to make—continue to be ornery and hard-headed, or be a good teammate. "I realized quickly: I'm a Division III player. Stop being an idiot and make it about everybody else," Stevens said. "So my senior year was really rewarding, and it wasn't because I played a lot or had a huge impact on our team. It was because I really enjoyed being a teammate."

Coach Fenlon believes that the internship experience was the catalyst for Stevens' metamorphosis as a teammate. "You're away from basketball, you're away from fraternity parties, you're going to work every day with adults who have expectations, and then you come back and you know you have a job," Fenlon said. "For a guy like Brad, who is pretty smart, at some point during that experience, he probably said, 'Oh, maybe basketball isn't all there is in life. Maybe I should just take it for the good things that it gives me and stop stressing about it so much.'"

In his 29 seasons, Fenlon never once gave out a Most Valuable Player Award. He preached the importance of teamwork, of striking the right balance between the little guy on one shoulder hoping for more minutes and the little guy on the other shoulder saying, "team, team, team." So he gave out a Coach's Award to the most dedicated teammate. For accepting his role and happily mentoring a promising freshman class, Stevens won the Coach's Award his senior year.

In some ways, it was easier for Stevens to put D3 basketball in perspective because of how much he had going on outside of the game. He pursued extracurricular activities and leadership positions with the vigor of a high school student hoping to pad their college applications. He served as head intern at the college's civic engagement center, volunteered as student coordinator for a series of weekend recreation events for local kids, chaired rush three times at the Alpha Tau Omega fraternity, and attended speakers and seminars as part of his Management Fellow work. In February of his senior year, the man NBA fans would glowingly refer to as "President Stevens" lost a narrow 314–282 vote in the election for student trustee.

But even with the full days of clubs and seminars and election campaigning, plus his newfound appreciation for a lesser role on the basketball team, not to mention the job waiting for him after graduation, Stevens still couldn't fully shut the door on his favorite sport. During his senior year, Stevens took two education classes. The state of Indiana required high school coaches to also teach. Just in case it didn't work out at Lilly, Stevens figured he could coach high school ball. He wanted to get a jump on the education degree that would make that option a possibility. It was the ultimate hedge, a sign that Stevens wasn't exactly burning the boats behind him when he accepted a spot in corporate America.

"You keep in the game"

When Frank Vogel decided to leave Juniata, he took the D3 axiom of "they don't recruit you; you recruit them" and gave it a whirl in the D1 world. Coming out of high school, he was barely a D3 player. During his three years at Juniata, he had grown into his body and improved his quickness. As a junior looking to transfer, Vogel believed himself equipped to play at the D1 level. He wrote letters to the head coaches at James Madison and George Mason pitching himself as a walk-on or student manager. Ultimately, though, James Madison and George Mason were fallback plans. To Vogel, the pinnacle of college basketball was the University of Kentucky and their magnetic coach, Rick Pitino.

The prospect of actually attending Kentucky seemed unlikely, and, to a kid who had barely left New Jersey and Pennsylvania, slightly terrifying. Still, if he was going to pursue this coaching thing, he had to give himself a chance to learn from the very best. Vogel typed out a letter explaining his path to D3 and his admiration for Pitino and mailed it to the Kentucky basketball office. Rather than begging for a spot, he made the case that Pitino could use a guy like him, someone with a strong aptitude for the game and an unmatched eagerness to learn.

Pitino, or someone in the Kentucky office posing as Pitino, replied with a form letter. The gist of it was: "Thanks but no thanks." Vogel also wrote to Kentucky's longtime equipment manager, Bill Keightley, who oversaw the student managers. It was a dead end. He kept looking for another angle, another way in. If only he had the chance to ask Pitino face-to-face, then maybe the coach would understand just how serious he was. That's when Vogel remembered Five-Star Basketball Camp.

Vogel attended Five-Star as a high schooler, witnessing firsthand just how many D1 coaches showed up to recruit. Pitino, one of the many Five-Star counselors whose career accelerated because he impressed Hubie Brown, stopped by every summer. So Vogel fired up his word processor once again. He penned a sappy, ass-kissing letter to Will Klein, the camp's cofounder, about how much he had learned at Five-Star and how special it would be to have the opportunity to pay it forward to the next generation. His plan worked. When he showed up to camp, Klein told him, "We don't normally take guys we don't know, but you wrote one hell of a letter, so we decided to take a chance on you." Vogel worked his tail off, coaching with an intensity and enthusiasm that was impossible to ignore.

Camp founder Howard "Garf" Garfinkel, who took a liking to Vogel's positive approach, set up an intro when Pitino was in town. "I was nervous—sure—but confident," said Vogel about the moments leading up to his meeting with Pitino. "I was really confident in myself at that age, secure in what I was trying to do and who I was. I really developed a strong level of self-confidence through the work ethic of the game of basketball."

As promised, Garf brought Vogel over to Pitino. Vogel jumped right into his pitch. He told Pitino he would love to walk on, but ultimately wanted to study coaching. "I really want to pursue this as a profession," Vogel said. "I know I can help you. I've got a good basketball mind and a relentless work ethic, like yourself."

Pitino told Vogel that they were all set with walk-ons and that he had nothing to do with student managers. Then Pitino made the most important introduction of Vogel's professional life. He called over his assistant coach, Jim O'Brien, to jot down Vogel's name as a courtesy. When O'Brien, a Philly native, found out Vogel was from South Jersey, he took an immediate liking to the kid. He sent Vogel off with no promises, but told him to get in touch when he arrived on campus.

For Vogel, that tiny sliver of a chance was too much to pass up. He decided he would transfer to Kentucky. His Juniata teammates were sad to see their captain leave, but also excited for him. "For the most part, there are pretty rational people who play Division III sports, who say this isn't a forever thing and you have to think about what's next," said Vogel's teammate, Casey Craig. "So I think there was a lot of admiration and respect for what he was embarking on."

Brad Stevens also harbored D1 dreams. Only he didn't choose to act on them until after already starting his full-time job at Eli Lilly. It's a well-known tale at this point—how Stevens quit the promising $40,000 a year gig at Lilly to take an unpaid position with Butler University's basketball team. "My own motivation to get into coaching was I liked the scoreboard, I loved being a part of a team, and I really wanted to compete in the NCAA Tournament at the Division I level," Stevens said. "When I was 23 years old, that's what I was thinking. And that's probably because I wasn't good enough to play at the Division I level, and that was like a dream to experience those moments."

Compared to Vogel, Stevens had a much easier time connecting with a D1 staff. While in college, Stevens landed a spot as a Butler summer camp counselor thanks to Fenlon, who knew Butler lead assistant Thad Matta. Stevens was then comfortable enough with Matta to call him directly and tell him he was interested in coaching and willing to work for nothing. Stevens also fit neatly into a loophole in college staffing. The NCAA limited how many coaches could be on the floor working with players, but there were no restrictions on the number of student managers. By enrolling in grad school and taking an unpaid position, Stevens was pure upside for the Butler program. He cost nothing and he could augment the existing staff.

The very same loophole came in handy for Vogel at Kentucky, but not until he hit a few more brick walls. Vogel hounded Keightley, the equipment manager, hoping to walk the tightrope between perseverance and annoyance. Keightley's answer never changed: "We don't take out-of-state kids." Vogel also attended the team's fall pickup games, which were open to the public. He shot on the side and watched how the team worked, figuring, worst-case scenario, at least he'd spend the year conducting a self-guided tour of Pitinoball.

He did have one last card to play: a visit to O'Brien. "Here's the thing," O'Brien said, according to Vogel. "All the student managers here? They're just excited to be a part of the program and be around the players because that's all they've known growing up in state here. But none of them have any interest in helping the coaches actually coach basketball. They just want to be around. And with NCAA restrictions, certain coaches can't do certain things. So I actually think I could use you."

A few days later, O'Brien called Vogel to let him know that he had spoken to Keightley. They would give him a trial as a student manager, with the understanding that, whenever time allowed, Vogel could work with O'Brien on special coaching projects.

"Progress is like electricity"

Once his trial run with the Kentucky program began, Vogel did everything he could to prove he was indispensable. He taught himself video editing software, thanks to many hours spent on the phone with customer support. He washed uniforms and filled water bottles. He chauffeured recruits to and from the airport and shuttled Pitino to speaking engagements. "I knew when I got that opportunity at Kentucky," Vogel said, "I had to work around the clock."

He basically never left the basketball office, doing anything and everything that was asked of him, aiming to prove he was the hardest worker in the program. "He just wanted to learn basketball," Pitino told ESPN's Kevin Arnovitz. "He worked tirelessly but never, ever looked for any credit, never looked for any approval, never looked to move up the ladder."

The driven and versatile Vogel became an essential staff member. When Pitino and O'Brien wanted their players to up their rebounding tenacity, they turned to Vogel to cut and splice together every single one of Dennis Rodman's offensive boards. When they decided to form a JV team to get extra reps for mountainous freshman Nazr Mohammed, Vogel played about 20 minutes a game at point guard.

All day every day, Vogel lived out his very own underdog story. At night, he often fell asleep to the movie *Hoosiers*, letting the message of the little school that could seep into his subconscious.

Hoosiers wasn't far from Brad Stevens' mind, either. The movie was stitched into the fabric of Butler University. The *Hoosiers* state championship scenes were shot at Butler's Hinkle Fieldhouse, the actor who portrayed Jimmy Chitwood grew up playing pickup at Hinkle, and Bobby Plump, the real-life basis for Chitwood, attended Butler on a basketball scholarship.

Butler was also, unlike Kentucky, a lovable underdog. When Stevens joined the program in 2000, they were more "mid" than "major." They hadn't won an NCAA tournament game in 39 years. In the 1970s, Butler even considered moving to Division III before ultimately sticking in Division I.

During the state tournament run in *Hoosiers*, Coach Norman Dale, played by Gene Hackman, has either one or two assistants on his bench, depending on the sobriety of Dennis Hopper's Shooter. Butler's 2000–01 staff was a little bigger. Matta had three full-time assistants and a director of basketball operations, all of whom were ahead of Stevens in the pecking order. Since he was serving in a volunteer capacity, Stevens planned to wait tables at Applebee's to cover rent.

When one of the assistant coaches got in some legal trouble and was subsequently dismissed, everyone slid up one seat, including Stevens. As director of basketball operations, he pulled in a salary of $18,000 per year. It was less than half of what he was making at Lilly, but at least he no longer needed to see to it that Indianapolis residents could "Eat Good in the Neighborhood."

In his new position, Stevens was responsible for the team calendar and smoothing out any potential operational frictions for the head coach. It gave Stevens, who very quickly realized he didn't know the first thing about coaching, a crash course in how to run a program. "The year that prepared me to be a head coach," Stevens said, "is the year when I was director of basketball operations."

Between Matta and assistant coaches Todd Lickliter and John Groce, Stevens had the opportunity to learn from three future Big Ten head coaches. Then there were the players, a dedicated group that was littered with future D1 head and assistant coaches. "I don't know that I understood how networking worked or how important it was to be surrounded by the right people," Stevens said. "But in retrospect I landed lucky."

Surrounding yourself with excellence has a compounding effect. Not only do you learn the profession from some of the very best, but they also tend to move into bigger jobs, creating new and better opportunities for their subordinates. After Stevens' first season, Matta took the job at Xavier. Once again, each staff member moved up a seat. Only one year after accepting a volunteer student manager job, Stevens was a D1 assistant doing D1 assistant things—recruiting, scouting and working with players on the floor. "I always tell people that as talented and smart as Brad is, there were a bunch of things that had to happen a certain way," Fenlon said, "or he might be a high school coach in Indianapolis right now."

Stevens agrees that, without the good fortune he had in quickly moving up the bench, his career would've taken a different direction. "I'm confident enough in myself to tell you I probably would've been a good high school coach or maybe gotten a Division III job," Stevens said.

Vogel also benefited from his boss' success. In 1997, exactly 10 years after Pitino jumped from college to the New York Knicks and unwittingly laid down the soil for the expansive Van Gundy coaching tree, he agreed to join the Boston Celtics as head coach and president of basketball operations. O'Brien, who joined the Celtics as an assistant, made the case to Pitino that Vogel should come with them. Pitino heeded O'Brien's advice and hired Vogel as video coordinator over another candidate. "Obi was critical in making sure that [Pitino] took me, which was not a lock," Vogel said.

"You expecting someone else?"

In 2007, Brad Stevens attended the Indiana regional high school tournament with his old college coach, Bill Fenlon. While taking in the action, they discussed the future. Stevens told Fenlon he would probably stay at Butler for a few more years, after which he hoped to find a small-college coaching job and put down roots.

A month later, Butler head coach Todd Lickliter left for Iowa. The school named Stevens, just 30 years old, their new head coach. Stevens then went out and proved himself to be one of the best coaches in all of college basketball. He won at a record clip and in 2010 became the youngest coach since Bobby Knight to make the Final Four. With an enrollment of just more than 4,000, Butler became the smallest school to reach the Division I title game in 40 years.

Newspapers and television networks across the nation couldn't get enough of the Division III kid, the guy who loved the game so much that he quit a pharmaceutical marketing job to get into coaching. The articles and human-interest pieces glommed on to the parallels between Butler's Cinderella run to the Final Four and *Hoosiers'* Hickory High. When the team arrived at the 70,000-seat stadium for their first practice, an administrator asked Stevens if he would reenact one of the movie's more popular scenes. They hoped he would, a la Gene Hackman's Norman Dale, use a tape measure to prove to the team that the height of the rim and length of the free throw line at the big stadium were the same as at their home gym.

Members of the team, who didn't embrace the underdog tag, said, "Hell, no."

The very next year, No. 8 seed Butler somehow reached the Final Four again. This time they were joined by another high-seeded mid-major, VCU, coached by Kenyon College grad Shaka Smart. Grantland later dubbed Stevens and Smart "Whiz Kids," the high-academic D3 guys who "seem to have cracked the code for postseason success" and are "committed to positivity on the sideline."

Years later, Smart recalled Stevens' unique ability to connect with his team. "He had a terrific way of creating a captive audience with his players, which I think is an attribute of the best coaches," Smart said. "And he had a really, really good command for how his team needed to go about being successful."

Stevens credited Lickliter with schooling him on the art of communication. Lickliter loved the quote, often falsely attributed to Mark Twain, where he apologizes for writing a long letter because he didn't have time to write a shorter one. If a scouting report were more than eight minutes long, Lickliter made Stevens re-do it. True genius, he would say, lies in simplicity.

"This is a hard game to play with a lot on your plate," Stevens said. "You've got to make sure that you can come up with gameplans and structures of practice plans and everything else that allows guys to play in games with a clear mind and fresh legs."

With the Boston Celtics, Vogel didn't need to worry about how to effectively communicate to an entire team. His role as video coordinator provided a soft landing. He didn't have to run drills in practice or contribute to on-the-fly strategic decisions during games. When he spoke to players, it was usually one-on-one, where Vogel was comfortable communicating and sharing his insights. "Your feet are not entirely to the fire when you're first getting started," Vogel said. "You're able to prove yourself behind the scenes."

Vogel was a part of that first generation of video coordinators, guys like Mike Budenholzer and Erik Spoelstra, who learned the NBA game in a film room rather than out on the road as a scout. In Boston, the three assistant coaches each handled a third of the scouting reports. But there was only one video coordinator, so Vogel had a hand in preparing strategic materials for every single game. The hours were long, the work was not glamorous, but Vogel excelled. "Frank has such a great demeanor about him and was so good at what he did that it made our jobs as assistant coaches a lot easier," said USC head coach and former Division III player Andy Enfield, a Celtics assistant at the time. "I always appreciated his expertise and work ethic."

During the season, Vogel would often return home after midnight. He ordered Domino's so frequently, the delivery guy started throwing in free pizzas as a thank you. For a time, Vogel lived in Watertown, Massachusetts, with a few Juniata classmates who had also made their way to Boston. As an experienced video coordinator, Vogel always made sure to record his favorite show, *Seinfeld*. He would watch the new episodes whenever his schedule allowed, memorizing the best quotes to rattle off whenever inspiration struck.

After a rough four seasons in Boston, Rick Pitino resigned in 2001. Jim O'Brien took over as head coach and promoted Vogel to assistant. Once he had a chance to run individual workouts, Vogel found that his years as a player prepared him well. As a teenager, he wasn't blessed with size or speed. If he wanted to keep playing, he had no choice but to spend hours in the gym experimenting with drills. "It's still the same game, still the same skills, and a lot of those [NBA players] hadn't worked at and developed the skills at the level that I had," Vogel said. "The knowledge of the NBA game came from the film room, and the knowledge of player development and skill development came from being a D3 player."

"We're way past big speech time"

The first time Vogel addressed a team as head coach wasn't at all how he had envisioned it. O'Brien, the man who had looked out for Vogel for more than 15 years and brought him along on multiple coaching stops, had been fired by the Indiana Pacers. Grabbing his mentor's still-warm whiteboard marker and taking over as interim head coach didn't sit right with Vogel. But O'Brien insisted Vogel make the most of the opportunity. If he was going to stick with the Pacers past that 2010–11 season, he was going to have to take a firm grip of the steering wheel. It would all start with that first speech. To win the team over, Vogel channeled the best public speaker he had ever witnessed—Pitino.

Vogel admired the positivity and power Pitino conveyed when speaking to the media. It was one of the many reasons he transferred to Kentucky in the first place. When Vogel drove Pitino to corporate speaking engagements, he didn't just sit in the car doing a Sudoku. He watched Pitino, studying what made his coaching idol such a convincing orator. "I've seen him and the conviction of his voice, the power of his voice, and the persuasiveness of it," Vogel said. "I just applied it at that moment."

Whatever he said, and however he said it, won the group over immediately. "When Frank started talking, I thought right away, he's grabbed the room—the energy, the positivity," longtime Pacers assistant Dan Burke told ESPN.com. "The room lifted up, and you could feel it."

The Pacers' fortunes turned. They qualified for the playoffs for the first time in five seasons and hung tough with the top-seeded Chicago Bulls. That offseason, Pacers president of basketball operations Larry Bird stripped the interim tag from Vogel's title. Vogel implemented one of the league's stingiest defenses and the Pacers emerged as a legitimate title contender.

In the 2013 offseason, just months after Vogel guided the Pacers to the Eastern Conference Finals, the Celtics attempted to lure the college wunderkind, Stevens, to the NBA. He was 36, just one year younger than Vogel was when he took over the Pacers, but he came with years of experience running a team.

Stevens had also been studying the NBA game. When Butler standout Gordon Hayward was drafted in 2010, Stevens bought NBA League Pass. He attended coaching clinics and retreats where most of the 50 to 60 attendees were NBA coaches. "I just got intrigued by the game," Stevens said. "It was hard, though. It was going to be hard to leave Butler."

Danny Ainge, then the Celtics president of basketball operations, first called Stevens early in the summer of 2013. Ainge said he wanted to discuss the team's coaching vacancy, but first he had to take care of some other matters. He then proceeded to trade most of his talented-but-aging roster for future draft picks. Even though coaching the iconic Celtics is, as Stevens said, "as good as it gets," the idea of overseeing a full rebuild was a challenging proposition.

Stevens thought back on his enchanted run at Butler, how he started out making less than $20,000 and playing lunchtime pickup with faculty members, many of whom were still on campus. Butler was also about to join the rebuilt Big East, presenting a new, exciting challenge. He told Ainge he was leaning toward staying put. Ainge, who Stevens called "a pretty persistent guy," kept the conversation going. The courtship lasted nine days. Stevens' wife told him, "You'll never be as good as you want to until you're uncomfortable." Then Ainge texted, letting Stevens know they would add some years to the contract offer. At that point, Stevens decided to take the job.

The two dads from the Indianapolis area playground were now NBA head coaches. And it wasn't some fellow D3 grinders who hired them—they had been knighted by Bird and Ainge, two former championship-winning NBA players. The latter was especially enamored of Stevens. Celtics co-owner Steve Pagliuca told Boston.com's Nicole Yang that Ainge's coaching wish list had Stevens first, second, and third. Three years before hiring Stevens, while sitting in the stands for the 2010 National Championship game, Ainge leaned over to Pagliuca and called Stevens "the best coach in college basketball." Given the fact that Stevens was facing Duke's Mike Krzyzewski, the winningest coach in NCAA history, it was quite the compliment.

Stevens' departure came as a shock to his Butler staff. Drew Cannon, who Stevens had hired as the first dedicated analytics staffer in all of Division I, first heard the news during Butler's summer basketball camp—the same camp where Stevens first connected with the school's coaches. Cannon went into Stevens' office to let him know they had run out of trophies and to ask if he should head to the store to buy more. With a friendly smile, Stevens told Cannon that he had just taken a job with the Celtics, so the trophy issue didn't really concern him anymore.

As Stevens built out his Celtics staff, he found a home for Cannon in the team's budding analytics group. Cannon believes the transition to the NBA was a smooth one for Stevens because, unlike many older college coaches who made the leap to the pros, he wasn't a domineering personality. "With Brad, it was always more respectful and even-handed, doing more talking to people instead of trying to scare them into doing the right stuff," Cannon said. "It was less of a transition for him than it might've been for other coaches."

Even Cannon, who had witnessed Stevens' approach firsthand at Butler, watched the first few practices at training camp skeptically. It took time for the players and coaching staff to feel each other out, but Stevens had the patience to work through it. "I was like, 'Brad, you've got to start yelling at these guys! Get them on the same page and pull them together!'" Cannon recalled. "Obviously, he didn't listen to me. That was a much better decision. It didn't take long before he had everybody's respect."

"I love you guys"

After the Celtics hired Stevens, he named just one Butler assistant to his coaching staff. Close friend Micah Shrewsberry served as Stevens' "translator," someone who could help filter and interpret messages between Stevens and his new coworkers. Then Stevens made what he calls his "key hire." He named Ron Adams, an NBA veteran coach, his lead assistant. Stevens thought of Adams as his "editor." "[Adams] told me that all the things I wanted to try had already been tried," Stevens said. "And they don't work."

Almost every time Stevens would bring the coaching staff onto the court to pitch new offensive and defensive wrinkles, Adams would say that the tactic wouldn't fly in the NBA. Stevens would welcome the feedback and move on to the next idea. "That shows Brad's humility," Shrewsberry said, complimenting a trait Stevens developed during his time at DePauw, "to not go, 'No, this is what we're going to do because this is what we've done in the past.' He listened and tried to figure out what would work best."

Stevens' successful acclimation to the NBA required more than just humbly scrapping some items from the Butler playbook. At Butler, his staff had three assistant coaches, a director of basketball operations, an analytics manager, and a couple of student managers. In Boston, he had to manage about double the amount of people—six assistant coaches, four video people, and a scheduling manager. He took a very intentional approach. "He's a great communicator," Shrewsberry said. "He lets everybody know what he needs from them for them to be successful and for the team to be successful. He makes everybody feel like their job is the most important thing. There are no small jobs. When you communicate that and people really feel that, then they want to work for you or they work so hard because they don't want to let you down because you believe in them."

Shrewsberry's words are straight out of an organizational psychology textbook on how to lead through prestige rather than with fear. "How seriously he takes being a good person and trying to do right by people is not an act at all," Cannon said. "That's 100 percent real all the time. He's been nothing but good to me for 11 years."

When it came to working with the players, Stevens might not have been able to directly relate to the pressures of playing in the NBA. He did, however, lean heavily on his own playing career, which enabled him to empathize with everyone from his starters to those plastered to the bench. Looking back on Stevens' time at DePauw, Fenlon believes the ups and downs informed the way he would eventually coach Butler and Boston. "It helped him relate to every single guy," Fenlon said. "The guys who aren't playing, the guys who are playing, the guys it's going well for, the guys it's not going well for, he literally had an experience for almost every single role you could have on a team."

Stevens also approached his players with humility, especially the veterans. He didn't come in looking to bowl them over with his famously sharp basketball mind. He approached each practice, film session, and game the same way he did at Butler—as another in a series of opportunities to prepare his team with a simple message. "I just felt a huge responsibility to be ready," Stevens said.

With the notoriously prickly point guard Rajon Rondo, for example, Stevens actively sought out input and advice. "Brad listens," Shrewsberry said. "He didn't come in saying, 'This is how we're going to do it.' He listened to those guys. Seeing his willingness to do that helped build relationships right away."

In a 2021 article entitled "A New Era," which ran on the popular basketball statistics website Cleaning the Glass, former NBA front-office strategist Ben Falk wrote that "the days of authoritarian coaches are fading." Rising up in their place, Falk argued, were a group who prioritized relationships with the players and the front office. Coaches who, he wrote, "can put aside their own ego and do what's best for the long term health of the franchise—those are the coaches best suited to the modern NBA."

Academic research backs up his claims. When psychologists Erica Carleton and Mark Beauchamp studied the leadership styles of 57 NBA head coaches between 2000 and 2006, they found that playing under an abusive coach who used ridicule as their primary motivation tactic caused a measurable decline in player efficiency. The adverse impact of those abusive coaches, according to their findings, lasted throughout a player's career.

The authoritarian coach persona was once so ingrained in the sport, it almost prevented Vogel from entering the profession. Part of the reason Vogel didn't consider coaching until the middle of college was because he thought of coaches as drill sergeants. The Bobby Knight approach wasn't a good fit with his personality. "I never really saw a guy who would approach it with charisma and positivity and laughter and 'Let's have fun but work our ass off,'" said Vogel.

That all changed when he started studying Pitino.

As a head coach, Vogel didn't publicly demean players. He rarely marched up and down the sidelines screaming and gesturing. In his world, it was okay to have a little fun. A film session staple of Vogel's was to keep the players laughing and engaged by splicing in clips from *Saturday Night Live* and *Wedding Crashers*.

Before he became a head coach—back in 2005, the same year *Wedding Crashers* was released—Vogel's future hung in the balance. His mentor, O'Brien, was between jobs. For the first time in his career, Vogel needed help from someone outside of his Kentucky family. Fortunately, another NBA video coordinator followed the first rule of Wedding Crashing—never leave a fellow crasher behind.

Vogel first met longtime Los Angeles Lakers video coordinator Chris Bodaken at the annual convention hosted by Avid Technology, a video editing software company. All the league's video guys attended. Officially, they were there to learn the new technology and give Avid feedback. But they also spent plenty of time golfing and trading war stories over drinks.

When it became evident that Vogel would not have a coaching job for the 2005-06 season, Bodaken helped him land a role as an advanced scout for the Lakers. For about $200 a game, he would scout upcoming opponents when they played in New York, New Jersey, Philadelphia, or Washington, D.C. Rather than just sending over a few play calls, Vogel wrote up full, detailed scouting reports.

The impression Vogel made as a scout stuck with Kurt Rambis, who was a Lakers assistant coach at the time. Years later, when Rambis was advising Lakers owner Jeannie Buss on the team's 2019 head coach search, he helped push Vogel's candidacy. "[Rambis] had a big hand with me getting hired with the Lakers," Vogel said.

Prior to his first season in L.A., Vogel decided to coach with reckless abandon. "'Just shoot your shot' is not really something that Frank Vogel says, but this is a once in a lifetime [opportunity]," Vogel said. "I'm the Lakers coach and I'm LeBron's coach...I put all my eggs into it. I was unafraid to take risks, to coach really hard on guys, and to just go for it."

Vogel approached the job with the same don't-give-a-damn mentality he had when he left Juniata for Kentucky. Rather than play it safe or dwell on all the ways it could blow up in his face, he instead threw everything he had at the opportunity in front of him. His team won the 2020 NBA championship, a remarkable capper to a coaching career conceived out of sheer force of will.

Willpower took Vogel far, but a healthy dose of humility helped him become a champion. Like Stevens, he, too, would check his ego at the door when it came time to hire. Where other coaches might worry about a powerful assistant undermining them or usurping their position, Vogel focused instead on building the best staff possible. "It starts with the top two—the head coach and the lead assistant," Vogel said. "To me, the perfect duo is two who are opposite of each other. I'm not talking about skin color when I say this, but diversity in experience and path, I think, is really important and really powerful in terms of checking all the boxes of your process. If a player is the head coach and he's never coached, then he should hire a grinder, someone whose path was coming up through the video group and knows all of the prep work inside and out to have that background [that] complements him. And me coming up as a grinder and not someone who played in Division I or the NBA, the best complement is someone who played Division I or in the NBA."

Vogel's lead assistants with the Pacers and Orlando Magic were respected former NBA players Nate McMillan, Brian Shaw, and Corliss Williamson. With the Lakers, Vogel had less say over his staff. Even though he didn't handpick Jason Kidd as his top assistant, it was still a former player with cache in the role, someone he trusted to have the pulse of the team. "[Vogel's] willingness to delegate was good, but his willingness to trust was elite," said Greg St. Jean, a player development coach on Vogel's Lakers staff.

As an example, St. Jean recalled a time when Kidd suggested that Vogel call off the next day's shootaround. Vogel asked why, and Kidd shared some comments from the team's star players. Even though Vogel would've loved to review some defensive miscues from the night before, he heeded Kidd's advice and canceled the shootaround. "And now players are like, 'They're listening. We have a relationship. We're able to get our voices heard,'" St. Jean said.

Vogel and Stevens' humbler management styles would have all been for nought without hard work and accountability. Their competitive fire burned deeply, pushing them to prepare diligently and expect a lot out of those around them. Competitiveness in coaching doesn't always manifest as chair hurling and clipboard tossing. Stevens is often lauded by his peers for his even-keeled demeanor. "His ability to keep his temperature down no matter what happened is what really sets him apart," said Will Hardy, who worked with Stevens for a season in Boston.

Stevens thinks his steadiness on the sidelines, while intentional and important, was overblown as a defining characteristic. "I like to think of myself first and foremost as competitive," Stevens said. Stevens' closest friends and family are intimately familiar with his deep desire to win. The high scores on the Ms. Pac-Man machine in the Stevens' family basement all belong to Brad. He has a tradition of bringing together a big group from high school and college for a reunion of sorts, one which always revolves around games like dodgeball. Shrewsberry, an attendee at those reunions, said that Stevens didn't just want to win. He wanted to dominate. "Playing cards or video games or anything else," Shrewsberry said, "he loves to compete and talk crazy."

Vogel is another fiercely competitive person—someone doesn't take the risks he's taken without craving a challenge. During his time as a Celtics video coordinator, Vogel played short-court games of two-on-two with Enfield, Kevin Willard (who played D1), and Lester Conner (who played in the NBA). When the games got close, any friendliness between coworkers went out the window. "On game point, [Vogel] would call some fouls occasionally that were not exactly fouls," Enfield said. Whenever Enfield happens to catch an NBA game and sees Vogel complaining to the refs, he's sure to remind him about his notoriously bad calls during those two-on-two games.

When asked about the movie *Hoosiers*, Vogel excitedly regurgitates a line that Hackman's Dale delivers during his first conversation with star player Jimmy Chitwood: "In my 10 years of coaching, I never met anybody who wanted to win as badly as I did." In the movie, it's more of a confession than a boast, but to Vogel, it's a mantra. "Yeah! That's how I feel," Vogel said about the quote. "I can relate to that."

Propelled by that intense passion, Vogel and Stevens resonated with NBA players by leading through inspiration, as opposed to fear. In a way, their coaching styles are reminiscent of Coach Dale at the end of *Hoosiers*. Dale only ended up at Hickory High because he was in coaching exile. Earlier in his career, he couldn't properly harness his competitive drive, leading him to hit one of his players. But he evolved. Before the state championship game, he doesn't scream or try to scare his team into playing well. The last thing he says before they take the floor? "I love you guys."

CHAPTER 11

G LEAGUE

*How the NBA's minor league helps outsiders
bridge the expanse between basketball's
hinterlands and the top league in the world*

In 2013, Andrew Olson drove to Las Vegas for what he thought would be the biggest meeting of his life. As promised, an Amherst friend with connections to the Houston Rockets organization provided the all-important introduction to general manager Daryl Morey. Morey, who was in Vegas for the NBA's Summer League, agreed to meet with Olson and hear what ASA was all about.

Olson ran Morey through the presentation he had spent months writing and rewriting, which was based on the data that took hundreds of hours to manually track. Morey listened politely, provided some feedback, and thanked Olson for his time. No consulting gig, no invitation to train James Harden in the offseason, just some constructive criticism and well wishes.

Rather than give up after one unsuccessful meeting, Olson kept pushing his idea forward. By working other connections, he got himself in front of more NBA teams. He even met with basketball analytics pioneer Dean Oliver, a former Division III basketball player at Cal Tech. The feedback all started to run together. They all said something about how the analytics community still had a lot to learn about shooting, and maybe the work would have value in a few years. Then, one piece of advice cut through the noise and gave Olson an idea for a way around the front-office gatekeepers: "If you could apply it to a player and actually see an improvement, that would be another story."

From 2011, Frank Vogel's first season as an NBA head coach, through 2018, NBA coaching demographics underwent quite a shift. Former NBA players, who held 21 of the 30 jobs in 2011, steadily fell out of favor. They were replaced by coaches who topped out at the collegiate level, many of whom played Division III—by 2017, seven of the 30 NBA coaches had played D3 ball.

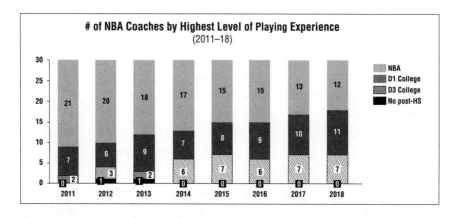

The surge in D3 alums was the result of several separate forces that coalesced at around the same time—Jeff Van Gundy providing a platform for D3 grinders from the Northeast, Gregg Popovich welcoming D3 players into his ideal NBA talent incubator, and Brad Stevens and Vogel finding their way from D1 programs to the league.

Then there was Dave Joerger, who played two seasons at D3 Concordia College in Minnesota before finishing up his career at a D2 school. Joerger represented a new and growing way to the NBA—the NBA Developmental League, now called the G League, yet another proving ground for D3 dreamers.

ABOUT ONCE A week, Nevada Smith would remember to check the voicemail on his rarely used Keystone College landline. When one day he heard a message from someone claiming to be with the Houston Rockets, he just assumed it was a joke. He texted his friends, most of whom were Division III basketball coaches like him, to see who the funny guy was.

When nobody fessed up, Smith did a little research. Jimmy Paulis, the man who left the message, was a very real person with a very real NBA job. Smith returned the call, and Paulis, a fellow former D3 player, explained that the franchise was hoping to set up an interview. Their minor league affiliate, the Rio Grande Valley Vipers, had an opening at head coach.

Following a phone call later that week, the Rockets flew Smith down to Houston for a full day of interviews. The conversations were far different than those he had had when applying for Division III coaching jobs, which tended to focus on how he would manage the academic responsibilities of his student-athletes. "This was the first time I got to interview for a job that was 99 percent about basketball," Smith said.

Rockets general manager Daryl Morey asked Smith how he would handle a variety of in-game situations. Would he go for a two-for-one if his team had the ball with 29 seconds left in the first quarter? That sort of thing. Smith, a self-described outside-the-box thinker, felt good about his answers. Apparently, Morey did, too. A few days later, he offered Smith the job.

The first G League game Smith coached was at the Los Angeles Lakers' practice facility. Multiple former NBA players were in the building, including A.C. Green, who was on the sidelines announcing. It was a far cry from the Keystone College gym Smith called home just a few months prior, where the side hoops still had wooden backboards.

Smith's sudden rise from Division III to the NBA's minor league was, to borrow a metaphor from another sport, completely out of left field. He didn't have a particularly well-connected network and he didn't win some bizarre contest like Whoopi Goldberg in *Eddie*. He did, however, coach a team that played a unique brand of basketball. Keystone's offense prioritized three-pointers and free throws. They avoided shooting from the midrange. In the early 2010s, before their style of play became mainstream, their stats would've jumped out to anyone who might be looking. And the Rockets were looking.

As he transitioned from D3 to the pros, Smith leaned heavily on Rockets assistant coach Chris Finch. Finch was better equipped than just about anyone at advising an outsider to the ways of the G League (which was then still called the D-League). When Smith fretted about an unfamiliar rule, like defensive three seconds, Finch told him not to worry. The refs never called it. Finch had a way about him, a calm demeanor that set Smith at ease. "I've been around a lot of different guys," Smith said. "And it's just weird. The Division III background guys are just regular human beings."

TO PARAPHRASE ONE of comedian Lewis Black's old bits, "If it weren't for those pet piranhas, Chris Finch wouldn't have spent those four years at a Division III college." Finch, a stellar high school player with a strong academic profile, had his heart set on Princeton. He had other Division I offers—Ivy League schools with less successful basketball programs, as well as some schools in the high-academic, no-scholarship Patriot League—but Princeton was interested in him, so he considered his recruitment closed.

Then Princeton coach Pete Carril called to deliver an unfortunate message. He apologetically but firmly informed Finch that another recruit, a talented big man from Chicago, was suddenly available. Kit Mueller, who went on to win two Ivy League Player of the Year Awards, had mistakenly stepped on the aquarium in which he kept his pet piranhas, slicing his Achilles tendon. The bigger Division I schools recruiting Mueller pulled their offers, and Carril pounced. The phone call caused Finch, who had always dreamt of playing Division I ball, to reconsider.

Franklin & Marshall College, a Division III school in Pennsylvania with a sterling academic reputation and competitive basketball team, had heavily recruited Finch. He figured (wrongly, it turned out) that his four years in college would mark the end of his basketball career. If it wasn't going to be Princeton, he didn't want to spend half that time on the bench at an Ivy or Patriot League school. "I wanted to go somewhere I knew I was going to play and where the team was good," Finch said. "At the time, F&M was rounding into a Division III national program."

When Glenn Robinson, F&M's head coach, received word of Finch's commitment, he was ecstatic. Robinson, whose 967 career victories make him the winningest basketball coach in Division III history, knew he was getting a complete player he could rely on from Day One. During the recruiting process, Robinson watched Finch play in a high school All-Star Game. Milling around the lobby afterward, the dozens of coaches in attendance made conversation, asking each other who they were there to see. When Robinson told them he had his eye on Finch, the other coaches were surprised. *What are you looking at?* Robinson thought to himself. *He's the best player here.* Finch didn't have eye-popping athleticism or a flashy ball-handling package, but he impacted winning in all phases of the game. "He just did everything," Robinson said.

As a freshman, Finch won his conference's 1988–89 Rookie of the Year award, helping F&M advance all the way to the quarterfinals of the Division III Tournament. Even though they were a top program, the life of an F&M basketball player was one with very few frills. Road trips officially ended only after you turned in your laundry in exchange for your $5 per diem. Home crowds were sparse, especially early in the season. The empty gyms stood in stark contrast to the jammed bleachers Finch played in front of throughout his high school career.

After his successful rookie season, Finch rightfully thought that he could play at a higher level. He even considered transferring to D1 American University. He would later call the decision to stay at F&M one of the best of his life. Over the next three seasons, Finch cemented himself as a top player in school history. He ended his career in the program's top 10 in assists, steals, and blocks. During Finch's junior year, his team went 28–3 and advanced all the way to the D3 title game, where they lost to Wisconsin-Platteville, coached by future University of Wisconsin coach Bo Ryan.

Each night, Finch took on the challenge of guarding the opposition's top perimeter player. One of his toughest covers was future Celtics assistant and current USC coach Andy Enfield, who played guard for Johns Hopkins. Enfield remembered Finch as "one of the best players I've ever played against." Their competitive matchups showcased the top-flight talent at elite D3 programs in the early 1990s. "The thing about Division III," Enfield said, "by the time you're a junior or senior and you're more experienced and you play one for the better teams, there are a lot of players that could slide into the Patriot League or Ivy League and be very good in those conferences."

On the court and with his teammates, Finch exuded the qualities of a future coach. "If you told him something, he remembered it and he would put it into action in the games," Robinson said. "He just competed every play. He didn't take plays off, he didn't get tired, he'd just keep grinding it out. He played offense like that, too. It wasn't sensational stuff. He would just do it right, do it right, do it right, never stop."

Robinson also admired Finch's competitiveness. The now-retired coach never felt as though he demanded more from Finch than Finch demanded from himself. Robinson's voice filled with glee when he relived the moment he walked into the locker room at halftime to see Finch pin the team's big man up against the wall, demanding him to play better. "He just didn't even stop to think for a second that if he challenged [his teammates]," Robinson said, "that that would create a long-term problem or a friendship problem."

Aside from that locker room story, which Finch laughingly said has reached Paul Bunyan status, he led with humility. After a not-so-great showing one night, he walked onto the team bus, pointed to a stat sheet, and said, "Look, Coach! I got a triple-double: points, rebounds, and turnovers!"

On a different team bus ride, assistant coach Mike McKonly sat with Finch and asked him about life after college. Finch thought he owed it to himself and to his parents to take his prestigious private liberal arts degree and apply it to a meaningful career, like a lawyer or FBI agent. McKonly told Finch he had all the makings of an excellent coach. "I always loved basketball," Finch said. "I always thought I'd have it in my life somehow, but I never verbalized that I wanted to be a coach. That was pretty much the first time I had done that."

Finch, like Vogel, understood that Division III in the 1990s was an insular world. He doubted he would have any luck landing a graduate assistant role at a higher level. "I never in a million years thought I'd be in the NBA or have a route to be in the NBA in any way, shape, or form," Finch said. "So I was focused on college. I thought that's where I would be and I just thought, naturally, it would be small college because that's all I'd ever known."

But before embarking on a coaching career, Finch had the opportunity to play overseas. Coach Robinson recommended him to a team in Sheffield, England, that signed Finch sight unseen. "Even though I knew coaching was what I wanted to do," Finch said, "I chose playing overseas because I thought it'd be a great life experience."

Little did Finch know, that decision would lead to him spending more than 15 years living across the pond. He played four seasons in Sheffield before taking over as his club's head coach, a role he held for another six years. He had success almost immediately. His second year, he won a league championship and was named the league's Coach of the Year.

He hoped that each trophy, each accolade, would be his ticket back home. But the right job never materialized. While still coaching Sheffield in the early 2000s, Finch was a finalist for a job at SUNY-New Paltz, a D3 college in New York not known for having a stellar basketball program. The position paid $24,000 a year—peanuts compared to Finch's six-figure salary in England. New Paltz chose another candidate, sending Finch into a bit of an existential crisis. *I'm better than this*, he thought. He stopped obsessing over how he could return to the States and focused instead on dominating in Europe.

Finch coached in Germany, then Belgium. Two of his teams went bankrupt in the middle of the season. He learned how to motivate players who didn't know when, or if, their next check would arrive. He coached road games in poverty-stricken former Soviet countries, never quite sure how shoddy the travel and accommodations would be. In Europe, personnel responsibilities usually went hand-in-hand with coaching jobs. With one, maybe two assistants, he had to structure an efficient program with minimal resources. "You've got to figure out what really matters to winning," Finch said, "what's important to your program, what resonates with players."

His teams played once or twice a week. On off days they practiced twice, giving Finch more teaching reps than he would have picked up as a college coach. He couldn't afford to cobble together much talent or height, so, through trial and error, he settled on a style of play that maximized his teams' chances. Instead of a rigid system with a lot of set plays, he implemented loose concepts. His players tended to be fast guys who could shoot, so he had them play up-tempo and chuck a lot of threes.

Unbeknownst to Finch, halfway across the world, the Rockets' front office was staging a mini revolution. Team owner Leslie Alexander hired Morey as general manager in 2007, the first pure quant GM in league history. It wasn't exactly a popular hire. "The media guys who sort of ran the opinion farm in Houston were calling me Deep Blue, after the chess computer," Morey said.

Within the league—and within his own organization—many doubted Morey's approach. "There was a lot of trepidation in our coaching staff," Jeff Van Gundy, the Rockets coach at the time of Morey's hiring, told *Sports Illustrated*'s Chris Ballard.

It didn't take long for Morey, whose data-based analyses raised productive questions, to impress Van Gundy. Despite earning some buy-in within his own walls, Morey felt the league as a whole was working to extricate him and his ideas. "The antibodies in the NBA were for sure trying to kick me out," he said.

Morey held strong beliefs about how the game should be played, concepts which he backed up with data. He wanted to take some of his ideas out for a test drive, but couldn't risk doing so with a playoff-bound team. So, in 2009, the Rockets partnered with the Rio Grande Vipers. The Vipers played in the Developmental League, the NBA's first attempt at an in-house minor league. As part of their arrangement, the first of its kind, the Rockets front office took control over Rio Grande's basketball operations. Morey now had his very own basketball laboratory.

"There's certain basketball factors that you can't evaluate at the NBA level because it's going to cost you wins and losses," Gersson Rosas, who took over as the Vipers general manager in 2009, told *Texas Monthly*. "But at the D-League level, you can experiment, you can try things, you can see the results and then apply it."

In Rio Grande, risk-taking was not limited to the style of play. With the Rockets, Morey only hired head coaches who had both played and coached in the NBA. "It's a pretty challenging job, so you want to grab people with some experience at the NBA level," Morey said. "But at the G League level, you can take a swing on a guy who's coaching in Belgium."

Morey and his team targeted the smaller leagues in Europe, where they compiled a list of a dozen or so coaches who played their desired style—fast-paced, spread out, and heavy on the three-pointers. Finch, whose teams played efficiently and, to Morey's eye, outperformed their talent level, made the list.

Finch walked into the 2009 interview without any idea what the Rockets were targeting. He was so immersed in European basketball that he barely knew anything about Morey. When Morey shared some of his ideas for how Rio Grande might play and the numbers behind them, they immediately clicked with Finch. "A lot of coaches during this analytics revolution have struggled to trust the numbers because it was forcing them to change how they played," Finch said. "Well, I had already played that way, so the numbers made sense to me."

Finch impressed Morey and ultimately won the job. Then, to Morey's surprise, Finch turned him down. It wasn't a negotiating ploy—Finch just wanted to make sure Morey and team were fully committed to their plan. "I didn't want to be a puppet for some sideshow," Finch said. "But I certainly wasn't afraid of being creative."

When Morey explained himself in more detail, Finch accepted the position, putting an end to his 17-year basketball exile. Finch's time in Division III and Europe prepared him for the realities of the G League. While NBA teams chartered planes to the nation's largest cities, G League teams rode buses to towns like Fort Wayne and Sioux Falls. Players and coaches coming from the high-D1 world had to acclimate themselves to a grittier, less glamorous basketball experience. Former D3 players, on the other hand, were well accustomed to an all-work, no-perk environment. "The cool thing about being on staff at that level is the responsibility that you have is so widespread because the resources are so limited," said Duncan Robinson, who played one year at D3 Williams College before kicking off an NBA playing career in the G League. "You might be picking a team from the airport up in a bus, cutting film, doing a scout, working with players on the court, doing the laundry. You're doing everything."

Kevin Hopkins, who played and coached at the Division III level, spent one season on a G League staff with the Santa Cruz Warriors. Members of the front office told him they preferred hiring former D3 players because, unlike D1 guys, they came in with a high motor and low expectations. "In the past, they hired D1 guys who, first day on the job, ask, 'Where's my gear?'" Hopkins said. "Versus D3 guys who come in and say, 'What can I do to help? And if I get a single T-shirt, great.'"

When Nevada Smith took over as Rio Grande's head coach, he learned that his staff would have to share one computer. On his last day, the team asked him to turn in any Rockets-issued electronics. His assistant had the computer, and the team never gave him a phone. He informed them that he didn't have anything to return.

The G League experience made up for its lack of swag with an abundance of opportunity. It was a welcome change for a former college coach like Smith, who no longer had to spend time recruiting or checking on classes. "It was like a basketball vacation," Smith said. "All you're doing all day, you're just doing basketball stuff. And you get to coach in a ton of games."

G League teams play 50 regular-season games, nearly twice the number on a college schedule. Plus, with players constantly getting NBA call-ups or shipping off to other opportunities, a team might cycle 25 players through their 12-man roster in a given season. All of those games and all of those players give a coaching staff plenty of reps to hone their approach through trial and error. "You get a lot of practice at teaching and reteaching and figuring out what works and what doesn't work," said Alex Lloyd, the former Pomona player who spent time early in his career as an assistant coach with the Spurs' G League affiliate. "The structure of the league is one that really lets you dive in and immerse yourself in how to teach things really effectively and how to teach things in a compressed time frame."

Beyond the X's and O's, G League coaches have to take a bunch of individuals primarily interested in getting called up to the NBA and somehow form a cohesive team. The G League is the only league in the world where 12 guys are thrilled to make the team on cut-down day and then—by the next morning—desperate to get the hell out of there. Finch learned that, by demonstrating his ability to help these pro players improve, they would respect him and listen to him, regardless of his background. "I would venture a guess that 99 percent of NBA players have never heard of Franklin & Marshall," Finch said. "But what matters is what I'm able to do when I'm with them while we're at the same point together."

After just one season, in which the Vipers won a G League title and Finch won Coach of the Year, Morey tore up Finch's two-year contract. He signed him to a longer deal that would eventually move him up to the NBA. "I was super fortunate to be with a team that valued the G League and was looking to develop coaching talent, which at the time wasn't really a thing," Finch said. "Now people are putting more emphasis on developing coaching in their own program."

Finch credits his two seasons in Rio Grande for helping him gain a crucial understanding of pro player psychology, lessons he has carried with him to the NBA. "They want to know that you care about their career as much as they care about their career," Finch said. "And you have to do that under the umbrella of trying to win as a team, too. These guys are all in a way their own individual business entities trying to grow their careers and maximize their earnings potential. One of the things I tell our guys on the very first day: this is really about two things—winning games and maximizing your opportunity in the marketplace, which is making the most money you possibly can. Oftentimes they go hand-in-hand. I think that honesty resonates with them."

Finch spent five seasons as a Rockets assistant, then bounced around to learn from other top coaches in the league, including the Denver Nuggets' Michael Malone and the New Orleans Pelicans' Alvin Gentry. In 2020, Finch joined the Toronto Raptors as an assistant coach, filling the spot left vacant by Nate Bjorkgren, a former Division III player at Buena Vista University. Bjorkgren, who coached multiple G League teams before finally making it to the NBA as an assistant, moved to Indiana to take over as the Pacers' head coach.

Bjorkgren, who only lasted one season with the Pacers, was the second former D3 player to use the G League as a stepstool to an eventual NBA head coaching job. With an increase in G League affiliations to NBA clubs, it's likely that this pathway will continue to grow. "The G League has probably changed coaching hiring," Morey said, "because people are more willing to take some risks down there."

Even in the organizations that aren't inclined to take big hiring swings, outsiders simply have more opportunities to break into the league. When coaching staffs were two or three deep, it wasn't always easy to find a place for an aspiring coach full of potential. But, as basketball's popularity grew, the business became more lucrative and owners were willing to support larger staffs. Jeff Van Gundy only reached the NBA because the Knicks needed a third assistant. Steve Clifford and John Hammond broke in as pro and college scouts, respectively. Mike Budenholzer and Will Hardy got their starts as video coordinators. G League jobs have become the latest improvement in the numbers game faced by those aspiring to work in the league. "At the very least," said Brad Stevens, when asked about hiring promising coaches from unconventional backgrounds, "the G League is hiring every year."

A job in the G League is more attainable and can very quickly help a young coach hit an NBA organization's radar. "You put two, three years of hard, hard work into a G League organization, you've kind of paid your dues in that sense," Duncan Robinson said. "And I think [NBA] organizations and people in the front office are eager to give those guys and girls opportunities."

Thanks in part to Morey's success in Houston, many of his staffers landed bigger jobs around the league. Rosas, the Vipers' GM during Finch's tenure as head coach, became the head of the Minnesota Timberwolves basketball operations department in 2019. When he dismissed head coach Ryan Saunders during the 2020-21 season, Rosas opted against finishing out the year with an in-house interim. Instead, he hired Finch off of Toronto's bench. It was a decision that sparked a controversy, one that illustrated how much had changed in NBA power structures—and how much had stayed the same.

PART IV:

Pipeline Complete

CHAPTER 12

D3 PLAYER EMPOWERMENT

How D3 alums reached prominent roles in the new NBA
power structure, and what that means for the league's
efforts to diversify their coaching staffs and front offices

After hitting multiple dead ends with NBA team officials, Andrew Olson shifted his attention to finding a pro player who could serve as a successful case study for ASA. He happened to train players in the same gym as Craig Wilcox, whose son, C.J., had just been drafted by the Los Angeles Clippers. So Olson asked him to coffee, where Wilcox told him, "You need to get this in front of the agents. They're the gatekeepers."

Wilcox introduced Olson to Aaron Mintz, who represented NBA players for Creative Artists Agency, one of the largest talent agencies in the country. After sharing his ideas with Mintz, the agent paused for a beat and told Olson, "You need to get this in front of GMs."

With that frustrating circular logic, Olson's latest quest was looking a lot like the D1 scholarship, the Summer League invite, and the call-up from the higher division in Germany—another dream just out of reach.

Mintz stepped out of the meeting to take a call. When he came back in, he mentioned offhand that it was Los Angeles Lakers general manager Mitch Kupchak, who had called to discuss one of Mintz's clients, Julius Randle. The Lakers had selected Randle with the seventh overall pick in the 2014 NBA Draft and then lost him for the entirety of his rookie season after he suffered a broken leg. Ever since the injury,

Randle had failed to live up to the Lakers' expectations. As the meeting wrapped up, Olson took one last shot, a desperation heave: "If there's anything I can do to help with Julius, I'll do whatever it takes."

After a few weeks of silence, Olson figured the meeting with Mintz was another staircase to nowhere. He shifted focus to marketing himself on social media and refining his shooting app. He was a little surprised when the phone finally rang and it was Mintz on the other end. Mintz tasked Olson with turning around a shooting report on Randle in 24 hours. Olson cleared the next day's schedule and pulled his first all-nighter since college (but only after playing in that night's men's league game...it was the playoffs, after all). The report was good enough to earn him an in-person meeting with Randle. Olson drove from San Diego to L.A. with both a suit and tie and workout clothes in his trunk, unsure if he'd have to prove himself in a conference room or on the court.

When Olson finally got some facetime with Randle, he remembers the big man slouching his 6'8" frame in his chair and barely responding to the presentation. Based on Randle's body language, Olson expected that their first meeting would also be their last. As they were wrapping up, the Lakers forward finally spoke. "Hey, if I end up working with you, you live in San Diego, I live in L.A. How will that work?"

"If you give me the opportunity," Olson replied, "I'll be there whenever you need me."

With the Lakers' blessing, Olson began training Randle at the team facility. Randle might've been bigger, stronger, and just plain better than any of his previous clients, but it didn't take long for Olson to realize he could still help. Regardless of the level, when you boiled it down, basketball was basketball.

Randle was a maniacal worker, even by NBA standards. He regularly put in three-a-days during the offseason. Over the summer, Olson trained Randle 80 times, driving the 200-mile round trip to L.A. and back as many as 26 days in a row.

The work paid off. During the 2017–18 season, Randle led the Lakers in per game scoring. He made 56 percent of his field-goal attempts—up from the 43 percent he shot prior to working with Olson. Despite Randle's success, Olson's NBA client list remained exactly one player long. Here and there, he did a consulting project for an NBA team, but the business was not accelerating at the degree he would've hoped.

On July 2, 2018, the Lakers announced they would not be re-signing Randle, one in a series of moves designed to clear enough cap room to sign LeBron James and rebuild the team around him. Randle, who ultimately signed a nice contract with the New Orleans Pelicans, had no choice but to leave L.A. Olson, whose only NBA client now lived across the country, became further collateral damage, a casualty caused by a ripple emanating from James' large wake.

Late on a February evening in 2021, the Minnesota Timberwolves did something that hadn't been done in the NBA in 12 seasons. Fresh off a loss to the New York Knicks, they announced that they had fired head coach Ryan Saunders. Instead of following standard mid-season NBA protocol and naming an interim replacement from Saunders' staff, Minnesota hired Toronto Raptors assistant Chris Finch to a multi-year deal, effective immediately.

To orchestrate a firing and hiring with that many moving pieces, and seemingly do so in one fell swoop, flew in the face of the league's mores. The move raised a lot of eyebrows, especially given the fact that the Timberwolves had a very qualified candidate in-house—associate head coach David Vanterpool, who had interviewed for multiple head coaching vacancies during his nine-year career as an NBA assistant. Michael Lee, a reporter for *The Washington Post*, tweeted that the sequence of events was "shadier than standing under a tree."

Lee wasn't alone in questioning the Timberwolves' decision. Journalists, activists, and other coaches came to the defense of Vanterpool, who is Black. Marc Spears, a Naismith Hall of Fame journalist and frequent chronicler of racial inequities in the coaching ranks, wrote in Andscape that the move was a "boiling point" for the league's Black coaches. Following a season in which NBA officials made a lot of highly publicized commitments to diversity and civil rights, Black coaches still felt they didn't have a fair shot at head coaching opportunities. "They use your skill set during the difficult times," an unnamed Black NBA coach told Andscape, "but when it's time to reward you with an opportunity, they always seem to find a reason to not, and then expect you to continue to be the good soldier." By bringing in Finch, who is White, in lieu of promoting the qualified assistant coach who was clearly next in line, the Timberwolves were rubbing rock salt in that wound.

The man behind Finch's hiring, Gersson Rosas, was the first Latino basketball operations lead in league history. He had a longstanding relationship with Finch, one that dated back to the Rio Grande Vipers, where Rosas was the general manager and Finch the head coach. As soon as Rosas took over in Minnesota, there were rumors that, should the team need to make a coaching change, Finch would be the pick. "There was no one I knew who was connected to the organization or to the league in any way who was surprised that Chris Finch was Gersson Rosas' choice," said Jon Krawczynski, a Timberwolves beat writer for The Athletic. "Ultimately, [Rosas'] decision was he believed that Chris Finch was the better coach than David Vanterpool. The way that Rosas viewed it was, 'I'm just making the best choice for this organization, and it has nothing to do with the color of anyone's skin.'"

According to Krawczynski, Vanterpool wasn't the victim of explicit racism. Rather, he just didn't have the same rich history with the decision maker as did the man who eventually landed the job. The story is illustrative of the quiet forces that have long prevented coaching staffs and front offices from reflecting the demographics of the players on the court. As their numbers and influence within the league grew, former Division III players became more and more tied in with the league's ultimate power brokers. Division III alums were no longer the lovable, plucky underdogs. They could now be perceived as just the latest in a series of White faces filling the league's media guides.

BY THE MID-2010s, D3 alums wielded more power than ever. Gregg Popovich, the frequent hirer of D3 grads, worked hand-in-glove with front-office lead RC Buford to keep the San Antonio Spurs dynasty humming. Stan Van Gundy and Tom Thibodeau, who toiled for years before getting their shot as an NBA head coach, were now in high demand. To successfully reel them in, the Detroit Pistons and Timberwolves offered Van Gundy and Thibodeau, respectively, full control over basketball operations. And in

2015, Mike Budenholzer stepped in to temporarily take over the Atlanta Hawks basketball operations department. With the exception of Doc Rivers, a former NBA player and championship-winning coach, the D3 trio of Van Gundy, Thibodeau, and Budenholzer were the only coaches in the league at the time who also officially held ultimate veto power over personnel.

It was a major departure from the mid-2000s, when most of the league's coaching and GM jobs belonged to former NBA players. In 2008, all but two teams employed a former pro as GM and/or head coach. One exception was San Antonio, where Popovich held both positions. The other was Oklahoma City, where two former Spurs staffers, Sam Presti and P.J. Carlesimo, manned the front office and the bench for the Thunder. At the time, the Thunder were a rarity—one of only four teams with a D3 alum in a top leadership role.

Then, in the 2010s, innovative and tireless assistant coaches from the Van Gundy tree started landing head coaching jobs, copycat NBA teams started poaching more talent from the Spurs D3 incubator, and other D3 alums rose to head coaching and GM jobs through various paths and networks. As a result, the D3 number nearly tripled. By 2015, 11 teams had a former D3 player running their front office, coaching their team, or both.

The path from small college to power position in the pros could no longer be ignored. This was a full-on infiltration. And it was coming mostly at the expense of former NBA players.

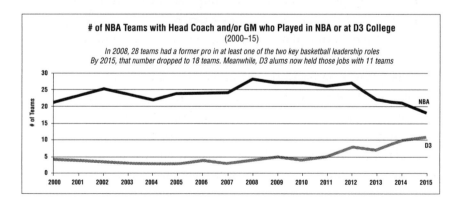

The trend is inherently racial. A decline in former NBA players in leadership positions directly correlates to a drop in Black leaders. In an

ESPN.com study, Kevin Pelton tracked the race of all NBA head coaches since the 1976 ABA merger. Of the 124 coaches who played in the NBA, 50 percent of them are Black. For the 113 who never played in the NBA, that number drops to just 12 percent. Between 1976 and 2021, only 14 Black men had ever coached in the NBA without having played in the league first. Data for front-office leaders is similarly skewed; from league inception through 2015, the number of Black GMs who didn't also play in the NBA could be counted on two hands, with fingers to spare.

It's a rather staggering figure, and it's one for which D3 alums historically haven't done many favors. From the NBA's founding through 2015, 31 former D3 players (including those who attended colleges that would eventually join D3) served as head coach or GM for at least half of an NBA season. Only one of those 31 individuals is a person of color, Ed Tapscott, who, as both a head coach and GM, was never able to shed the "interim" tag.

Now, nobody is accusing D3 players of banding together and conspiring to supplant Black former players in the name of White supremacy. Among their ranks are individuals who have loudly spoken out on issues of civil rights and diversity. One of the most vocal, Stan Van Gundy, acknowledged his skin color must be mentioned alongside the other factors outside of his control that positively impacted his career. "Even though my background coming from Division III is still relatively rare for NBA coaches, I still always have the privilege of being a White man in America," Van Gundy said. "That's just a reality. It's not just basketball; it's just a fact of life in America. You're born a White man here, you're quite a few steps up the ladder on everybody else."

One salient example of the White privilege Van Gundy describes can be found in D3 sports. Colleges that don't offer athletic scholarships seem to have fewer opportunities for student-athletes of color. According to the racial report cards compiled by The Institute of Diversity and Ethics in Sport, Division III athletes who are now old enough to hold leadership positions are a Whiter bunch than their Division I counterparts. In 2004-05, across all sports, 25 percent of D1 athletes identified as Black, compared to just 8 percent of D3 athletes. That large gap, while slightly less dramatic, persists to this day. Television personality Chris Broussard, who played

D3 basketball at Oberlin College in the late '80s, put it more succinctly. "Keeping it real," he said, "Division III is mostly White players."

In 2000, Mark Cuban bought the Dallas Mavericks for $285 million, unofficially ushering in a new era of NBA ownership. Unlike any other owner before him, the T-shirt clad tech billionaire treated his team like both a business and a toy. He invested heavily in facilities, shot around with the players, and racked up fines for heckling refs from the sidelines. Financial penalties notwithstanding, the Mavericks have been one of the *Shark Tank* panelist's best investments. Cuban offloaded a large chunk of his ownership stake in December of 2023 at a reported valuation of $3.5 billion. "I've seen the league go from what I call 'ma and pop,' where you had wealthy owners, to very wealthy owners, to multimillionaire owners, to billionaires," said NBA executive Rick Sund, who began his front-office career in 1974.

Of the 21 current majority owners who purchased their team between 2000 and 2022, 16 made their vast fortunes in either tech or finance (private equity, venture capital, or mortgage lending). Meanwhile, of the nine holdover owners from the 20th century, all but the late Paul Allen worked *outside* of tech and finance. "With the influx of finance people into sports ownership, that has led to an increase in owners with a mindset that is more open to statistical analysis than may have been the case for the barons of industry who tended to own teams in a prior era," said Seth Partnow, The Athletic's NBA writer and the former Milwaukee Bucks analytics lead.

On the hook for hundreds of millions or billions of dollars, the new generation approaches ownership differently than their predecessors, all of whom bought into the league for eight figures. "Ownership is coming in and buying a team for a lot of money, so optimization matters," said Philadelphia 76ers president of basketball operations Daryl Morey. "They're coming in with quant backgrounds, like venture capital, like software, ones that generally will value STEM backgrounds. Ownership changing has led to hiring changes, which has led to folks in power who are going to look to different backgrounds than what was there before."

Morey, one of the few GMs in NBA history with a quant background, is a bit of an anomaly. Even though the new generation of data-loving owners coincided with basketball's *Moneyball* revolution, not a lot of teams were in a hurry to hand over their entire operation to a GM who was comfortable running regressions. They were more likely to hire someone like Sam Presti, a leader with a rich basketball resume who was also data- and process-driven. These new owners, as illustrated in Chapter 9, were also far *less* likely to hire a lead executive who played in the NBA.

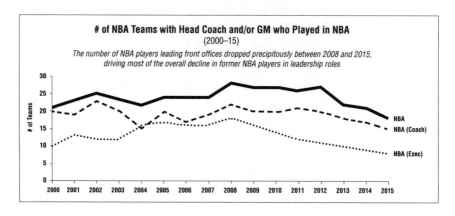

of NBA Teams with Head Coach and/or GM who Played in NBA
(2000–15)

The number of NBA players leading front offices dropped precipitously between 2008 and 2015, driving most of the overall decline in former NBA players in leadership roles

With so much new data available, basketball started to resemble any other business optimization problem. The NBA was no longer an unknowable black box better left to those who played the game. So, when former players like Isiah Thomas had very public front-office failures, owners felt increasingly comfortable turning to lead executives who walked and talked like businessmen. The new wave of owners come from industries where decisions are made after reviewing data-laden PowerPoint presentations. They expect their basketball executives to speak the same language. "When you talk to GMs, they say, 'I've got to show a deck,'" Weitzman said. "Was [former NBA player and executive] Rod Thorn showing his owner 30 years ago a deck of his free-agency plans? I don't think so. You've got to walk them through these things with data."

Twenty years ago, when owners had less data at their disposal and hadn't invested nine or 10 figures on their team, it was more palatable to risk empowering an iconic player without any experience. Now, the potential downside to such a hire can be too much for an owner to undertake. As former players fell out of style, D3 alums were well positioned to step into the void. "[The new owners] are pushing the envelope to run these franchises more like a Fortune 500 company, and I think D3 student-athletes fit the bill," said Matt Bollero, who held front office jobs with both the Timberwolves and Bucks.

D3 student-athletes all carry a full academic load, unlike many of their D1 counterparts, especially those who leave college early to go pro. In lecture halls and seminars, D3 students are surrounded by young people who will go on to work at companies like those run by NBA owners. Then, in their 20s and early 30s, when a pro athlete is still competing, the former D3 student-athlete is gaining valuable experience in the business of basketball. Instead of taking hundreds of jumpers and watching film, they are learning the intricacies of the salary cap and honing communication strategies geared toward owners and executives.

In high school, future D3 players often fought an uphill battle against the bigger, faster, stronger, and more talented players—the ones who earned the scholarships. Now, when faced with a former pro in the front office, the seasoned former D3 players are often the ones with the upper hand. Organizations still value NBA players' unique perspective and aptitude for the game, but they are now expected to work their way up to top leadership roles. The bridge directly from an NBA roster to a GM job has been detonated.

There are, however, still paths to the top of an NBA organization for those without coaching or front-office experience. But these new entry points are not for former pros. They are yet another way in for basketball junkies who never played at the highest level.

THE SO-CALLED "PLAYER Empowerment Era" began on July 8, 2010, with nine now-infamous words—"I'm going to take my talents to South Beach." Live on ESPN, LeBron James told Jim Gray, along with the nearly 10 million people tuning in, that he planned to leave the Cleveland Cavaliers and sign with the Miami Heat. Over the next 10 years, James would play for the Heat, the Cavs again, and the Los Angeles Lakers. At each stop, he negotiated short-term deals to maximize his leverage and flexibility. And at each stop, he led his team to at least one championship.

In a *The New York Times Magazine* article about Kevin Durant, another super-duper star who exercised his free agency and hopped from team to team, Sam Anderson described the post-"Decision" NBA as one where "the league's center of power swung from executives in front offices to group texts among superstars. 'The Player Empowerment Era,' people call it. Other superstars now routinely do the things James did: they tailor their contracts for maximum flexibility, influence the hiring and firing of coaches, and—above all—scheme to play together."

"The Player Empowerment Era" is a bit of a misnomer. A better term would be "The Superstar Empowerment Era." The average rotation player doesn't necessarily wield more influence than before, but James, Durant, and the other elite players of their generation have bent franchises to their will more than any other generation in league history.

If "The Player Empowerment Era" is misnamed, so too was "The Decision." James wasn't making up his mind right then and there on live television. The moves behind his announcement had been put into motion years earlier by Creative Artists Agency (CAA) and James' agent, Leon Rose.

It was Rose who convinced James to sign only a three-year deal in 2007 so his free agency would align with Dwyane Wade's and Chris Bosh's. It was Rose who convinced the CAA Sports honchos to bring Wade's and Bosh's agent under the CAA umbrella. And it was Rose who first showed James how it could be possible for Miami to sign all three players. His fingerprints were all over the move, from its very inception to its airing on TV; he even reviewed Gray's final list of questions prior to taping.

Behind each bolting superstar, another group was enjoying more power than ever—the agents. On his Substack, former Warriors beat reporter Ethan Strauss has written extensively on the recent symbiosis between teams and agents, especially in the major markets that tend to attract star players. During a March 2022 appearance on *The Bill Simmons Podcast,* Strauss said, "[LeBron James] brought this mercenary era that is very much tied in with agencies and getting represented and leveraging meetings and flexing your power."

Agents pulling a front-office's strings is not a new phenomenon. David Falk, who represented Michael Jordan and several other top players during the 1990s, regularly helped orchestrate trades for his clients. But there's a significant difference between an agent acting like a GM and an agent actually *becoming* a GM, which Rose did in 2020 with the New York Knicks.

WHEN CHERRY HILL East's head basketball coach, John Valore, was looking to name a godfather for his son, he didn't turn to a lifelong friend,

nor did he ask a trusted relative. Valore could think of no better role model
for his son than Leon Rose, his senior point guard. That's how much Valore
respected his sub-six-foot co-captain. "At his size he had to be competitive,
and that is what he was," Valore told the *Courier-Post*.

South Jersey sportswriter Walt Burrows couldn't help but compare the
tenacious Rose to a local star from a different sport—Pete Rose, who played
for the Phillies at the time. "He's a leader, dives for loose balls, makes the
big plays, and does a slow burn when things aren't going right for his Cherry
Hill East High School team," Burrows wrote in the *Courier-Post*.

Following high school, Rose attended Dickinson College, a private
Pennsylvania liberal arts school whose athletic teams competed in the same
conference as Juniata, Frank Vogel's alma mater. Rose, who attended college
more than a decade before Vogel, played JV basketball as a freshman and
sophomore before contributing some minutes at point guard for the varsity
team as an upperclassman.

After college, he wanted to coach, but could never fully take the plunge.
His father, an attorney, recommended law school, so Rose enrolled at Temple
Law. Between classes, he served as an assistant coach at Cherry Hill East
High, his alma mater. He then took a job as a county prosecutor, a position
that afforded him enough time to also moonlight as an assistant coach at
D3 Rutgers-Camden.

Yogi Berra once said, "When you get to the fork in the road, take it."
In 1988, Rose reached a point where he could no longer travel on both
Basketball Boulevard and Lawyer Lane. Forced to choose between coaching
and law, he shelved his dreams and joined a private practice. After a few
years, he joined his father's law firm, where he made partner. Rose's cases
ran the gamut. Among his most notable clients were the 83-year-old dentist
accused of telling a 31-year-old newspaper carrier to "give him some sugar"
before allegedly fondling her, the local radio personality who had an affair
with a prominent rabbi accused of killing his wife, and the family of a
teenage boy who died after eating yogurt laced with cyanide.

The work kept him busy, but he still carved out time to play hoops. As
part of the JCC league, he competed in runs all over the Jersey suburbs of
Philadelphia, where he regularly dropped in more than 20 points a game.

Even though he stayed closely tied to the Philly basketball scene, Rose
had no long-simmering master plan to marry his passion for basketball and

talent as a lawyer. His career as an agent began when Bill Simmons (not to be confused with the founder of The Ringer) asked Rose to negotiate an NBA contract for his nephew, local Philly product Lionel Simmons. "Wow, this is like the perfect combination," Rose said. "It brings together the law and the coaching aspect because it would give me the chance to be involved with basketball players as their coach with regard to the next phase of their life."

Through word-of-mouth referrals, Rose's agency business grew, one client at a time. First came Temple alum Rick Brunson, which led to relationships with other Temple products like Aaron McKie and Eddie Jones. The Temple niche became a Philadelphia 76ers niche, which eventually led to Rose signing his biggest client to date, Allen Iverson, in 2002. Three years later, Rose landed an even bigger fish—LeBron James.

Rose's business didn't grow because of his ability to pour in points in over-30 leagues ("Most of them tell me to keep my mouth shut and worry about everything else," Rose responded when Kevin Collier of the *Courier-Post* asked if he gives his clients jump-shooting advice). Instead, he impressed the game's best players with the same qualities that impressed his high school coach—his leadership abilities and aptitude as a teammate. Clients all praised his loving diligence. Both Brunson and Dajuan Wagner, a Rose client from nearby Camden, New Jersey, said their agent "is like family."

Shortly after Rose signed James, CAA—one of the most influential agencies in entertainment—decided to expand into sports. They purchased several smaller agencies, including Rose's. With CAA's resources behind him, Rose built himself into one of the largest agents in basketball, with a client list that included James, Iverson, Wade, Chris Paul, Carmelo Anthony, Joel Embiid, and Devin Booker.

SUPERSTARS WIN CHAMPIONSHIPS. It's the number one truism in NBA team building. Without one superstar, you're drawing dead. Without two, the odds are stacked heavily against you. Teams need that top-flight talent, who they can acquire in one of three ways—through the draft, through a trade, and through free agency. The draft is the one route to a superstar that is actually available to all 30 teams. Players have little say over who picks them, especially at the very top of the draft. For small markets like Oklahoma City and San Antonio, a high lottery pick is the best bet to bring in a transcendent talent. It's the reason teams loath the dreaded middle of the pack. If you're not competing for a championship, best to press the reset button, lose a bunch of games, and hope for a high pick.

For the big-market destinations, however, the other two paths to a superstar—free agency and trade—are wide open. The very best players have historically sought out opportunities to play in a big city, preferably one with good weather. When LeBron James and "The Decision" signaled the beginning of the so-called "Player Empowerment Era," the trade/free agency road to acquiring a superstar transformed from a two-lane urban side street into a six-lane superhighway. A year after "The Decision," Carmelo Anthony pushed for and received a trade from the Denver Nuggets to the New York Knicks. Then, in 2016, Kevin Durant left the Oklahoma City Thunder for the Golden State Warriors in free agency, where his new super team would win the next two championships.

Bob Myers, who presided over Durant's successful recruitment, joined the team's front office after spending more than a dozen years working as an agent. Naturally, other big market teams hoping to land the next disgruntled superstar began to wonder if they, too, should consider a former agent to lead their front office. "Team-building in the post-Decision NBA had become more about recruiting than scouting," Ethan Strauss wrote in an article on his Substack. "And so hires were made on that basis. This was the natural evolution of letting player agents into NBA ops."

One year after the Durant decision, the Lakers tabbed Kobe Bryant's agent, Rob Pelinka, to step into their vacant general manager seat. Shortly thereafter, the Lakers signed James in free agency and acquired Anthony Davis, who had forced a trade from the New Orleans Pelicans.

When Durant and Kyrie Irving banded together to sign with the Brooklyn Nets in 2019, it forced the New York Knicks, the city's marquee franchise, to take a long look in the mirror. If the Nets were attracting top free agents over them, then maybe they needed to hire a powerful agent too. So they reached out to Leon Rose.

In a business that breeds animosity, Rose made very few enemies on his rise to the top. He is more Jerry Maguire than Ari Gold. "Everyone really respected him as a basketball guy, everyone from other GMs to the grouchiest *Moneyball* type of scout," said NBA writer Yaron Weitzman.

Austin Brown, an agent who worked under Rose and now co-leads CAA's basketball business, said that Rose is "the ultimate leader, ultimate glue guy, ultimate locker room guy. He keeps your team right. You want him on your team. He makes everybody feel better and he makes everybody around him better."

Brown, like Rose, played D3 basketball and attended law school before combining his passions into a dream career. At CAA company retreats, Brown and Rose would try to relive their glory days during the staff three-on-three games. According to Brown's scouting report, Rose is a high-IQ player, someone who is great to have as a teammate and frustrating to play against. Having experienced life as a D3 student-athlete himself, Brown believes you can draw a straight line from Rose's college days to the skills that helped him win over so many clients and peers in the NBA. "It goes back to that Division III mentality," Brown said. "Doing the little things, not taking everything for granted, making sure that you do what's needed to be successful."

Rose, according to reports, did not have designs on parlaying his successful career as an agent into the chance to play fantasy manager with an NBA team. Then the Knicks made him an offer he couldn't refuse (the good kind, not a horse's head in his bed) and Rose accepted.

He wasted no time in assembling a trusted staff of associates with whom he went way back. William Wesley, better known as "World Wide Wes," joined the team as an executive vice president. Wesley and Rose, both South Jersey natives, had known each other for more than 40 years. A connector and mentor to NBA players, Wesley joined CAA soon after Rose, where he represented Tom Thibodeau and University of Kentucky coach John Calipari. As soon as the Knicks announced Rose and Wesley's hiring, Thibodeau, whose stint as Timberwolves head coach and president of basketball ops ended unceremoniously after two-and-a-half seasons, was linked to the Knicks open head coaching job.

Thibodeau had spent the 2019–20 season doing his usual between-jobs routine. "What Thibs does on a year off, he's not, like, going to beaches," said Boston Celtics executive Brad Stevens. "He's going to Boston for five practices and three games, and then San Antonio for six days, and then Utah for 12 days. He's just wrapped up in the game."

Despite staying closely involved, Thibodeau was no lock to land another head coaching job after the Chicago Bulls and Timberwolves both let him go. His win-at-all-costs mentality during the regular season stood at odds with the championship contenders who paced themselves in order to peak come playoff time. "I did wonder if he was going to get another shot because his approach to doing the job is different than the 'modern way' that coaches do things," said Timberwolves beat writer Jon Krawczynski.

According to Nick Friedell, who covered Thibodeau in Chicago and Minnesota for ESPN, Leon Rose could overlook Thibodeau's supposed warts because he knew the coach "completely."

"In order to bring Tom on at this stage, you have to have an understanding of exactly who he is and what kind of coach he is and what he brings every day," Friedell said. "In that regard, the fit was right for the time, place, and for where the Knicks were as they tried to get back to respectability."

To nobody's surprise, Rose and the Knicks named Thibodeau their head coach in 2020. He then guided them to an unexpected playoff berth, earning his second Coach of the Year award along the way. In just one year, Thibodeau went from nearly exiled from the NBA's head coaching ranks back to the top of the profession. None of it would've been possible without his connection to Rose, a fellow former D3 player.

WHEN IT CAME to the day-to-day aspects of his job, Rose played to his strengths and delegated the rest. "The staffs are so big now that you're going to get the input of your scouts, your GM, your director of player personnel, and I think Leon does a good job," said "third Van Gundy brother" Andy Greer, who is back with the Knicks, this time as one of Thibodeau's assistants. "He gets them all together, he lets them speak their minds, and ultimately he makes the final decision."

Greer also noted that Rose isn't just soliciting opinions from an ivory tower and handing down a decree. He leads with the same personal touch that made him such a successful agent. "He's really caring," Greer said. "You can tell he was a great agent because of his ability to connect with people. I think everybody who is in the organization, the basketball ops side, feels the same way I do. He really cares about you as a person outside of basketball."

In a way, the ballooning front offices allow someone like Rose, who possesses the right people skills and also the wherewithal to solicit opinions and delegate, to more seamlessly step into the role without any experience. With cap experts, analytics whizzes, and scouts at his disposal, Rose can focus on leadership and recruiting free agents. "If it was 1995 and Leon Rose got hired by the Knicks and you were a mom-and-pop small basketball operation, I might say, 'Wait a minute: you're in trouble here from an experience standpoint,'" said Bobby Marks, ESPN's front office insider. "But now it goes back to staffing. There are a group of people under him who have worked for a team. He doesn't have to be a guy who has an A+ understanding of the CBA."

What Rose does have is an A+ understanding of the importance of relationships. In the 2022 offseason, Rose, who placed a high premium on surrounding himself with "family," poached his first marquee free agent—Jalen Brunson, the son of Rick Brunson, Rose's very first client.

Rose, like Thibodeau, is one in a series of improbable underdogs who managed to work their way from D3 to the top of the NBA. On a micro level, stories like theirs are happy little tales of success in the face of long odds. But from another perspective, especially when amalgamated together, they weave a potentially problematic tapestry. The Knicks hired a White man without front-office experience to run their basketball operation. He then hired a close associate to coach the team, another White man who didn't perform up to expectations in his last job. Are these happy little underdog stories just perpetuating the lagging diversity in NBA front offices and coaching staffs? Or is the D3 infiltration actually leading to a more inclusive and meritocratic NBA?

CHAPTER 13

GOT NEXT

*How D3 programs at elite liberal arts colleges
became the new feeder to the NBA, and how the
fully mature pipeline to the pros is doing its part to
diversify NBA coaching staffs and front offices*

When it became clear that Julius Randle would be leaving the Lakers, Andrew Olson, reckoning with the realization that he couldn't drive across the country on the chime of a text, made a move of his own. As luck would have it, Olson's college coach, David Hixon, had been exchanging emails with a high-ranking NBA executive. Hixon sent a note describing ASA and Olson's work with Randle. The now-intrigued exec, who also happened to have played ball at a D3 school, invited Olson to fly in and meet with his team.

Prior to the trip, Olson called a friend for advice—former Amherst graduate assistant Koby Altman. After leaving Amherst, Altman coached a few college teams before joining the Cleveland Cavaliers. He quickly scaled the organization's front office and, in 2017, was named general manager of the Cavs. Throughout the years, Olson kept in touch with Altman and even did some consulting work for the Cavs. They maintained a lukewarm courtship, which, thanks to the presence of another suitor, was about to heat up.

Altman invited Olson to Cleveland for Game Three of the 2018 NBA Finals. Prior to the game, Olson met with analytics staffers and behind-the-bench assistant coaches. He watched draft prospects work out and even played pickup at the practice facility during a pregame lull. It was a mix of guys, some who played in college and others who never played competitively. Olson later learned that the young man he was guarding, who everybody was being so nice to, was team owner Dan Gilbert's son. After watching the Cavs blow a double-digit lead to fall behind 3–0 in the series, Olson thanked everyone for their time and flew home to San Diego wondering what, if anything, would come next.

Not long after the Warriors completed their sweep of the Cavs, Altman called Olson and officially offered him a job. It was originally a hybrid opportunity, where Olson could stay in San Diego and travel in from time to time. Throughout the process, Olson always envisioned a consulting job that wouldn't require him to uproot his life. But after his trip to Cleveland, he knew he'd be selling himself short by remaining remote. After another discussion with Altman, Olson agreed to relocate so he could be the team's full-time shooting coach.

It didn't take long for Olson to acclimate to life as an NBA coach. He learned that days of the week were irrelevant—there were only travel days, game days, and practice days. As a coach hired by the front office, and someone who had never had a "real" job, he came face-to-face with organizational politics for the first time. He learned the importance of building strong bonds with coworkers and forming relationships with players. Most of all, he discovered that his work with Randle was not a fluke. He could help the very best in the world get even better.

Despite Olson's immense basketball gifts and dogged work ethic, it's safe to say that, without the inroads made by other D3 alums, he would still be training kids in San Diego, always wondering why he never had what it takes to play or work at the highest level. Instead, he's coaching All-Stars and sitting behind the bench for playoff games. The game he loves so much finally loved him back, without any caveats or contingencies.

On the evening of October 29, 2003, the Cleveland Cavaliers were about to open their season against the Sacramento Kings. Koby Altman scrambled to make it to The Grille, a little eatery located in the Middlebury

College student center, for the 10:30 PM tip. After sliding into a seat just in time, Altman and some friends munched grilled cheeses and chicken tenders and watched in awe as LeBron James—just 18 years old, younger than they were—made his NBA debut. "You could see how he moved and how easy it was for him," Altman said. "We were like, 'Oh my gosh.' And then you think about what I've gone on to do: work with LeBron, win a championship with him. To trace it all back to watching his first basket at The Grille at Middlebury, it's pretty remarkable."

Altman's basketball story begins in his hometown of Brooklyn, New York. When the New York Knicks won the 1985 draft lottery and the right to select Patrick Ewing, Altman's mom, a school social worker, shouted so loudly she woke little Koby up in his crib. It wasn't the last time the Knicks made Altman and his mom scream, either in delight or in agony.

Growing up, Altman cut his teeth in the intense pickup games played in the neighborhood parks. The city was especially adept at churning out elite point guards. To play that position in the Brooklyn parks and public schools, swagger was just as crucial as a tight handle. Altman possessed both. He harbored dreams of competing in the public school city championship at Madison Square Garden, the world's most famous basketball stage. Then, like all of the top local players, he hoped to continue his career in the Big East, the nation's premiere college basketball conference. "Unfortunately," Altman said, "I was 5'10"."

St. John's and Georgetown weren't offering Altman a scholarship. But the Posse Foundation was. Today, Posse pulls students of color from most major metro areas, but back in 1999, the program was geared toward racially diverse New York City kids like Altman. After applications and rounds of interviews, those who displayed exemplary leadership potential received full scholarships. They were then placed in groups of 10 at one of Posse's partner schools. Posse's goal, according to their website, is to "identify young leaders who might be missed by traditional admissions criteria but who can excel at selective colleges and universities." To set each 10-student group up for success, they undergo rigorous leadership programming and regular meetings before and during their four years of college.

As Altman moved through the extensive Posse interview process, he honed in on one partner school in particular, Middlebury College in Vermont. Middlebury head basketball coach Jeff Brown was alerted to the fact that a potential Posse scholar was also a pretty good basketball player. Brown traveled down to New York City to watch Altman play and left feeling as though he had found someone who could contribute to his program.

After arriving on campus, Altman discovered that Middlebury might as well have been on a different planet than Brooklyn. "It was very White, very rich, private, and elite," Altman said. "If you don't come from that ecosystem, you do feel out of place."

At a Division III school like Middlebury, basketball players are not as separated from the general student body as they are at a major D1 program. Altman lived in dorms, worked on group projects, and ate in the dining hall with non-basketball players. Thanks to the social standing that came from being on the basketball team, along with a helpful nudge from his Posse training, he quickly settled in and began to comfortably interact with students from all different backgrounds. "For me, basketball has always been my comfort zone," said Altman. "So being able to go there and play basketball certainly helped me grow and be much more outgoing."

Small colleges like Middlebury have proven to be better than large universities at fostering socialization across diverse groups. A few years after Altman graduated in 2004, Wellesley College psychology professor Angela Bahns conducted a study comparing social trends at different sized colleges. Since students at a big university are exposed to more peers of differing backgrounds and beliefs, it seems intuitive that they would more frequently form diverse social circles. Instead, Bahns found that larger schools provided students with the luxury of only needing to befriend others like them. On the other hand, the small-college environment promoted more intermingling between races, political beliefs, and prejudices. "At a smaller college with fewer people," Bahns wrote, "there is less overall diversity. But this means that it is almost impossible to find someone who thinks or looks exactly like oneself. You have to compromise, to accept some minimum level of difference."

Altman had an innate ability to connect with his classmates, which his coach noticed "right from Day One." It's a skill that, along with the leadership chops he sharpened in the Posse program, helps Altman to this day. "The strength of being a connector and really being able to interact and walk in different spaces," Brown said, "is the key to his success right now at the professional level."

On a given day, an NBA head coach or general manager has conversations with owners, staffers, coaches, and players, who together represent a wide range of cultures and upbringings. Learning to walk in new spaces and find common ground might not be on a course syllabus, but it can be a big part of the residential, small-college education.

During his time at Williams College in the early 2000s, Utah Jazz coach Will Hardy discovered that the small student body was full of different people from different cultures. The environment helped him hone the people skills that have set him apart as a coach. "Not everybody's the same, and I can't treat everybody like they're the same," Hardy said. "I have to figure out who they are, what's important to them, what makes them tick. I think that Williams, for me, was such a big step in that direction."

Of course, liberal arts college grads also acquire valuable skills and lessons *inside* the classroom. The actual coursework is often applicable to today's NBA. Altman, for instance, wrote hundreds of papers en route to a sociology major. In doing so, he learned how to structure a sound argument and back it up with data. Even though he didn't major in a quantitative field like economics or computer science, Altman still said he "learned to become really analytical in my decisions. I've learned to try to get every ounce of data you can possibly get before making one of those big decisions."

In other words, Middlebury taught Altman and his classmates how to "speak the language" of the modern franchise owner. Pairing that ability with his experience both playing and coaching college basketball made him an ideal candidate for today's NBA front office.

Excluding Lou Mohs, Carl Scheer, and Norm Sonju—those who worked in other industries before transitioning into basketball—most of the small-college alums who assumed NBA leadership positions prior to the early 2000s majored in education-related fields at small state colleges. They essentially trained at vocational schools, which prepared them to teach, lead, and coach.

Recently, however, the former D3 players rising to the ranks of head coach or general manager are overwhelmingly graduates of elite liberal arts colleges. Since 2018, NBA teams have hired five D3 alums as general managers, all of whom attended a top-tier liberal arts school. The same trend is also emerging in coaching, where three of the newer D3 first-time head coaches—Chris Finch (Franklin & Marshall), Wes Unseld Jr. (Johns Hopkins), and Hardy (Williams)—all attended top academic schools.

A liberal arts college's primary objective is to teach its students how to think. They eschew plug-and-play majors like accounting or marketing in favor of a more holistic education, one that gives students the tools they need to learn on the job. Liberal arts grads may not appeal to entry-level hiring managers, but once they learn their chosen craft, they tend to possess the soft skills that accelerate mid-career growth.

The tricky part about receiving a liberal arts education is figuring out where to apply it after graduation. Schools like Middlebury and Williams effectively allow students to take the "What will I be when I grow up?" question and kick it a few years down the road. In some ways, it's liberating to graduate college with a nearly endless buffet of career options. But that wide array can lead to paralysis by analysis.

For those considering pursuing a lower-paying career, there's also the matter of opportunity cost. Elite liberal arts schools often serve as feeder programs for top-paying investment banks and consulting firms. "When you graduate from these kinds of schools," Altman said, "you feel you have to justify it with making money."

Altman's quest for cash led him to a New York City real estate brokerage. A couple years in, he was brokering multimillion dollar purchases, making six figures, and living on Fifth Avenue. He came to realize that, while he might've been living *a* dream, it wasn't *his* dream. "I just knew something was missing," he said. He started volunteer coaching at a high school four blocks from his office. One hour a day suddenly stretched into two or three. A mentor reassured Altman that it was okay to walk away from the real estate job. Coaching could be a career, too. Altman applied to UMass' Sports Management program and interviewed at Amherst College for a graduate assistant job.

Compared to the older generation of small-college alums, Altman was behind the curve. By the time Garry St. Jean was 24, he had already been a high school head coach for three seasons. John Hammond also started coaching while still in college. Then there were the Fratellos and Van Gundys and Thibodeaus of the world, all of whom made a beeline right to a coaching career.

At Amherst, Altman did what he could to make up for lost time. His competitiveness, basketball IQ, and ability to relate to the players all stood out to head coach David Hixon. Some graduate assistants would, here and there, ask out of coaching responsibilities to take care of their schoolwork. Not Altman. He was in the office all day and spent many nights on the road scouting. On those scouting trips, he learned the art form from Amherst's longtime assistant, Ron Buelow, whose trained eye could watch a set play in real time and perfectly capture each piece of the action on a notepad, all while carrying on a conversation.

During practices, Altman's modern approach to individual skills work injected new life into Hixon's repertoire of drills. "Koby was not afraid to challenge something I was talking about because he had basketball experience and basketball IQ," Hixon said. "And that made me better, too."

By the end of his first season, Altman was the pied piper, gathering most of the guards and forwards at one hoop prior to practice for what he dubbed "The Melo Drill." It was a king-of-the-court style, one-on-one game where the offensive player caught the ball on the wing and had three dribbles to score. He lovingly named the drill after that era's master of the jab step, Carmelo Anthony. Altman would serve as entry passer, score keeper, and MC. He would encourage the offensive players to "put 'em in the popcorn machine!" and made sure all the participants knew who had scored the most buckets. When a player got on a roll, Altman would start shouting "Reynolds!"—as in, that's a wrap.

Off the court, the UMass graduate program hooked Altman into a powerful network. His assigned mentor—Sean Ford, USA Basketball's Men's National Team Director—set up Altman with a summer job as manager for the gold medal-winning U19 National Team. That second summer, with grad school and the Amherst job behind him, felt rockier. Altman pieced together basketball camps to stay busy and stay connected, but during the downtime, he started questioning his decisions, wondering where he would land next.

Fortunately, through connections he made at USA Basketball, Altman managed to break into D1 basketball as an assistant coach. He was happy in the D1 world, but he pined for the NBA. When David Griffin, a Cavaliers executive he had gotten to know, offered him an internship with the video staff, Altman passed, but asked that Griffin please keep him in mind for anything bigger that might open up. Sure enough, the next summer the Cavs decided to add a pro personnel position.

Altman got the job. Twenty days a month, he would hit the road scouting NBA games. It was isolating work, far removed from the day-to-day interactions with players he so enjoyed. But it helped him quickly familiarize himself with the league.

After a year he was promoted to director of pro player personnel. He spent more time in the team offices, where he built strong relationships with both Griffin, who would eventually preside over his wedding, and team owner Dan Gilbert. "[Gilbert] always has been grooming me for upper management, which is huge," Altman said. "Obviously, you want diversity in your pipeline and you want to elevate from within. Those are nice things to say. The only way to do that, really, is to be in the room."

Altman sat in on hundreds of conversations. The subjects ranged from personnel to tax payments to investments to coaching hires. In the 2017 offseason, just one year removed from winning an NBA title, the Cavs failed to reach contract extensions with both Griffin and his top lieutenant, Trent Redden. To fill their empty GM seat, the team broke with league trends and courted recently retired player Chauncey Billups. Talks ultimately reached an impasse. All the while, the highest-ranking remaining member of the front office, Altman, called the shots. Eventually, Gilbert opted to officially name Altman the team's new GM.

His first six seasons as GM involved navigating a Kyrie Irving trade demand, one last trip to the NBA Finals, and a full rebuild. Through each challenge, Altman has repeatedly convinced Gilbert to sign off on aggressive and opportunistic deals. "What Division III and Middlebury gave me is the ability to make an argument and be able to negotiate with real sound data," Altman said. "And then get it to your owner so he can make it a reality by saying yes."

Altman is a successful GM today thanks to the traits he acquired on each step of his journey—the confidence of a New York City point guard, the leadership of a Posse scholar, the sound reasoning of a liberal arts student, the scouting knowhow of an Amherst assistant, and the many lessons he learned by having a seat at the table during a volatile period for an NBA franchise. But the missing ingredient—Altman's secret sauce—might have come from his time *away* from basketball. "The part that I think people miss is you have to have the negotiation savvy," he said. "How far can I take a negotiation to get to a point where it's actionable and then I can go to [Gilbert] and make it a reality?"

That process of back-and-forth conversations—understanding when the offer is ripe, and then selling it to the person who must ultimately sign off on the deal—bears a lot of similarities to the job of a real estate broker. As roles in basketball leadership, especially on the front-office side, have increased in complexity, it makes sense that experience in other competitive industries would prove beneficial.

Altman isn't alone in having both basketball and professional jobs on his resume. Leon Rose practiced law before blending his passion and expertise as an agent and GM. Brad Stevens, who transitioned from coaching to leading the Celtics front office in 2021, uses his brief time at Eli Lilly to inform his management style. "Anybody that's been in marketing would probably tell you they just hated the days when they see their entire day is all scheduled in meetings," Stevens said on the *Slappin' Glass Podcast*. "I like to communicate what's needed and give people the time to do their work appropriately."

Houston Rockets general manager Rafael Stone is another D3 alum who started his career outside of basketball. Like Altman, Stone is a biracial former point guard from a top liberal arts college. Stone, originally from Seattle, followed the advice of some high school counselors and visited Amherst and Williams on an East Coast college tour. He ultimately determined that Williams would put him in the best position to achieve what he wanted both athletically and academically. "I really wanted to keep playing," Stone said. "And that level of basketball was probably the right level for me."

According to Stone, Williams wasn't as integral to his growth as Middlebury was for Altman. He left with lifelong friends and a great education, but when it came to interacting with people from all walks of life, he already felt equipped. "I'm pretty comfortable no matter what situation you toss me in," Stone said. "There are definitely people I don't vibe with, but as far as people from different socioeconomic backgrounds, I grew up knowing people with all the money and people who had absolutely none of it and being comfortable. And my mom's White; my dad's Black. I've grown up with two very different communities that way."

After graduating from Williams in 1994, Stone figured law school was the next best step. He could keep forging ahead, while still calibrating what he actually wanted. Even though he was the son of a lawyer, he hadn't given the profession much thought. Since the age of 12, all Stone really wanted was to be an NBA general manager.

In the legal world, Stone, who oozes competitiveness and confidence, found a new game. He was good at it, and the rewards for winning were bountiful. "I was much more interested in being rich," Stone said. "I left basketball behind at that point in my life."

Stone became the youngest partner in his firm in 2005. A week later, the Rockets called. "The call literally came out of nowhere," Stone said. "They wanted a lawyer, and they wanted a really strong one evidently."

The Rockets brass also figured that, out of the pool of fast-rising attorneys, Stone's basketball background might make him more interested in the job. Three key things happened before Stone would agree to be the team's general counsel. First, the Rockets doubled the salary from their initial offer. Second, they agreed to Stone's provision that he would not be siloed off from basketball operations—he would handle all contracts and participate in collective bargaining agreement conversations. Third, Stone wanted to have a talk with the owner, Leslie Alexander. "You don't work for the president or the GM; you work for the owner," Stone said. "These businesses are owned by a guy. It's not the same as working at IBM or Microsoft. So that was an important part for me, and we hit it off right away."

Once he realized he would have the owner's support, Stone accepted the job. He figured, at the very least, it would be a fun break before jumping back to a law firm. "The appeal of the job was to get back into basketball, which I love," Stone said. "It put me in closer proximity [to a general manager role]. So if I'm as good as I think I am, I'll be able to carve out an opportunity at some point in time."

A year into Stone's tenure with the Rockets, Alexander hired Daryl Morey. When Morey took over the franchise's front office, it spelled trouble for many of the existing basketball operations folks. They were used to the tried-and-true process, and Morey was looking to shake things up. He and Stone, a fellow outsider, clicked right away. "To be frank, a lot of people were annoyed that I was involving a lawyer in stuff," Morey said. "To me, I'll just take smart, hard-working people wherever I can get them. I don't care how they came in the door. If you can add value, if you have good ideas, I'm going to use it. Just based on how confident and how good he was, that's what dictated that he got a bigger and bigger role over time."

According to Morey, Stone possessed a "killer combo" of skills—knowing basketball at a high-level, thanks in part to his experience as a player, and being a really smart negotiator, thanks to all of the deals he had orchestrated during his legal career. For 14 years, Stone worked in Morey's inner circle, helping him reshape the Rockets and, in many ways, the very game of basketball. Most of Morey's top capos moved to bigger positions with other teams, but Stone stayed put. When Morey's time ran out in Houston in 2020, Stone, then the executive vice president of basketball operations, was the natural successor.

Even though his journey to eventually living out his pre-teen GM dreams was circuitous and accidental, Stone actually sees it as making a ton of sense. When asked about his unconventional route to the GM seat, he said, "A lot of what we do is negotiating, and contracts, asset value, and stuff where, if you have a pure basketball background, you're not necessarily great at it. I think [my background] is more conventional than you think."

In a way, Stone is right. Altman, Rose, and Stevens also started their careers outside of basketball. Altman and Stevens, who both course corrected after just a year or two, came to the NBA armed with valuable basketball experience, impressive educations (augmented by special leadership programs), and short stints in the professional world.

Stone had a slightly different resume, one with a long track record of professional success, followed by an equally healthy dose of the NBA. It harkens back to the ABA era, when small-college guys like Scheer and Sonju imported their professional skills into pro basketball. It's just one of many ways the latest generation of D3 alums in the NBA contains echoes of the past.

DESPITE ALL OF his success, Stone still isn't even close to being the highest-paid Williams grad in basketball. That would be Duncan Robinson. "I always give [Stone] shit that he didn't transfer to Michigan," Morey said, "and become a player making $80 million in the NBA."

As a freshman, Robinson, a 6'8" wing with a deadly jumper, helped lead Williams to a D3 national title game appearance. When Robinson's coach, Mike Maker, took a D1 job that offseason, he set into motion a series of events that eventually led to Robinson transferring to University of Michigan, where he would play for Maker's old boss, John Beilein. A few solid Big Ten seasons and a stint in the G League later, Robinson was earning millions bombing threes for the Miami Heat.

In the early '90s, when Stone played at Williams, a tall tale about a player transferring from the NESCAC to the Big Ten would've been good for a few laughs during a team meal in the dining hall. If someone decided to take the story even further, and say that the player would carve out a long and lucrative NBA career after transferring, their teammates probably would've pelted them with whatever scraps of food were left on their tray.

A decade after Stone's time at Williams, when Altman played for Middlebury, most onlookers weren't confusing his games for the NBA on NBC. During a particularly dull Saturday afternoon affair between Middlebury and Bowdoin, one of the 15 or so fans in the stands decided to voice his displeasure. While Altman was lining up a free throw, the fan yelled, "Koby, you have been an epic disappointment!"

Disappointing or not, Altman's career did overlap with the New England Small College Athletic Conference's rise to national basketball prominence. In 2003, Altman's junior season, one in which he missed the entire first semester while studying abroad in Australia, Williams won the conference's first D3 national championship. Four years later, Amherst rode Andrew Olson to a title of their own.

But not everyone on NESCAC campuses was cheering the conference's athletic success.

In 2004, Middlebury president John McCardell helped draft several NCAA proposals whose purpose was to affirm that "athletics is not something one does apart from the rest of the collegiate enterprise." At the time, some NESCAC leaders even considered joining other like-minded schools around the country to create a Division IV. They hoped a separate division geared toward residential liberal arts colleges would free them from the arms race purported to be raging between the universities under the D3 umbrella. "I wouldn't say that NESCAC drifted away from the rest of

Division III," Andrea Savage, the conference's executive director, told *The Middlebury Campus*. "I would say that they have drifted away from us."

A few years before McCardell's proposals, Amherst rounded up a committee of professors, students, and trustees to take a holistic look at the role of athletics on campus. The 2002 study—titled "The Place of Athletics at Amherst College: A Question of Balance"—grappled with the fact that recruited athletes' median SAT scores were 120 points lower than non-athletes, and that non-athletes were complaining that a culture of "anti-intellectualism" among athletes was "devaluing their Amherst degrees."

After conducting dozens of interviews and having an economics professor crunch some numbers, the committee agreed upon the value of a successful athletic program. But they also acknowledged that success on the playing field comes at a cost. The committee proposed, among other items, that the school place more of an emphasis on racial and socioeconomic diversity in athletics. They also implored administration to work with the NESCAC to reduce and standardize the number of each team's "slots"—free passes through admissions for slightly less-qualified students. Finally, to avoid the temptation of competing with colleges that might have different priorities, they strongly recommended actively pursuing the formation of a Division IV.

Ultimately, NESCAC schools did not deprioritize athletics to the extent that McCardell and the Amherst committee recommended. Without a D4 of their own to call home, the conference evolved into one of the nation's premiere D3 basketball leagues, regularly receiving multiple at-large bids to the NCAA Tournament.

Ivy League basketball has also improved over the last decade, attracting more talented players than ever before. The deeper and more competitive Ivies are squeezing high-academic basketball players who may have previously joined their ranks down to the D3 level, with many heading to the NESCAC. Starting around 2010, many Ivy League coaching staffs began hosting prospect camps on their campuses. The summer clinics draw kids from all over the country. NESCAC coaches flock to the camps in droves. "Our access to watch players who are academically qualified and really good has never been at this level," said Wesleyan University coach Joe Reilly, who has coached in the NESCAC for over 25 years. "It's because of the Ivy League camps."

Over the last 15 years, the NESCAC's improvement as a basketball conference coincided with a shift in the NBA's idea of a prototypical GM or coach. As a result, the elite New England colleges have formed a special branch of the D3-to-NBA pipeline, one that continues to grow.

DUNCAN ROBINSON ACTUALLY had his sights set on the NBA from the moment he enrolled at Williams. He knew all about the former D3 players working in the league and hoped a successful career at Williams would unlock a front-office internship or job in the video room. *Man, this is awesome,* Robinson thought. *I have the opportunity to play basketball at a high level and then also get exposed to a network that can potentially get me access to the NBA.*

When Robinson transferred to Michigan, he found himself in a starkly different basketball situation. If he wanted to get shots up, there was always an open gym with a student manager eager to rebound. For his teammates, schoolwork took a backseat to basketball—if it even had a seat at all. It was a stark contrast to Williams, where his friends eschewed summers in the gym for competitive corporate internships. Every now and then, as he shot around in Michigan's pristine facility, Robinson would think of his first collegiate game at Williams, when an NCAA Tournament volleyball match forced his team to play at a neutral site off-campus.

Robinson's ascension to the NBA did a lot to validate the talent at the D3 level. In his one season at Williams, he averaged 17 points per game—solid numbers that put him on a trajectory to be one of the level's best, but nothing that indicated a LeBron James vs. preschoolers type of situation. Other D3 players piggybacked off of his success and signed G League contracts, although none have joined Robinson in the NBA (…yet).

In 2020, the year Robinson signed his $90 million dollar contract, Rafael Stone took over as the Houston Rockets general manager. The next season, Will Hardy accepted the Utah Jazz head coaching job. The trio made Williams the first D3 school that could boast an NBA player, head coach, and general manager as alums.

One of Williams' longtime rivals, Wesleyan University in Connecticut, had an impressive claim to fame of their own. In 2021, Wesleyan alum Jordan Sears won a championship ring as a video coordinator with the

Milwaukee Bucks. The year before that, a fellow alum, Greg St. Jean, got a ring of his own as a behind-the-bench assistant coach for the Los Angeles Lakers.

If the name Greg St. Jean sounds familiar, it's because he is the son of former Sacramento Kings head coach and Golden State Warriors general manager Garry St. Jean.

Second-generation NBA employees like St. Jean, Donnie Nelson and Jeff Weltman are peppered throughout the D3 pipeline to the NBA. In 2021, another legacy, Wes Unseld Jr., became head coach of the Washington Wizards. Unseld Jr., a Johns Hopkins alum, is the son of Hall of Fame center Wes Unseld. Unseld Jr.'s ascension is notable in several respects—he is the first D3 alum with an NBA father to be named a head coach and he is the first Black D3 alum to serve as head coach on a non-interim basis. To the uninformed, Unseld Jr.'s story might reek of nepotism. Like Donnie Nelson and Jeff Weltman, he leapt directly from a D3 college to the NBA at a time when that was incredibly rare. He is, after all, the son of one of D.C. basketball's most beloved icons, a man who won a Finals MVP and later served as the then-Bullets head coach and general manager.

But that charge of nepotism would ignore the 24 years Unseld Jr. grinded away, beginning with stints in some of the more grueling NBA jobs—personnel scout and advanced scout. It would disregard the fact that, as he started making a name for himself as a Denver Nuggets assistant coach, Unseld Jr. unsuccessfully interviewed for at least five jobs before landing the Wizards position. It would turn a blind eye to the unsolicited endorsements the Wizards received from the Nuggets head coach, team president, and several players, including Nikola Jokic and Jamal Murray. And perhaps most importantly, it would ignore the bias persistent throughout league history against Black coaching candidates who never played in the NBA.

At Johns Hopkins, Unseld Jr. left his mark on and off the court, overcoming a torn ACL that truncated his sophomore season. In 1997, he graduated in the top 15 in program history in points, free throws made, minutes played, rebounds, steals, and field-goal percentage. Most of all, Unseld Jr. impressed others with his maturity. "Wes was the adult in the room," said Bill Nelson, Unseld Jr.'s coach at Johns Hopkins. "What's the old saying? 'The best thing about a freshman is they become sophomores?' Well, Wes came in as a sophomore."

It's certainly fair to argue that without the cache of the Unseld name in D.C., Wes Jr. would still be working as an assistant coach, waiting for his opportunity. Nepotism in a world like the NBA is a bit more complex than in other, less public professions. NBA fathers can pass down knowledge and open up opportunities. They provide a head start, but it is only a few miles into an ultramarathon.

If anybody would besmirch a legacy for how easily they got into the league, it would be Frank Vogel, who had to sacrifice so much and take so many risks just for a shot at a video coordinator job. Instead, he focuses more on just how much work legacies have to put in to get to the top. "Maybe somebody gets a door open because he's somebody's son or because he played," Vogel said. "I don't hold it against people in any way because once they get there, if they don't do the work and they don't know what the fuck they're talking about, they're going to fall right out of it. So I feel like everybody who has succeeded has grinded the way that I grinded."

Vogel practiced what he preached when he hired Greg St. Jean onto his Lakers staff in 2020. St. Jean landed with the Lakers through a mishmash of connections—he and Vogel shared an agent, and St. Jean's dad had coached Kurt Rambis, the man who endorsed Vogel for the Lakers job.

Growing up, St. Jean spent so many years as a Warriors ballboy, his dad thinks he might've broken a record. On weekends, Garry would bribe Greg with candy and popcorn to get him into the office for some quality time. Sometimes Garry would look up, and Greg would be gone. He would inevitably turn up on the court, where he would be running through drills with Chris Mullin and Mitch Richmond. Most young basketball players are lucky if they have a coach who can teach them some effective plays. Then there was Greg, who learned the Princeton offense from its inventor, Pete Carril.

Economist David Laband, who helped explain how the Van Gundy brothers acquired valuable human capital from their dad, believes that a childhood spent observing the pros and cons of an NBA lifestyle serves as a sort of screening process. Some sons may see how hard Dad needs to work in order to succeed as an NBA coach and decide it's not the life for them.

"On the other hand," Laband said, "if you have a complete picture of what it takes to be a successful ball coach, and you say, 'Not only can I do that, but I can do it pretty well and thrive in it,' then you have a real advantage over someone who just walks in the door."

When he began to seriously consider a coaching career, Greg's mother sat him down and explained to him the strain the profession can put on a family. It was one of a handful of ways he was able to observe what Laband refers to as the "dark side of the force." Gene DeFilippo, Garry St. Jean's dear friend and college roommate, had a similar interpretation. "Greg grew up in the fire," DeFilippo said. "He couldn't leave the fire. I think it's a tremendous advantage."

When it came time for college, Greg knew he wanted to continue playing basketball. Based on his skill level and academic profile, he zeroed in on the NESCAC. On his visit to Wesleyan, Greg told the coach, Joe Reilly, that he ultimately wanted to work in the NBA. So Reilly worked with Greg to formulate a plan. "If a guy wants to get into finance, we're going to find a mentor for him to learn more about the finance world and to try to get the network established," Reilly said. "For a kid who wants to get into coaching, the first step for us is to loop him into what we're doing."

During the season, Greg would visit Reilly's office almost daily, where they would experiment with new plays and counters on a magnetic coaching board. In the offseason, when contact is restricted between players and coaches, Greg would run workouts, which helped him establish his coaching voice.

Occasionally, future Orlando Magic GM Rob Hennigan, then with the Oklahoma City Thunder, would email NESCAC coaches like Reilly and ask if they had any candidates for internships. With Reilly's blessing, Greg began contacting Hennigan and Sam Presti, hoping the D3 network could help augment his father's NBA connections.

Greg began his NBA career in the video room with one of his dad's old teams, the Kings. Greg is very open and almost apologetic about the inherent advantage he had. "I'm not naive," he said. "I was given an opportunity because of my last name."

A few stops later, he was in L.A. with Vogel on his way to winning a championship. One of his responsibilities with the Lakers was to decipher the other team's hand signal, formation, or play call, and then yell out whatever action the defense should expect. Most of the time, he could tip off LeBron James or Rajon Rondo and help them jump the play. But one time, Denver coach Michael Malone called a brand new play Greg had never seen. When Rondo looked to the bench, Greg had to shrug. Rondo then shot a dirty glare to James, who slumped his shoulders in disappointment. Greg sunk down into his seat, realizing just how high the expectations were when coaching basketball geniuses.

To keep improving, Greg aggressively sought out advice wherever he could find it. He went to Vogel to find out about how to establish a coaching presence out of the video room. He spoke with other coach's sons, like David Adelman, Coby Karl, and Casey Hill, to ask how to embrace their father's legacies while also stepping out of their shadows. And he continued to build and develop connections with other D3 alums, especially those from the NESCAC.

There's a stark difference between D3 alums who graduated in the 2000s and their older counterparts. Even though he's as proud a D3 booster as there could be, Jeff Van Gundy was surprised when he was told the number of D3 coaches and executives in the league. Rafael Stone was unaware of the fact that Chris Finch, with whom he overlapped in the Rockets organization for seven seasons, played D3 ball. Meanwhile, Greg can rattle off D3 head coaches, GMs, and assistants as if he was reading off of a cheat sheet.

It helps that the D3 world is smaller and more accessible than ever before. Thanks to Pat Coleman and Dave McHugh, the men behind the essential website D3Hoops.com, the sport is covered professionally and extensively. There are podcasts dedicated to D3 basketball, Twitter accounts that regularly share clips and insights, individuals who crank out D3 analytics and win probabilities, and resources that help prospective student-athletes navigate D3 recruiting and admissions. Most games stream online, making it easier for alums to stay connected and for D3 junkies to watch the best teams from around the country. "You get a great sense of what level of basketball it is," said Reilly, Wesleyan's coach. "You used to have to drive to see it or you'd be watching the game on someone's camcorder, and someone's head with a baseball cap is in the way half the time."

When he could find the time in between his busy coaching schedule, Greg would watch webcasts of Wesleyan games from across the country. One player in particular, Jordan Sears, stood out as an impactful defender. Besides that, Greg knew nothing about the kid. Then his old coach reached out with a request.

When Greg was seeking out NBA opportunities, he sent plenty of emails and messages that went unanswered, even with his recognizable last name. Now that he's on the inside, he's hoping to do whatever he can to help guide the next generation of prospective coaches. He's especially drawn to people like him—D3 players or D1 student managers—anyone who has shown a willingness to do hard, unglamorous work. "I'm going to bet on that small-college guy because in the fall, in the spring, and in the summer in Division III, there is no coach," St. Jean said. "They're not allowed to work with the players. You've got to work with yourself. You've got to come back at night and get shots for yourself. You have no rebounders. You rebound for each other. So any job you're going to give them, more likely than not they're not feeling entitled to it."

St. Jean is also conscious of how that bias toward the D3 guy could set himself up to making a crucial hiring mistake. He is well aware of the importance of the type of diversity that helped make the San Antonio Spurs such a potent organization. "It's not just diversity of race, diversity of gender, diversity of experience," he said. "It's also diversity of thought and mentality, trying to find that blend and figure out how we can give opportunities to those who might not get one if we don't do a little digging on our end."

Unlike Greg, Sears enrolled at Wesleyan with every expectation of going into business. Basketball, he figured, would only last another four years. Then he'd head off to the real world. During his senior season, a year in which Sears took a tremendous leap on the court en route to winning the 2018 NESCAC Defensive Player of the Year, he started spending more and more time devouring film in the basketball office. He also became conscious of people like him who were excelling in the world of basketball. "You start to see the Prestis, the Koby Altmans, a couple of the other lesser-known guys in our conference specifically, all working in the NBA," Sears said. "And obviously Greg St. Jean was always around our program."

In February, with his senior season nearly finished, Sears looked at Reilly during one of those film sessions and said, "Coach, I'm not ready to give this up. I'm loving this side of it."

So Reilly texted Greg, who, before his time with the Lakers, was coaching at St. John's University under Chris Mullin. Greg spoke with Sears, encouraged him to apply for a graduate assistant role at St. John's, and then hired him.

Sears lasted just one season at St. John's before Mullin and his staff were let go. While Greg was scrambling to make his way back into the NBA, he worked just as hard on Sears' behalf. Greg landed in L.A. with Vogel, and Sears ended up in the Bucks video room. As a former D3 player, Sears fit right in. Both the head video coordinator (Blaine Mueller) and the head coach (Mike Budenholzer) were also D3 alums.

Since Budenholzer had come up as a video coordinator himself, he held the group to the highest of standards. It wasn't out of the ordinary to receive a 2:00 AM text message asking for new clips to be organized and trimmed in time for that morning's practice. When he wasn't editing and tagging film, Sears, who is 6'5" with long arms and tremendous defensive instincts, also proved valuable during practice. He could hop into drills and reasonably simulate an NBA wing defender, affording him the opportunity to get reps working with players.

During one scrimmage with a few members of the team, Sears threw down a lob dunk. Everyone in the gym went bonkers. It's a moment that will literally stay with Sears for as long as he's alive. "The players, they gas you up, they shit talk in general either way, so it's pretty funny," Sears said. "But that's the thing: you're the video guy. You can actually manage the clip. You can grab the clip and hold onto it forever."

In 2021, Sears landed the head video coordinator job with the Dallas Mavericks. Once again, the assist went to Greg St. Jean, who had joined the Mavericks after his time with the Lakers and recommended Sears for the opening. Two years later, Sears took over as head coach of the Texas Legends, the Mavericks' G League affiliate. As his coaching star rises, Sears hasn't forgotten his D3 roots. Like Greg, he, too, can rattle off the D3 alums, and NESCAC guys in particular, working their way up in front offices and coaching staffs around the league.

Sears is also conscious of the role he can play in showing young people of color that, even though they weren't good enough to play in the NBA, they can still find a home in the league. He speaks to the importance of reaching kids earlier in their college careers and providing guidance and access to an expanded network. "What you see in the NBA, whether it's front offices, video rooms, whatever it may be, is that it's overwhelmingly White," Sears said. "I would say the tables are turning a little bit in that regard. It's more so just spreading knowledge and outreach. We don't have as many connections as White people do traditionally, especially when we're not the ones who are playing."

Sears is correct—the tables are beginning to turn. In 2023, for the first time in NBA history, White head coaches were in the minority. When it comes to mirroring the demographics on the court, however, front offices are still a ways away. As of 2023, seven of the league's front-office leads are people of color. Of those seven, two—Altman and Stone—played D3 basketball. Growing up, Altman only had one role model for a Black front-office lead who never played in the NBA—Bernie Bickerstaff. Seeing a fellow D3 guy like Presti helped him start to believe. "When [Presti] achieved that goal, it gave me hope that I could achieve that goal," Altman said. "Even though he doesn't look like me, we had the same experience."

Stone, who joined the Rockets prior to Presti becoming a GM, is both hopeful and pragmatic about the future for other aspiring Black executives. "I'm definitely going to do what I can, but you also just have to live in the world you live in," Stone said. "Just because your hill is a lot higher doesn't mean you don't climb it."

Presti, among others, gave D3 alums hope that one day they, too, could work in the NBA. Altman, Stone, and Unseld Jr., as well as up-and-coming leaders like Sears, are providing a different kind of D3 representation. They are showing the next generation that you don't need to look like the team owner to be able to speak their language. Both explicitly and implicitly, they are doing their part to convey that the NBA has a place for the hardest working and brightest basketball minds, regardless of skin color or playing background.

IN THE LAST decade, Division III alums have built a sturdy, covered bridge to help protect other small-college players on their journey to the pros. As this newest generation of D3 grads grows into bigger roles, they continue to mine talent from colleges like their own. Tom Thibodeau and Mike Budenholzer both spent time grooming Matt Bollero, the DePauw grad who worked in the Milwaukee Bucks and Minnesota Timberwolves front offices before breaking off to start his own sports agency. Wherever Bollero ends up, he will undoubtedly hire and mentor former D3 players. "If you're a Division III student-athlete and you have some fairly good recommendations or work experience," Bollero said, "you're going to get, whether it's for internships or lower-level positions, an extra check mark."

Leon Rose mentored Austin Brown, now the cohead of CAA's basketball business and, like Bollero, a DePauw basketball alum. Brown, who worked in investment banking and earned a law degree prior to jumping into the player representation business, is now one of the top five NBA agents in terms of player salary. His clients include Zion Williamson, Donovan Mitchell, and Jaren Jackson Jr. According to Brown, his D3 playing days are integral to his success.

"You see guys at the Division III level who have superior basketball IQs because you have to think the game the right way," said Brown, who is rumored to be a likely candidate to one day hop over to the team side.

Brown found that, even though his career peaked at D3, he's still able to talk the game. As a result, he can relate to both his clients and the teams he's negotiating with better than a rival agent who never played at a high level. "Just to have that kind of connectivity and understanding has been super beneficial for me," Brown said.

Today's young D3 alums are finding more opportunities than ever to show off their basketball acumen in the NBA ecosystem. Sure, more D3 players are leading basketball operations and coaching staffs, but the widening and lengthening of NBA organizational charts is equally important. Now, there are D3 alums in the middle and lower rungs of coaching staffs and front offices across the league. Generally, they are more than happy to help guide a fellow D3 grad to one of many entry-level jobs. When Koby Altman was coming up, it might've been hard for him to just pick up the phone and call the general manager of the Oklahoma City Thunder. But now Sam Presti has D3 alums up and down his staff, who might be more inclined to spend 20 minutes on the phone with a student-athlete from their school or their conference. "At each level you can find that person to reach out to," Altman said. "It was so daunting to be like, 'Okay, how do I get to Sam [Presti]?' Now, I don't necessarily have to get to Sam. Maybe I just reach out to Glenn [Wong, an Amherst graduate and Thunder chief of staff]."

There are also more opportunities than ever for current D3 players to build connections with NBA head coaches and executives. Many are active alums who donate time and money to their alma maters. Altman is on the

Middlebury Board of Trustees and has called recruits to help lure them to the college. Brad Stevens holds preseason Zoom Q&As with the DePauw basketball team. Jeff Van Gundy and his wife paid for new locker rooms for the Nazareth men's and women's basketball teams. Van Gundy's support also extends far beyond just writing a check. Unsurprisingly, he has been quick to reach out on behalf of former Nazareth players who are looking for coaching opportunities. He watches games online and provides informed feedback during his regular chats with the team. "The first time he ever talked to my team," said Nazareth head coach Kevin Broderick, "I remember our best player was Steve Gabel, and he said, 'I watch the games. Gabel, if you're not going to defensive rebound better, we're not going to win a championship. Let's start there.'"

Even if there isn't that alumni connection, with more D3 grads doing the hiring, a small-college playing background in and of itself can be enough to qualify for a competitive entry level NBA job. Plus, as more D3 players become aware of others like them spreading throughout the league, more will chase after a job that, even 10 or 15 years ago, might've seemed like a fairy tale.

The journey of one current NBA mid-level executive (who, showing that trademark D3 humility, asked to remain anonymous) best illustrates the new reality. As a D3 student-athlete, the future executive realized that the Thunder GM had played D3, just like him. He did more research, had more conversations, and ultimately figured that maybe he, too, could work in the NBA. To prove how serious he was, he volunteered as a video coordinator for his school's men's and women's team…while also playing for the men's team. If he attended a D1 school, they would've already had a dedicated video coordinator, and he wouldn't have had time during the season to take on two jobs. Instead, he was able to add some unique bullets to his resume, all because he played D3.

When a D3 alum working for an NBA team reviewed the anonymous future executive's application and read about the triple duty he pulled during the season, the team scheduled him for an interview. They subsequently hired him as an intern. He's been in the league for more than a decade now, and is well on his way to one day leading a team of his own.

By the early 2020s, the D3 pipeline was complete. The combination of a top-notch education and a still-pretty-decent basketball experience has proved itself to be an ideal training ground for today's NBA. D3 athletic programs are no-scholarship and no-frill. The reward for playing a D3 sport is almost entirely intrinsic. It's an environment that self-selects athletes with a deep passion for their game of choice. That love is often strong enough to propel a young person through the NBA's entry levels, with their long hours of grunt work and very little pay. Anecdotally, D3 programs are also teeming with athletes who fit the more modern profile of a leader—humble, diligent, open-minded, prideful, and full of humanity, like Brad Stevens and Frank Vogel.

Several recent developments have made the NBA more hospitable to former D3 players. Coaching and front-office staff sizes are growing. That, paired with the newer G League affiliations, has increased the number of potential entry points. Also, with changes in ownership and advances in basketball analytics, fewer teams are hiring former players as GMs, opening up more opportunities to D3 alums at the very top. But even with the increase in jobs and potential for advancement, former D3 players still require a hiring manager to take their background seriously. This latest and greatest influx began just before the turn of the century when, through hard work, immense ability, and fortuitous connections, a few pioneers managed to break into the league. They then hired other D3 grads, who subsequently landed leadership opportunities of their own. The ripple effects of Jeff Van Gundy and Gregg Popovich's success continue to emanate throughout the league.

In previous eras, a former small-college player's coaching or management career would go only as far as the connections they made and the skills they acquired. Today, those hoping to work in the NBA benefit from a rather shocking development—by simply playing basketball at certain D3 schools, they inherently have both the valued skills *and* the necessary proximity to power required to land one of the league's coveted jobs.

D3 alums in the head coaching ranks peaked in 2019, at eight. Numbers remain strong. Entering the 2023–24 season, there were six former D3 players serving as head coach. These six coaches—Tom Thibodeau, Steve Clifford, Frank Vogel, Will Hardy, Chris Finch, and Wes Unseld Jr.—all traveled very different paths from their D3 school to the NBA. They are living proof of the many viable entry points available to today's aspiring coaches.

Meanwhile, D3 representation in the basketball executive ranks is peaking. The 2023–24 season is the fourth in a row with six D3 alums running a franchise's basketball operations. Interestingly enough, the paths they are taking resemble the same ones small-college alums have been walking since the pre-D3 days. Presti and Jeff Weltman followed in Bob Whitsitt's footsteps, joining the NBA right after school and learning from the ground up. Stevens followed in Garry St. Jean's footsteps, turning a coaching career into one as a front-office lead. Rose and Rafael Stone parlayed legal careers into GM jobs, just like Carl Scheer. And Altman—who worked in business like Norm Sonju, assisted on college staffs like John Hammond, and then bounced around different front office roles like Whitsitt—took a little bit from all three. The journeys look the same, but with ownership now more open to different backgrounds, there are more opportunities than ever for former D3 players.

Those D3 alums who now preside over NBA organizations embrace diversity as a competitive advantage. They are changing NBA hiring—not by exclusively hiring others with backgrounds like theirs—but by opening their doors to a wider array of candidates. Succeeding because of (and not in spite of) an unconventional background can prompt someone to target and develop other talented men and women who might be hiding in plain sight. In his long tenure leading the Thunder, Presti has taken a page out of the old San Antonio Spurs playbook. He built a diverse staff, filling his front office and coaching bench with everyone from women to former NBA journeymen to ex-bloggers to, of course, D3 alums. In a story written by The Athletic's Erik Horne, Presti referred to his organization's diversity as a "catalyst," something that is "a means to an end" and "not the end itself." Altman concurred. "The thing that Sam did, and we're doing as well here, is to look across the spectrum of talent that we can get," Altman said. "Certainly, Division III talent, whether you played there or coached there, brings a lot to the table. Part of a diverse staff is the level of where they played in college."

Before flying the "Mission Accomplished" banner, it's important to remember how quickly preferences shift in a copycat league like the NBA. Dynasties crumble, others rise up in their stead, and the blueprint for success suddenly looks a lot different. Even if the D3 background is now so prevalent as to be impossible to fully eradicate, there are still risks upstream.

Even the sturdiest of pipelines can spring a leak, preventing the flow of materials from one end to the other.

A variety of forces can throw the D3 world, with its ideal blend of basketball and academics, off-kilter. Administrators at top liberal arts schools can make another push to deprioritize athletics, which, if successful, could cause the basketball-loving kids who grow into NBA leaders to go elsewhere. The professionalization of D1 football and basketball, whose television and tournament proceeds help fund D3 tournaments, could trickle down and adversely impact the D3 experience. Or, perhaps NIL money, growing social media followings, and the trappings of the modern-athlete experience could chip away at that trademark D3 humility.

If the pipeline were to burst, sending D3 alums once headed for the NBA spraying across basketball's lower levels, all hope would not be lost. Years of evidence and dozens of examples have proven one simple fact— former D3 basketball players have a place in the NBA.

Even if macro forces clog up today's shortcuts, there is a particular road to success that can never be completely barricaded. To create a pipeline, sometimes all it takes are a few individuals who manage to get themselves in front of powerful decision makers and accumulate the right skills to impress those gatekeepers. The entryways and their keys have changed over the last seven decades, but, as much as the NBA has evolved, who gets to work in the league has always boiled down to talent and connections. And not always in that order.

EPILOGUE

One summer day, sometime between his 2007 National Championship and his 2013 National Championship, Amherst College basketball coach David Hixon was mowing his lawn when he felt a buzz in his pocket. Normally, he would've ignored the call, but something about the mysterious number from Oklahoma implored him to turn off the mower and answer.

On the other line was Sam Presti, general manager of the Oklahoma City Thunder. Hixon and Presti were familiar with each other—Hixon had actually coached against Presti when he played for Emerson—but this was unexpected. Presti was calling to ask Hixon his opinion on a former Amherst graduate assistant who was a final candidate for a role with the Thunder. The call was a little muffled, but Hixon assumed he knew about whom Presti was asking. Hixon started into his spiel, Presti asked some follow-up questions, and then the pair realized something—they were talking about two different people. So the Thunder decided to interview both. Neither of the former graduate assistants ended up landing that particular job, but they both went on to work in the NBA shortly thereafter.

Over the course of the 2010s and into 2020, Hixon gradually started to notice the once-gargantuan gap between his program and the NBA shrinking. In October of 2022, he traveled down to Oklahoma City for a Thunder preseason exhibition against Maccabi Ra'anana, a top Israeli team. One of his former players, Willy Workman, had carved out a 10-year career in Israel and was one of Ra'anana's starting forwards. On the Thunder side, two recent Amherst alums—assistant coach Connor Johnson and basketball operations chief of staff Glenn Wong—worked in Presti's organization. After the game, the group of Amherst alums now living this pro basketball life enjoyed a dinner with their college coach.

Then, in March of 2023, Hixon traveled down to Houston for the Division I Final Four. Throughout his career, Hixon, along with most college coaches, made the annual pilgrimage to the Final Four to network and attend National Association of Basketball Coaches meetings. This trip, however, was different. Hixon received a call earlier that week that his presence was requested for a ceremony to officially announce his acceptance into the Naismith Basketball Hall of Fame. He became the first coach enshrined in Springfield for accomplishments at the D3 level.

The Hall of Fame Class of '23 was full of superstars with D3 ties: Dirk Nowitzki, who was drafted by Donnie Nelson; Dwyane Wade, who was drafted by Randy Pfund and first coached by Stan Van Gundy; Tony Parker, the pick that helped put Sam Presti on the map, and Gregg Popovich, the former D3 coach who would go down as one of the game's best ever. During his acceptance speech, Popovich wondered aloud about how he ended up on that stage, receiving the highest honor in basketball. "It's hard to describe," Popovich said. "Because I'm a Division III guy. Guys like Coach Hixon are my idols. That's real basketball."

Hixon's Amherst roommates, teammates, former assistants, and former players all joined him to celebrate his induction. Koby Altman—Hixon's graduate assistant who, no matter how high he ascended, never turned down an opportunity to give back—was there. So was Andrew Olson, a top player in program history, who was now also with the Cleveland Cavaliers, thanks to Altman.

In his 40-plus years, Hixon had his fair share of players come through the program who were natural coaches but decided to pursue other careers. A humble life coaching prep school or small-college ball often didn't stand a chance against the allure of a high-paying career or the obligation the young men felt to use their Amherst degree to pursue some combination of money and status. When they would come back to campus as young professionals or middle-aged men with kids of their own, Hixon would size them up in their button downs and slacks and think about how unnatural it looked, about how they belonged in warmup pants and a T-shirt, whistles around their necks.

Hixon figured Olson would be another one of those alums, a born coach who put his aptitude for the game aside in the pursuit of the almighty dollar. But this was a new era, one in which a former D3 player could realistically find a home at the game's highest level. The pipeline to the pros changed the old career calculus. These competitors, who couldn't get enough of the game and didn't mind their time in the fire, could now access base camp. Whether or not they would make it to the summit would take some skill and a whole lot of luck. But they were just happy to finally have a place among the game's very best, to get their chance to show the world, and more importantly, themselves, that a small-college kid could be capable of big things. To prove what everyone in the D3 community already knew—these nobodies were somebody special.

ACKNOWLEDGMENTS

The seeds of this book were first planted in 1995, when Joanne Dages forced us to be friends. The Parkins family had just moved into town, and Joanne told her eight-year-old son, Matt, and his best bud, Ben, that they were to hang out with the new kid named Danny. Thus began a friendship between not only the three of us, but also our parents and siblings. Only one word can sufficiently describe that bond: family.

To our agent, Joe Perry, who answered a cold email from a nobody pitching a memoir centered around Division III basketball and, for whatever reason, decided to respond, thank you for helping us shape this idea into its final form, iterate on the proposal, and guide us through the literary world.

To the team at Triumph, Jeff Fedotin, Josh Williams, and everyone behind the scenes, thank you for taking a chance on us and believing that a Division III book would have an audience.

As a couple of newbies, we required plenty of help and handholding from people who were not professionally connected to this project in any way. Fortunately, we encountered a bunch of generous folks who were happy to help. Thank you to all the coaches, executives, coworkers, and friends who took the time to answer our questions. Thank you to everyone who helped introduce us to interview subjects—K.C. Johnson, Adam Lefkoe, Nick Wright, Nick Friedell, Tim Frank, Brian Baskauskas, James Romey (hockey assist), Stacey Moragne, Yaron Weitzman, Peter and Julia Steinberger, Bill Nelson, Kevin Broderick, Bill Fenlon, Lorn Foster, David Hixon, John Halas, Joe Reilly, and Matt Bollero. We were also lucky to speak with several writers who generously shared advice and feedback throughout the research and writing process. Thank you Jeff Passan, Damon Agnos, John Lombardo, Chris Herring, Chris Ballard, Seth Partnow, Mirin Fader, and Pete Croatto.

We would thank the Stains, but since most of you have so generously assured us that, even though you'd buy the book, you probably wouldn't read it, we don't want to waste the ink.

Second-to-last, but certainly not second-to-least, thank you to our families. To our wives, Alex and Steph, thank you for encouraging us, for picking up the parenting slack, and for saying you'll still love us, even if the book sells nine copies. To our boys, Cade, Coley, James, Owen, and Eli, thank you for playing nicely (most of the time) while your dad conducted interviews, read old newspaper articles, and edited rough drafts. To our moms, Nancy and Patti, and our sisters, Alyson, Megan, and Amy, thank you for your endless love and support.

Most of all, we wanted to thank this book. Thank you, book, for giving us an excuse to interview so many impressive and fascinating people. Thank you, book, for providing a distraction from the illness and loss our families faced these past few years. And thank you, book, for the opportunity to work on a fun project with an old pal.

Sources

Unless cited below or otherwise noted in the text, all quotations are from interviews conducted by the authors between May of 2022 and July of 2023. All coach and executive charts showing information pertaining to the head coach or lead basketball executive, who oversaw each team for all or a majority of a given season, are from Basketball Reference.

Prologue
"Oh well..." *Bubbleball*, Ben Golliver

Chapter One
"Go out there and don't let me..." "Growing to Greatness" *Sports Illustrated*, William Leggett, 10/29/62
"Ask anybody around here..." *100 Things Lakers Fans Should Know Before They Die*, Steve Springer
"West would have been in a position..." *The Whittier News*, 9/21/60, p. 11
"not necessarily for the team..." "St. Thomas' 1960s connection to LA Lakers" 2017 Tommie-Johnnie Football Program
"Too bad he didn't score five fewer points..." *Tall Tales*, Terry Pluto
"The salaries you pay the Jerry Wests..." *100 Things Lakers Fans Should Know Before They Die*, Steve Springer
"Don't sign anyone..." "Morning Briefing" *Los Angeles Times*, 12/9/84, p. 2
"His statistics last year showed..." "Lakers Buy Don Nelson From Bullets" *Los Angeles Evening Citizen News*, 9/6/63, p. 14
"That son of a gun came in with literally..." *Jerry West: The Life and Legend of a Basketball Icon*, Ronald Lazenby

Chapter Two
"I have half a mind I want to…" *Cavs From Fitch to Fratello: The Sometimes Miraculous, Often Hilarious, Wild Ride of the Cleveland Cavaliers*, Joe Menzer and Burt Graeff
"I'm your coach, Bill Fitch." *When the Game Was Ours*, Larry Bird, Magic Johnson, Jackie MacMullan
"the most lopsided in history" *The Selling of the Green: The Financial Rise and Moral Decline of the Boston Celtics*, Harvey Araton and Filip Bondy
"Our goal in 1983 wasn't to…" *When the Game Was Ours*, Larry Bird, Magic Johnson, Jackie MacMullan
"by far the best coach I've…" "Bill Fitch, Hall of Fame coach who rebuilt the Rockets into 1986 NBA finalists, dies at 89" *Houston Chronicle*, Jonathan Feigen, 2/3/22

Chapter Three
"I've got no idea what marijuana…" "Taking Over" *The Charlotte Observer*, Frank Barrows, 8/9/70, p. 4D
"We wanted to get the best man…" "Ex-NBA Man As New GM" *The Charlotte Observer*, Harry Lloyd, 7/15/70, p. 19
"Next time, you guys will come to me…" "How Early Hornets Architect Carl Scheer Left a Lasting Legacy on All-Star Weekend" NBA.com, Sam Perley, 2/15/19
"Dealing with Donald was impossible…" "Proposed Celtics Trade Could Send Rivers to the Clippers" *The New York Times*, 6/17/13

Chapter Four
"Montclair State made so much sense…" "Playing to Win" *Montclair*, Steve Politi, Spring 2014
"We see the NCAA…" "NCAA Reorganization Gains Support At Convention" *The Asheville Citizen*, Herschel Nissenson, 1/6/72
"Why should Michigan…" "Sports Seen" *The Daily Dispatch*, Paul Carlson, 1/26/73

Chapter Five
"I wasn't a chemistry major..." *Jail Blazers*, Kerry Eggers
"I was so impressed with his energy..." "Whozit? Whitsitt?" *The News Tribune*, Mike Kahn, 10/29/86
"Bob was by far the best one..." *Ibid*
"Bob walked in here very organized..." "Whitsitt's super Sonics job" *The News Tribune*, Mike Kahn, 5/11/87
Marty Blake called the odds against Kemp "astronomical" *Hoops Heist*, Jon Finkel

Chapter Six
"I had the chance..." "A D-III School's NBA Crusade" D3Hoops.com, Jason Bailey, 7/1/06

Chapter Seven
"owner of the boards" "'Canes Stun Hartford As Mel Kline Scores 29" *Hartford Courant*, Woody Anderson, 2/11/76
"schleps with a D3 background" "How Stan and Jeff Van Gundy Became an influential duo on and off the court" *New York Business Journal*, John Lombardo and John Ourand, 10/18/17

Chapter Eight
"The X's and O's are the same..." "Coach Learns From Hoop Giants" *Los Angeles Times*, Gary Klein, 2/26/87
"The small-college level is the place..." *Ibid*
"My whole life, I've been taught...""The ballad of Larry Brown, Pop and the Kansas staff that changed basketball" *The Athletic*, Rustin Dodd, CJ Moore, Alex Schiffer, 7/10/20
"I'm delighted..." "Ex-Pitzer Cage Coach Taking Shot at Pros" *Los Angeles Times*, Mitch Polin, 8/11/88
"There's a real genuine care..." "From division iii to the nba with mike budenholzer '92" Pomona College Sagecast, 3/12/21
"a breakthrough" "Pro Basketball Notes" *The Boston Globe*, Peter May, 9/21/03

Chapter 10
Zauzig blamed the slow start… "Greyhounds Need OT to Get Away from Indians" *The Morning Call*, 12/5/93

Chapter 12
"Wow, this is like the perfect combination…" "S.J. agent Rose on the rise" *Courier-Post*, Kevin Callahan, 6/26/02
"is like family" *Ibid*

Chapter 13
"Liberal arts grads may not appeal…" "The Workforce Relevance of Liberal Arts Education" MIT Open Learning, Vijay Kumar, Ramji Raghavan, George Westerman, Susan Young, 8/4/22
"athletics is not something…" "Division III Votes on Recruiting" *The Middlebury Campus*, Peter Yordan, 1/15/04, p. 28

Newspapers

The Whittier News
Valley Times
The San Bernadino County Sun
The Minneapolis Star
Los Angeles Times
Los Angeles Evening Citizen News
St. Cloud Times
The Bismarck Tribune
Coe College Cosmos
[Coe College] Courier
Houston Chronicle
The Charlotte Observer
The Dallas Morning News
The New York Times
The Atlanta Constitution
The Record
Paterson Evening News
The Asheville Citizen
The Daily Dispatch
The Herald-News

The Atlanta Journal-Constitution
Detroit Free Press
Quad-City Times
The Rock Island Argus
Oakland Tribune
Chicago Tribune
The Gleaner
Contra Costa Times
New York Post
Hartford Courant
New York Daily News
The Student Life
Billings Gazette
San Antonio Express-News
The Boston Globe
The Washington Post
The DePauw
Courier-Post
The Middlebury Campus

Websites

tommiesports.com
bizjournals.com/newyork
scholarworks.bgsu.edu
NBA.com
The Ringer
Grantland
GoUpstate.com
www.montclair.edu

Cleaning the Glass
kornferry.com
Pacers.com
ESPN.com
Andscape
The Athletic
House of Strauss

Podcasts

The Woj Pod
Pomona College Sagecast
Coaching U Podcast

The Bill Simmons Podcast
Slappin' Glass Podcast

Books

100 Things Lakers Fans Should Know & Do Before They Die
Tall Tales
Jerry West: The Life and Legend of a Basketball Icon
Joe Tait: It's Been a Real Ball
When the Game Was Ours
Forty-Eight Minutes: A Night in the Life of the N.B.A.
*Hoops Heist: Seattle, The Sonics, and How a Stolen Team's Legacy Gave
    Rise to the NBA's Secret Empire*
Unguarded
Reynolds Remembers
*The Selling of the Green: The Financial Rise and Moral Decline of the Boston
    Celtics*
Tip Off: How the 1984 NBA Draft Changed Basketball Forever
Jail Blazers
From Hang Time to Prime Time
The Great Nowitzki
Blood in the Garden
Agile Talent
Think Again: The Power of Knowing What You Don't Know
Giannis

Magazines
Sports Illustrated
ESPN The Magazine
GQ
Texas Monthly
The New York Times Magazine

Academic Research
Group Processes & Intergroup Relations